The Best Boring Book Ever™ *of*
Tableau *for* Healthcare
fourth edition

by

Daniel Benevento
Katherine Rowell
Janet Steeger

The Best Boring Book Ever™ of
Tableau *for* Healthcare
fourth edition

Copyright @ 2021 by HealthDataViz

ISBN 978-0-578-77792-4

Designed by:

Breviloquent
Charlottesville, Virginia
www.breviloquent.com

More information:

www.healthdataviz.com

Contents

Introduction

1

Introduction

A Book Designed for Health and Healthcare Professionals

Designed specifically for health and healthcare professionals by the health, healthcare, data-visualization, and report-design experts at HealthDataViz, this updated volume introduces and describes in detail Tableau 2020´s features for analyzing health and healthcare data and creating dashboards and reports.

As we have done for all prior editions of Tableau for Healthcare, we have used health and healthcare data (real, but rendered neutral and anonymous) from a wide range of sources (public health, hospital, clinical, operational) to demonstrate Tableau´s functionality in concrete, practical ways immediately useful for real-world application by health and healthcare professionals.

What's new in Tableau since our 3rd edition?

DATA PREPARATION AND MANIPULATION

- Relationships Data Model
- Hyper
- Multiple table storage for extracts

ANALYTICS

- Nested sorting
- Join calculations
- Table calculation assistance

DESIGN AND USER INTERFACE

- Set Actions
- Parameter Actions
- Viz Animation
- Viz in Tooltip
- Export to PowerPoint
- Show/Hide dashboard containers
- Customizable tooltips for Reference Lines
- Show/Hide Sort control
- Dashboard navigation buttons
- Automatic mobile layouts
- Dashboard extensions
- Dashboard grids

What's new in the latest edition of Tableau for Healthcare?

In addition to covering the latest enhancements and features available through Tableau 2020, we have also updated the fourth edition of this book with:

- Four brand new chapters
- Five new and eight updated data sources
- 13 improved step-by-step walk-throughs

Using Vision to Think – The Power of Tableau™

The power of visual displays (and by extension the power of Tableau™) is that they help us use what we see to improve the way we think—how we comprehend, reason, deduce, and respond. Tableau empowers users to quickly grasp the stories and potential opportunities buried in the bottomless oceans of data that surround us.

As with all truly great technology and design, the apparent simplicity of Tableau™ belies the complex concepts and mechanisms used to create it. Building on a new technology that combines Structured Query Language (SQL™) for databases with a descriptive language (Visual Query Language|VizQL™), Tableau translates a user´s actions into a database query, then expresses the response graphically. Tableau´s drag-and-drop and "Show Me" functionality, as well as its high-quality graphics, are the products of complex engineering built on a solid foundation of substantial research into visual intelligence and information visualization, and their connections to vision, perception, and visual cognition.

No Tool is the Total Solution: Knowledge of the Subject and Visual Intelligence Required!

Clearly, we are Tableau fans, but we also know that no tool is a total solution. Designing and building transparent, revelatory dashboards and reports requires subject-matter expertise in health, healthcare, and statistics; knowledge of best practices; and awareness of current research in visual intelligence.

None of these abilities are intuitive; data-visualization skills in particular, often assumed to be instinctual, must be honed over time. Additionally, while it is unnecessary for every team member to become an expert in visual intelligence, each should be aware of it to avoid working at cross-purposes with those members who specialize in data visualization best practices. (That is, everyone should know better than to ask for 3D red, yellow, and green pie charts.) Building a team with these multiple and complementary knowledge areas has enabled us to become even better at creating effective visualizations, and will help you "See how you're doing©."

How to Use this Book: Tips & Tricks

Each chapter begins with a brief discussion of a chart or other display type and its appropriate use, illustrated by a graphic of the finished chart to be built in the chapter, coupled with a brief description of the health and healthcare data´s source and significance. The main body of the chapter contains meticulous, logical, step-by-step instructions on how to build the chart, with frequent screenshots and other images to help orient the reader and clarify each action.

>> Directions formatted like this (with a yellow arrow bullet) indicate an action to be performed by the reader.

Key information is highlighted in call-outs containing images or side-text in the following categories:

Tableau Call-outs ▶

Call-outs formatted like this (black header; orange italic body type) indicate Tableau-specific information and functionality.

Best Practice

Blue boxes display data visualization best practices.

Refreshers ▶

Call-outs formatted like this (orange header; blue italic body type) contain reminders of information discussed in previous chapters.

We have also included introductory overviews of how Tableau connects to data, and of Tableau Server—emphasis here on "introductory." More in-depth explanations, tutorials, forums, and online Tableau communities are found at https://www.tableau.com/resources.

Downloading and Using the Datasets

Although you can successfully and effectively use this book without working with the datasets we have created for its teaching | training exercises, we believe that completing a visualization using the same data is a terrific, hands-on way to see how Tableau works. To that end, we have stripped the datasets included of all formatting or other distractions, freeing you to fully immerse yourself in learning, step-by-step, how to create visualizations using Tableau.

To download the datasets you'll need, please visit HealthDataViz at:

`http://www.healthdataviz.com/Tableau-for-Healthcare`

and follow the instructions we have posted there.

On a Personal Note:

A couple of us at HealthDataViz (HDV) remember the first time we encountered the beta version of Tableau. It was not quite ready for prime time but intriguing all the same. As we watched it develop, becoming easier to use and more powerful with each release, our imaginations were captured by the promise of being able to explore our data faster and easier than ever before, and of creating beautiful, enlightening visualizations. We were nothing short of ecstatic about an emerging application that would empower us to display the stories buried in the mountains of health and healthcare data we worked with every day—revelatory data that (we were certain) had the power, once it had been clearly presented, to improve health and healthcare across the board and across the globe.

Using our substantial experience with and broad knowledge of health and healthcare data, and advanced skills in data visualization and the use of Tableau (our team includes a Tableau Zen Master and Tableau Certified experts), we designed both Beginner | Intermediate and Advanced Tableau training courses for health and healthcare professionals.

A book to reach an even wider healthcare audience was the next logical step. *The Best Boring Book Ever™ of Tableau for Healthcare* (now in its 4th Edition) is the result, and this ever-evolving curriculum has been used to train thousands of students across the health and healthcare space and at universities across the nation. Each learning unit walks a reader through one of many types of visualizations or tasks from start to finish, with particular emphasis on clarity, logic, simplicity, and the smooth flow of ideas. Reading these chapters in order allows a user to build on what has already been accomplished, however, doing so is not mandatory: each unit stands alone to teach one type of lesson fully.

To learn more about the research behind the best practices of data visualization along with lots of helpful methodologies and examples for creating clear and compelling displays of health and healthcare data, we encourage you to check out another of our books, *Visualizing Health and Healthcare Data*, by Katherine Rowell, Lindsay Betzendahl, and Cambria Brown. It is a perfect companion to this book. To learn more about the different types of health and healthcare classification systems and databases, we encourage you to take a look at our award-winning work, *The Best Boring Book Ever™ of Select Healthcare Classification Systems and Databases* (available from Amazon). And we invite you to join the ongoing conversation about health and healthcare data and data visualization by subscribing to our free newsletter, *Unleash Your Inner Healthcare Data*, at http://www.healthdataviz.com.

Equipped with these resources, our hope is to empower a generation of health and healthcare professionals to communicate their data clearly, to make better decisions, and to make the world just a little bit better.

This book and the three editions preceding it would not have been possible without the tireless work of a host of wonderful, creative, passionate individuals. We extend our sincerest thanks to Ann Cutrell, Marnie Morales, Anne "Grammar Lady" Jackson, the designers at Breviloquent, and the entire HealthDataViz extended team who have shaped the many iterations of this book.

And, of course, to you. Thank you for your interest in this book—for supporting our mission and sharing our vision of creating clear and compelling dashboards and reports that create opportunities to improve our health and healthcare systems and move people to action.

Sincerely,

The HealthDataViz Team

CHAPTER 2

Tableau Desktop Interface and Navigation

This chapter lays the foundation for working with Tableau Desktop, beginning with an overview of its interface and operational workflow, followed by a discussion of the core concepts that govern how visualizations are displayed. The rest of this chapter—layout, workflow, and field attributes—will help you become familiar with Tableau, so you can use its rich and powerful features with confidence.

Tableau Desktop Layout

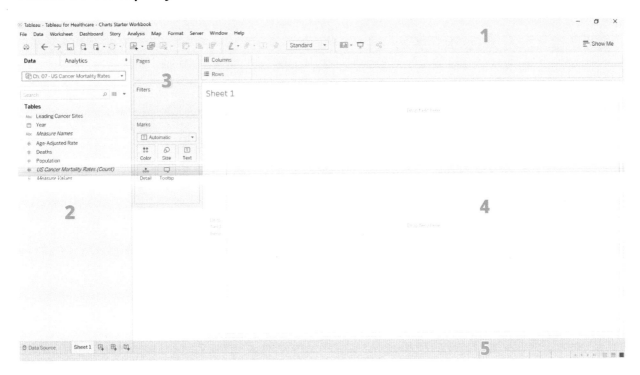

1 - Workbook Title, Menu Bar, and Toolbar

In the image above, a workbook title is displayed at the top of the space. Below it, a Menu Bar and Toolbar (with icons for most commonly used features) extend across the top of the workspace.

2 - The Side Bar

This multi-purpose pane on the left side of the screen contains different features and controls, depending on the task being performed. The Data pane (shown above) is the default display; it shows the list of connected data sources with corresponding fields organized under the Tables label (discussed later in this chapter). The images below show a selection of other possible content of this pane, depending on what function the user chooses.

▲ Collapse, Show, or Close the Side Bar

Each Side Bar has either a double caret or an 'x' in its upper right corner. Click the double caret to collapse the Side Bar to the bottom left of the screen. Click it again to re-display the pane. Click the 'x' in Format and Map panes to return to the default view.

3 - Shelves and the Marks Card

Shelves (Columns, Rows, Pages, and Filters) and the Marks card (Color, Size, Text/Label, Details, and Tooltips) are landing areas for dragging and dropping data fields to build and format visualizations.

4 - The View

The View is the work area where the visualization is displayed. Data fields can be added directly to the View in any of the "Drop field here" locations as well as to the shelves and to the Marks card.

5 - Data Source tab, Sheet tabs, New Worksheet/Dashboard/Story tabs, Navigation Tools

The Data Source tab contains the data sources and their corresponding connections to Tableau. Data connections are covered in Chapter 3.

Each workbook contains three sheet types:

1) **Worksheet** allows the creation of individual charts.

2) **Dashboard** displays one or more worksheets in a single view.

3) **Story** organizes worksheets and/or dashboards into a narrative presentation.

Sheet tabs are a quick path to individual worksheets, dashboards, or stories created in a Tableau workbook. Every newly created sheet has a corresponding sheet tab. Dashboard tabs display a small "window" icon, Story tabs an "open book" icon.

Three small icons at the bottom right of the workbook enable toggling the sheet tab view between a sheet sorter, a sheet filmstrip, and the default sheet tabs.

Data Sources and Fields in Tableau

The top of the Data pane lists all available data sources and their designated connection types. The fields from a selected data source appear below it and are organized by Table with Dimensions residing above the thin gray line and Measures below it and, if applicable, Sets or Parameters. These are the building blocks of any Tableau visualization.

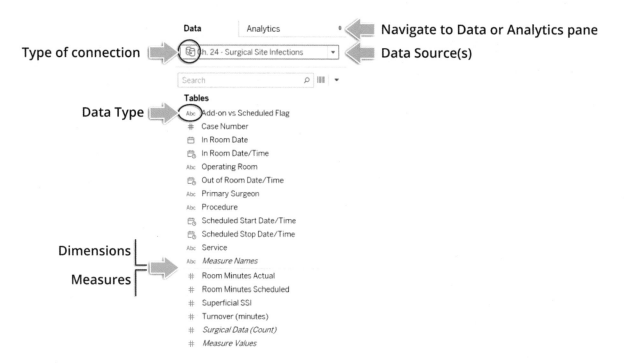

Each data field displays an icon to its left representing its data type, and is colored accord-ing to whether it is discrete or continuous (discussed later in this chapter). The three itali-cized field names shown—Measure Names, TableName(Count), and Measure Values—are auto-generated by Tableau and serve valuable functions, discussed throughout this book.

Data Sources

Datasets imported into Tableau appear in the Data pane. The icon to the left of each data source indicates the type of data connection.

⬚ Live connection to a relational data source.

⬚ Connection to an extract of the data source.

⬚ Connection to a multidimensional or cube data source.

A **blue** checkmark superimposed on the data-source icon means that the source is the *pri-mary* one for the worksheet; an **orange** checkmark indicates a *secondary* source used in data blending.

Data Types

Each field is automatically assigned a Data Type reflecting the kind of information stored in that field. Types might be integers (932), dates (1/23/2017), or strings ("General Hospital"). The Data Type is identified by a unique icon placed to the left of each field in the Data pane.

Icon	Value Description
Abc	Text
#	Numerical
📅	Date
📅🕐	Date and Time
T|F	Boolean
🌐	Geographic

◄ **Data Type Icons**

An = sign preceding any icon denotes a user-defined calculated value field or a copy of another field—for example =# or =Abc .

Sometimes Tableau matches a field with an incorrect data type—for example, a field that contains dates may be identified as Numerical rather than as Date. To correct this, click the incorrect data type icon, and choose the appropriate type from the appearing menu.

Mechanics of Data Field Placement in the Workspace

The layout of any chart created in Tableau is controlled by the placement of data fields from the Data pane in specific locations on the worksheet. Possible targets for data fields include the Columns or Rows shelf, the Filters or Pages shelf, or the Marks card. Tableau offers several ways to place data fields on the shelves and Marks card:

- *Drag and Drop.* Drag a field from the Data pane and drop it directly onto the View in any of the "Drop field here" locations, or onto any shelf or Marks card. A field present in the View can also be dragged from one location to another. Alternatively, drag a field with the right mouse button to generate a Drop Field menu with shortcuts to additional field options.

- *Double-Click.* Double-clicking a data field prompts Tableau to add the field to the shelf it deems most appropriate based on the field´s data properties. If the location is undesirable, it can be dragged and dropped onto any location.

- *Type-In.* Double-click any blank space in Rows, Columns, or on the Marks card, to type in a field name. Tableau auto-completes field names.

- *Show Me.* The Show Me window suggests visualization type(s) for data selected in the Data pane or data fields already present in the View. Tableau evaluates the chosen fields and determines what chart options are appropriate based on the data´s attributes.

Hovering the cursor over each thumbnail in the Show Me dialog box displays, at the bottom of the box, a chart name and the number of Dimensions and Measures required to generate the chart. Click the thumbnail to create the desired chart. It is possible to build an enormous variety of charts in Tableau; Show Me is a one-click option, not a comprehensive list of all possible choices.

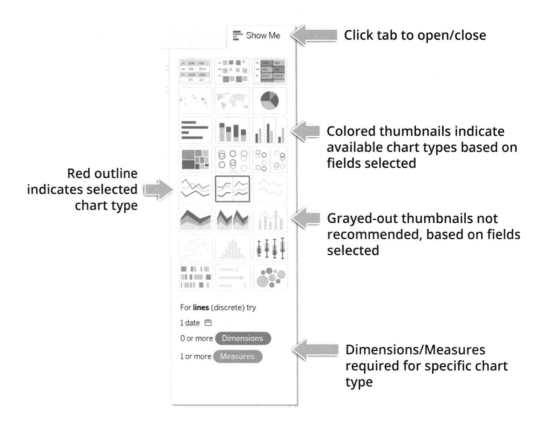

Click tab to open/close

Colored thumbnails indicate available chart types based on fields selected

Red outline indicates selected chart type

Grayed-out thumbnails not recommended, based on fields selected

Dimensions/Measures required for specific chart type

Marks Card

The Marks card controls the type of chart rendered and its display properties. The drop-down menu displays the default or "Automatic" chart type as determined through Tableau logic or the Show Me selection, but can be manually edited if needed.

Marks Card ▷

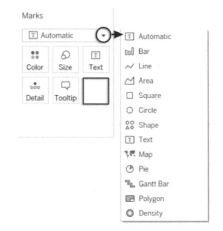

The Marks card offers these display-customization options:

Color and Size: can be manually set or dynamically calculated by a field dropped onto either of these buttons.

Label and Tooltip add written information to the View. Text/Label (the header varies by data type) displays information directly on the marks; Tooltip does so in a pop-up box when the cursor is hovered over marks in the View.

Detail affects the level of granularity for the chart. Dimensions added to the Detail shelf are part of the chart's level of aggregation and Measures added to the Detail shelf can be used in chart elements like reference lines..

The blue box outline is an area that changes depending on the chart type selected. For example, if a Line or Polygon chart type is chosen, a Path button appears; if Shape is selected, a Shape card does.

Dimensions vs. Measures

When connecting to a dataset, Tableau evaluates each field, then places categorical data in the Dimensions section—above the light gray line— and quantitative data in the Measures section—below the light gray line.

DIMENSIONS	MEASURES
Categorical Data, Independent Variable	Quantitative (numerical) Data, Dependent Variable
Organize data into groups	Are used in calculations, (Sum, Average, Count)
Answer: • Who? • What? • Where? • When?	Answer: • How much? • How many? • How long?
Dimensions group or slice Measures. The combination of values of all Dimensions in the view defines the lowest *Level of Detail* for that view by default.	Measures aggregate in real-time and recalculate with every Dimension incorporated into the visualization.
Dimensions are not typically aggregated.	Measures are most often aggregations.
Each Dimensions field displays as its field name. Hospital Service Line	Measures fields display the aggregation along with the field name. SUM(Discharges)

Aggregation and Reassigning Dimensions and Measures

Aggregation is the task of combining multiple values (individual numbers) into a single result by, for example, summing values (SUM), counting the number of values (CNT), averaging values (AVG), or displaying the smallest individual value for a group of rows (MIN). In a worksheet, performing an aggregation on a Dimension field requires it to be changed or treated as a Measure.

Aggregate a Dimension in one of three ways: 1) right-click the field on the worksheet and change its default selection to Measure and choose the desired aggregation; 2) drag the field from the Dimensions section to below the gray line to the Measures section; or 3) right-click the field in the Dimensions section and select Convert to Measure. The last two approaches can be used conversely to convert a field from a Measure to a Dimension.

If Tableau is connected to a cube data source, Dimensions and Measures are predefined in the database and cannot be reassigned.

Basics of Granularity | Level of Detail | Aggregation

Tableau returns results by aggregating data in real time based on the Dimensions present in a worksheet. Every time a new Dimension is incorporated into a visualization, Tableau recalculates the aggregation of the Measure(s). The most common aggregations are Sum, Average, Minimum, Maximum, Count, and Count Distinct.

The first image below, using data from a sample patient data source with 167 records, shows a count of patients by the Dimension "Gender." The second image adds another Dimension, "Race," increasing the granularity of the visualization.

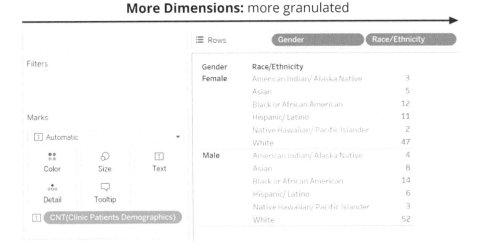

Discrete (Blue) vs. Continuous (Green)

Besides the Dimensions and Measures distinction, fields are also either Continuous or Discrete, a contrast signaled by **blue** for a discrete field and **green** for a continuous one.

"Discrete" and "Continuous" are mathematical terms. "Discrete" means individual, separate, countable, finite. Such fields can be reordered and still make sense. "Continuous" means a range (containing an infinite number of values). Reordering these numbers renders them meaningless.

Field data type icons are either blue or green, discrete or continuous. When a field is moved to the worksheet, it becomes an oval shape of the same color as the icon.

In many cases, Dimensions are discrete (blue) fields that create category headings, and Measures are continuous (green) fields that create axes along a continuous scale. If required, Dimensions (only date or numeric fields, or those aggregated to produce counts) can be changed to continuous; all Measures can be changed to discrete, producing a list of all the distinct values of the field.

◀ Blue and Green Fields

Date and numeric Dimensions can be either discrete or continuous, as can all Measures. A field's background color indicates whether it is discrete (blue) or continuous (green).

Right-click a field to change discrete to continuous or vice versa. This change can also be made from the Data pane: right-click a field and select the "Convert to" option.

When a field is placed on a worksheet, Tableau creates headers for Discrete fields and axes for Continuous fields.

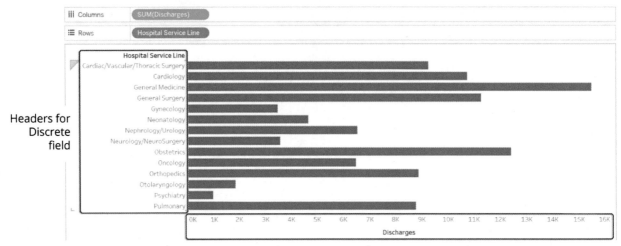

Headers for Discrete field

Axis for Continuous field

There are other functional differences between leveraging discrete and continuous fields in a worksheet; these will be discussed in future exercises.

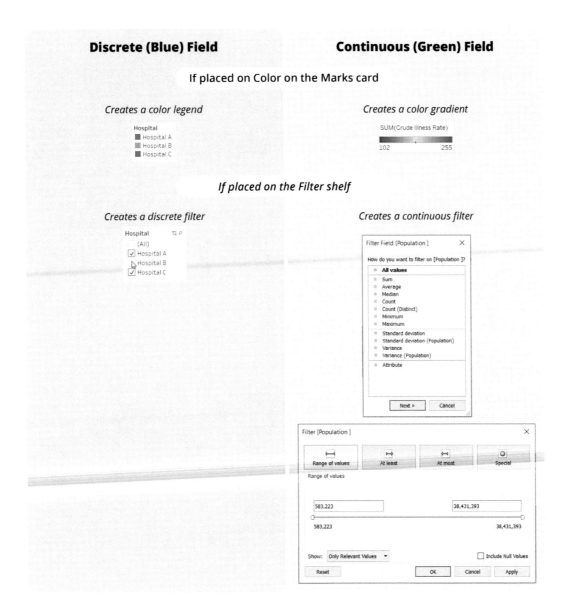

Tableau-Generated Data Fields (*Italicized Font*)

Italicized field names—Measure Names, Measure Values, and TableName(Count)—are Tableau-generated fields and not part of the underlying data source. Tableau creates them when the data source is created.

Measure Names and Measure Values

These Tableau tools allow two or more Measures to be compared side by side along the same axis. Tableau automatically adds these two fields to every dataset, placing the Measure Names field at the bottom of the Dimensions list, and the Measure Values field at the bottom of the Measures list. "Measure Names" contains multiple Measures´ names in a single, discrete (blue) field. "Measure Values" contains multiple Measures´ values in a single, continuous (green) field. These unique fields make it possible to build data views involving multiple Measures.

Measure Names and Measure Values

The Measure Values field represents all user-selected Measures; however, since they are not visible in the field itself, a shelf appears below the Marks card listing all field names that the field contains.

If user chooses to display only certain Measures, a Measure Names field appears on the Filters shelf. Right-clicking this field and selecting Edit Filter shows a list of both excluded and displayed Measures.

⚠ Data Exploration Tip

Measure Names and Measure Values allow easy exploration of a dataset by creating a text table. Moving "Measure Names" to the Rows shelf, and Measure Values to Text on the Marks card gives effortless access to the data.

TableName(Count)

This field represents the number of rows in the data source. It is a Tableau-generated field counting the number of rows of data in the dataset. When working with a new dataset, use TableName(Count) to determine the size of the data source and to understand what one row of data in the dataset represents.

Latitude and Longitude

In fields that have a Geographic role (these can be used to create maps), Tableau automatically geocodes the data and includes Latitude (generated) and Longitude (generated) fields. These fields can be used to overlay data on live maps.

File Types and Saving

Work can be saved as several different Tableau-specific file types described below.

Tableau Workbook (.twb)

This file format is Tableau´s default way of saving work. Tableau workbooks contain one or more worksheets, dashboards, or stories, as well as all the information required to draw visualizations, such as fields used in each view; measure-aggregation methods; and style and formatting applied. Workbooks also include data-source connection information and any metadata created for that connection (see .tds file type below); however, they do not include the data itself.

To create a .twb file:

> » On the Tableau Menu Bar, select "File."
>
> » Select "Save."

Tableau Packaged Workbook (.twbx)

A Packaged Workbook bundles the information in a workbook with any associated files including local data (any data not on a server). This file type is for sharing work with those who do not have access to the data source. (Note: .twbx files are the only format viewable in Tableau Reader.)

To create a .twbx file:

> » On the Tableau Menu Bar, select "File."
>
> » Select "Save As."
>
> » At the bottom of the Save As dialog box, choose the ".twbx" option from the drop-down menu.

Recovered Tableau Workbook (.twbr)

Tableau's autosave feature runs every few minutes; however, if Tableau crashes, a recovered Tableau workbook (.twbr) file is saved in the same location as the original file or in the My Tableau Repository/Workbooks folder. When Tableau is reopened, a recovery dialog box appears containing a list of the recovered files to resume or delete. Autosave is turned on by default, but can be disabled from the Help menu.

Tableau Data Source (.tds)

This file type contains only the information needed to connect to data sources, such as data source type, location, and metadata. If local file data sources (Excel, Access, Text, extracts)are used, the file path is stored in the data source file.

Tableau Packaged Data Source (.tdsx)

A Packaged Data Source (.tdsx) contains all the information in the Data Source (.tds) file as well as any local file data sources. This file type is a single zipped file and is good for sharing a data source with people who do not have access to the original data source.

>> On the Data menu, select a data source, then choose Add to Saved Data Sources from the context menu.

>> Complete the Add to Saved Data Sources dialog box by specifying a file name and type of data source file. The new .tds or tdsx file is then listed in the Saved Data Sources section of the Connect pane

Tableau Data Extract (.tde)

Data Extracts are a local copy of an entire data source or a subset of that source. They are highly compressed and can be used to share data, work offline, or speed up database performance. Connecting to data using Tableau can be either "Live" or "Extract"[ed] into a .tde file. The disadvantage of using an Extract is that the Tableau visualization no longer points to the Live data source; however, the ability to refresh an Extract is only a few clicks away, and can be scheduled using Tableau Server.

To create a .tde file:

In an initial connection,

>> Select the "Extract" radio button.

If the live connection has already been established,

>> Right-click the data source connection.

>> Select "Extract Data."

Tableau Bookmark (.tbm)

A Tableau Bookmark file contains a single worksheet and provides an easy way to quickly share work.

Tableau Preferences (.tps)

A Tableau Preferences file includes the color palettes used across all workbooks for a given user. It is typically shared to maintain a consistent color aesthetic within a group of report creators.

SECTION 2

Connecting to Data

21

CHAPTER 3

Connecting to Data

3.1 Common Data Source Connections

The first step toward creating a visualization in Tableau is to connect to the desired data source. Most organizations have data stored across multiple systems, often including live databases and static files. Tableau connects to these in a variety of ways, enabling fast development of dashboards and reports. These visualizations can then be distributed to other users through multiple channels (described in the chapter "Report and Dashboard Distribution").

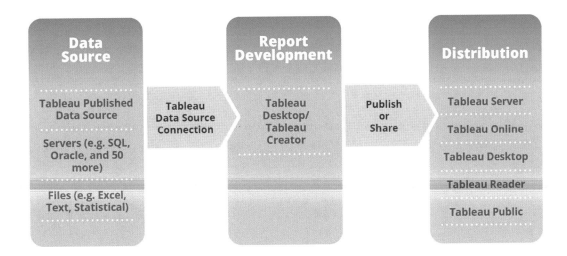

There is no limit to the number of data source connections Tableau can have in one workbook, making it possible to analyze data from multiple sources in the same report. A given data environment may have several tables of related information needed for a report. Tableau can combine these tables into a single data connection, or work with them separately. Once a connection is created to the desired data table(s), it can be kept as a live connection to the data source, or a subset or "snapshot" of the data can be extracted from the data source and saved as a local (.hyper) file.

Connections to data sources are created and modified on the following two pages:

- The **Tableau Start Page** allows the user to select the appropriate connector for the specified data source.

- The **Data Source Page** displays additional details to validate and modify the data connection.

Each page is explained below, along with instructional examples of how to connect to two common data sources: CSV files and MS SQL Server.

The Tableau Start Page

The Start Page contains three sections, shown in the screenshot below. From this central location, the user can (1) **Connect** to data, (2) **Open** most-recently used Tableau workbooks, and (3) **Discover** resources such as training materials, Viz of the Week, and other content produced by the Tableau community.

Connect   **Open**   **Discover**

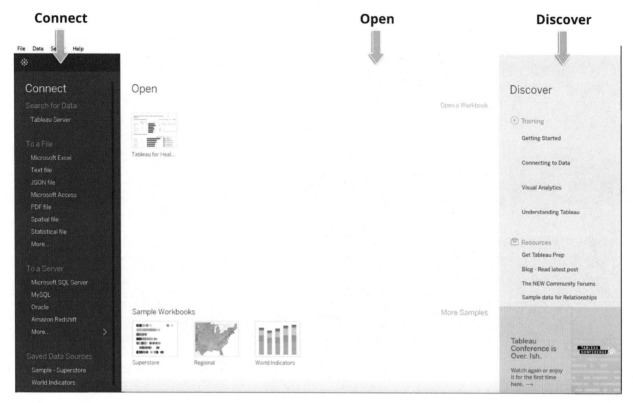

▲ **Tableau Editions**

In the Tableau Personal Edition, the menu title To a Server is not visible on the screen. Only Tableau Professional Edition allows the user to connect to data on a server.

Connect

◄ **Connect**

The small Tableau logo icon at the top left of the Connect pane is a handy button to toggle between the Tableau Start Page and any active Worksheet.

The left pane lists connections to an ever-expanding library of file- and server-based data source types. It also displays a list of shortcuts to saved data sources for quick access.

1) **Search for Data:** Search for Tableau-published data sources by name when connected to Tableau Server.

2) **To a file:** Connect to data stored in Excel, text files, PDFs, statistical files, etc.

3) **To a server:** More than 50 server-based data source connections are available here. Each connector has been optimized for performance when working with the capabilities of the particular data source. If the desired data source is not listed, it may still be possible to connect to it using an Open Database Connectivity (ODBC) standard connector.

4) **Saved data sources:** Access frequently used data sources quickly and easily through shortcut links created by saving Tableau Data Source (.tds) files. Saved data

sources allow the user to set up data source customizations once for reuse across multiple reports and analyses.

Open

Open

Open a Workbook

Tableau for Heal...

The Open pane facilitates quick access to workbooks:

1) **Recently viewed workbooks** – These can be pinned (kept on the recent workbook list), unpinned (removed from that list), or opened from this pane.

2) **Open a workbook** –This link opens a navigation window to select other workbooks than those displayed.

3) **Sample workbooks** –Tableau displays these at the bottom of the Open pane for demonstration and learning purposes.

Discover

This pane contains training materials from Tableau and Resources, such as Blog posts, Tableau Conference information, and Forum links.

How To Connect To A New Tableau Data Source

All Tableau data source connections occur via these five steps:

Step 1 - Choose a Connector. Under "Connect" on the Start page, click a type of file or database and, if required, enter authentication information to open the Data Source page.

Step 2 - Locate the Data. Select the file, database, or schema, then choose the data table(s) within it to be used for analysis.

Step 3 - Validate. Preview and edit metadata if needed.

Step 4 - Customize. Select connection options.

Step 5 - Begin. Go to worksheet to start analysis.

The Data Source Page

After the initial connection to the data is established, Tableau automatically navigates to the Data Source Page. This Page can also be accessed from any location in a Tableau workbook by clicking the Data Source tab at the bottom left of the workbook screen. The Data Source Page can look different according to the type of data connection; however, it will contain the same sections in all cases.

In this image, the four sections of the Data Source Page have been numbered to show workflow sequence and direction.

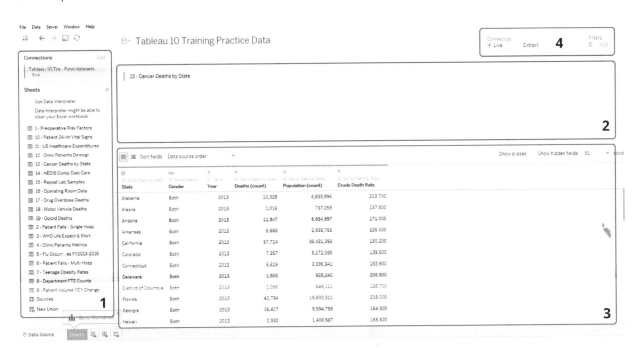

Section 1 - _Data Source Information._ Displays the default title of the data connection as inherited from its file or database name, as well as details of the connected data. This section´s display may differ slightly depending on the capabilities of the connected data source. If prompted, choose the desired database to see its data tables displayed in a list below. Connect to desired tables by double-clicking or dragging and dropping them to Section 2, the Canvas or Work Area. To retitle the data connection, highlight the title and type in a new one.

Section 2 - _Canvas or Work Area._ Choosing a data table from the list in section 1 and placing it here connects to its data. Multiple tables with related data can be placed here to specify Relationships, Joins, and Unions. More information on Relationships, Joins, and Unions is in section 3.2, below. Once selected, the data will populate the data grid area.

Section 3 - _Data Grid._ Here the dataset can be previewed, modified, and validated. The Data Grid is a preview of rows of data values. When multiple tables are present and configured using the Relationship Model, only one table is previewed at a time and the previewed table can be changed by clicking a different table on the canvas. The view can be changed to a Metadata Grid—which is a simplified list of the columns in the data source and their properties—by clicking the icons in the upper left corner of the section.

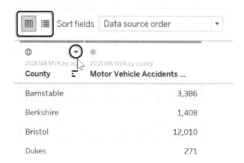

Either the Data or the Metadata Grid can be used to modify column/field proper- ties. To hide or rename a field, hover over the field header and click the caret that appears. Select the appropriate option from the drop-down menu. To change the data type, click the icon by the field name, then select the correct type from the menu.

For data sources including Excel, Text files, and Google sheets, columns of data can be pivoted and split into new fields. These tools are explained in section 3.3 "Re- shaping Data Files; Using Data Interpreter, Pivot, and Column-Splitting."

Section 4 - Customize Connection & Filters.

- **Connections** are either Live or Extract. "Live" connects directly to the data source; "Extract" imports data into Tableau´s fast data engine.

- **Filters** can be used to define a subset of the data, reducing the number of records in the data source. Filters can be applied to both Live and Extract connections. Data Source Filters limit the number of records queried; Extract Filters limit the amount of data extracted into the .hyper file.

▲ Data Connection: Live vs. Extract

The decision to create a live connection to the data or to extract data from the data source into Tableau's data engine depends on user requirements and available network resources.

Live: Tableau connects directly to the data source and queries this source in real time as the report is rendered. This is the best choice when data is constantly updated and time-sensitive analysis is required. With Live connections, the queries' speed will depend on the performance capabilities of the source system.

Extract: Tableau takes a snapshot of the data and puts it into a .hyper file, a proprietary, columnar data format optimized for querying by Tableau. Once an Extract is made, queries are directed to the .hyper file rather than the originating data source. The Extract can then be refreshed manually or via Tableau Server on an automated schedule. As of Tableau 2018.3, extracts can now be saved in a single .hyper extract file as multiple tables mirroring the underlying data structure by selecting "Multiple Tables" from the extract creation menu. This may result in smaller extract files, faster extract creation, and even faster queries.

Best Practice

There are many reasons to consider extracting data when developing and distributing Tableau reports.

1) If a Live connection is slow, a Tableau Data Extract may enhance performance.

2) End users may not have access to the underlying (possibly remote) data source. An Extract file (.hyper) can be combined with a .twb workbook file to create a Tableau Packaged Workbook file (.twbx) that can be distributed and used for offline analysis.

3) Data Extracts can aggregate data for visible Dimensions and hide unused fields to improve performance and enhance security.

If real-time analysis is needed or the data is too large to extract, a Live data connection can be used.

Go to Worksheet. Once a data connection is set up appropriately, click "Go to Worksheet" or "Sheet 1" to start the analysis or to trigger the creation of the extract.

Data Connection Examples

The following examples are intended to be conceptual walk-throughs, illustrating the steps required to connect to a single table from common data sources.

EXAMPLE 1: CSV FILE CONNECTION

This example illustrates connecting Tableau to a text data file to set up a single table data source.

Choose a Connector

» On the Tableau Start page, in the Connect section, To a File section, click "Text file."

Locate the Data

» Click the desired data source title, then click "Open."

» On the Data Source page, drag and drop the selected table from the left pane onto the canvas. (If there is only one table in the left column, Tableau automatically places it in the canvas.)

Validate

» Preview the data.

Customize

  » Rename column headers, hide columns, and/or edit data types as needed.

  » Under "Connection," click the radio button for "Live" or "Extract" as desired.

  » Replace the pre-assigned title with a descriptive one of your choice by highlighting the title field (upper left corner of the workspace) and typing in the chosen name.

Begin

  » Click "Go to Worksheet" to start analysis or to trigger the creation of the extract.

> **Note:** Dragging and dropping more than one sheet to the white canvas activates Tableau's Relationship, Union, and Table Join functionalities. These processes are explained in sections 3.2."Relationships and Table Joins."   This example assumes that only one table is needed.

EXAMPLE 2: MICROSOFT SQL SERVER

Connecting to server-based data sources, like Microsoft SQL Server, requires additional steps for user authentication and locating the desired data tables.

Choose a Connector

  » On the Tableau Start page under "Connect," go to the "To a Server" section, and click "Microsoft SQL Server."

Locate the Data

  » Enter the name of the server.

  » Provide login credentials for the server by specifying whether to use Windows Authentication or a specific Username and Password.

  » Check the "Require SSL" box if connecting to an SSL server.

  » Specify whether to "Read uncommitted data."

  » Click "OK."

  » On the Data Source page, choose a database from the "Select Database" drop-down menu.

  » Drag and drop the desired table onto the Work Area.

Validate

  » Preview the data.

▲ Data Grid Preview

To minimize queries to the database, the data grid may not update immediately— in which case an "Update Now" button will display. Select it to preview the data.

Customize

>> Rename column headers, hide columns, and/or edit data types as needed.

>> Under "Connection," click the radio button for "Live" or "Extract" as desired.

>> Replace the pre-assigned title with a descriptive one of your choice by highlighting the title field (upper left corner of the workspace) and typing in the chosen name.

Begin

>> Click "Go to Worksheet" to start analysis or to trigger the creation of the extract.

3.2 Relationships & Table Joins

Relationships provide a new approach for combining multiple tables into a single Tableau data source using common fields. Data tables can also be combined using an advanced technique called data blending, covered later in the book, which merges data from multiple data sources; however, creating a single data source requires a Table Join or a Relationship. This chapter will discuss the new Relationship Model, review the legacy Table Join approach, and discuss the key points to know for each technique.

Tableau's New Relationship Model: In Tableau 2020.2, Tableau released a new method for combining tables into a single data source: Relationships. This new data model is a flexible way of merging tables without some of the limitations inherent in the legacy approach using table joins. Unlike with Table Joins, Relationships do not physically combine the data to create a single data source; instead, the data is merged when utilized in a worksheet for analysis. In order to learn this new approach and its benefits, a deeper understanding of Tableau's legacy approach is needed.

Table Joins: This technique merges two tables into a single data source. Joining Tables means combining them based on one or multiple common fields between the tables. Conceptually, it is useful to imagine the result of a table join as a new table containing fields and values from both of the original tables.

The mechanics for using Table Joins and the new Relationship model will be outlined below, but first a functional understanding of how these two approaches work is helpful.

Here are two data sources used to create a compelling map visual later in this book:

Table 1: 2018 MA MVA by County

County	Motor Vehicle Accidents with Injury (counts)
Barnstable	3386
Berkshire	1408
Bristol	12010
Dukes	271
Essex	10928
Franklin	656
Hampden	12165
Hampshire	1453
Middlesex	16877
Nantucket	59
Norfolk	9567
Plymouth	9516
Suffolk	5600
Worcester	11970

Table 2: MA Trauma Hospitals

Trauma Hospital	Trauma Level	Location	County	Latitude	Longitude
Baystate Medical center	1	759 Chestnut Street, Springfield,MA	Hampden	42.1215221	-72.6030062
Berkshire Medical Center	3	725 North Street, Pittsfield, MA	Berkshire	42.4600752	-73.2492796
Umass Memorial Medical Center	1	55 Lake Avenue North, Worcester, MA	Worcester	42.2774799	-71.7616699
Anna Jaques Hospital	3	25 Highland Avenue, Newburyport, MA	Essex	42.8136933	-70.8909165
Lawrence General Hospital	3	35 Prospect Street, Lawrence, MA	Essex	42.7081477	-71.14724
Beverly Hospital	3	85 Herrick Street, Beverly, MA	Essex	42.5641506	-70.8751358
Lowell General Hospital	3	295 Varnum Avenue, Lowell, MA	Middlesex	42.6478028	-71.3422337
North Shore Medical Center	3	81 Highland Avenue, Salem, MA	Essex	42.5112107	-70.9051624
Beth Israel Deaconess Medical Centr	1	190 Pilgrim Road, Boston, MA	Suffolk	42.3382078	-71.109713
Boston Medical Center	1	751 Albany Street, Boston, MA	Suffolk	42.3351263	-71.0713925
Brigham & Women's Hospital	1	75 Francis Street, Boston, MA	Suffolk	42.33568	-71.1060436
Lahey Medical Center	1	41 Mall Road, Burlington, MA	Middlesex	42.512247	-71.189462
Children's Hospital	1	300 Longwood Avenue, Boston, MA	Suffolk	42.3373469	-71.1057172
Mass General Hospital	1	55 Fruit Street, Boston, MA	Suffolk	42.3628604	-71.068753
South Shore Hospital	2	55 Fogg Road, Weymouth, MA	Norfolk	42.1755371	-70.9539143
Tufts Medical Center	1	800 Washington Street, Boston, MA	Suffolk	42.3495588	-71.0634112
Steward Good Samaritan Medical Center	3	235 North Pearl Street, Brockton, MA	Plymouth	42.098054	-71.0609587

The common field between these tables is "County," but notice that the granularity of the data is different. Table 1 has one record for each of the 14 counties; Table 2 has multiple records for eight counties representing the different Trauma Hospitals.

Combining via Table Join: Performing a Table Join (here, an Inner Join) on County will result in the following data source:

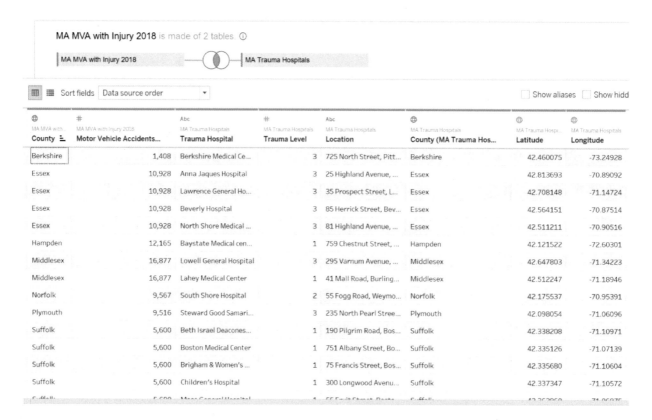

Using this data source and placing the Tableau-generated field "2018 MA MVA by County (Count)" onto Text generates the table below, displaying the number of rows of data per county in the dataset. Of the eight counties displayed (counties present in both Table 1 and Table 2), three have more than one trauma hospital.

County	Count of 2018 MA MVA by County
Berkshire	1
Essex	4
Hampden	1
Middlesex	2
Norfolk	1
Plymouth	1
Suffolk	6
Worcester	1

When displaying the measure "Motor Vehicle Accidents with Injury (counts)" (table below), the results are summed multiple times for those counties with multiple trauma centers, resulting in incorrect results. For example, in "Table 1: 2018 MA MVA by County" above, Middlesex county has 16,877 motor vehicle accidents with injury. However, in our joined table below, the results for Middlesex are doubled to 33,754 because there are two Middlesex hospitals in the "MA Trauma Hospitals" table.

County	Motor Vehicle Accidents with Injury (counts)
Berkshire	1,408
Essex	43,712
Hampden	12,165
Middlesex	33,754
Norfolk	9,567
Plymouth	9,516
Suffolk	33,600
Worcester	11,970

Even if no fields are used in our worksheet from the MA Trauma Hospitals table, the data source has been "physically joined" before any analysis takes place, so the repeated rows cannot be summed accurately. This repetition can be addressed with a more complex Level of Detail expression (discussed in more detail in Chapter 23), however, Tableau's new Relationship model offers a simpler solution.

Combining via Relationships: With Relationships, both tables are brought onto the canvas and connected via a "noodle," the Tableau term for the line relating tables via a common field(s).

Notice that the preview will not show a combined table with the new relationship model—the tables are not physically joined at the data source level (each table in the two images below are highlighted to display their corresponding data). Instead, these tables are "logically" related but remain separate until they are queried on a worksheet during report development. If no fields from a table are present in a worksheet, the table is not joined or queried on that worksheet.

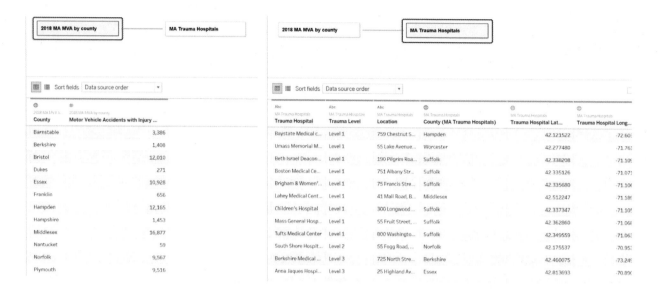

This Relationship Model has several benefits:

- **Improved Performance:** A table is queried only when its fields are utilized in a worksheet, which results in more efficient queries to the data source.

- **Reduced Complexity:** Relationships will not duplicate data in the query if the more granular table is not used in the analysis, thus avoiding the need for complex Level of Detail expressions to account for repeated data.

Performing the same SUM(Motor Vehicle Accidents with Injury)" aggregation using the related tables does not duplicate the data because no fields from the MA Trauma Hospitals are used (or needed) for this analysis.

County	Motor Vehicle Accidents with Injury (counts)
Barnstable	3386
Berkshire	1408
Bristol	12010
Dukes	271
Essex	10928
Franklin	656
Hampden	12165
Hampshire	1453
Middlesex	16877
Nantucket	59
Norfolk	9567
Plymouth	9516
Suffolk	5600
Worcester	11970

This is the accurate Motor Vehicle Accident with Injury count for MA in 2018.

Here are some key points from each approach:

Table Joins – Key Points:

- Must be defined when the data source is first created and before analysis is performed.

- Must define a specific join type/clause (inner, outer, left, right).

- Changing a table join impacts all sheets in the workbook leveraging that data source.

- Physical joining can cause rows to drop or duplicate depending on join criteria.

- Even with the new relationship model, joins can still be performed in Tableau when necessary, I.E., when using row-level-security.

- Joins are represented with a Venn diagram and accessed by "opening" an object in the Data Model logical layer to reveal the physical table join layer.

Relationships – Key Points:

- This is the new connection method that occurs at the logical layer, not the physical.

- Relationships are represented by noodles between different data objects (tables or joined tables) on configured fields.

- Does not require tables to be joined when creating data source. Instead, data is joined at the time of analysis when fields are added to individual worksheets.

- Does not require join type selection. The joins are determined by the collection of fields on individual worksheets.

- The dimensions and measures present in the worksheet determine the type of join Tableau is performing.

- This simplifies calculation complexity and improves performance by preventing data from being duplicated unnecessarily. This limits the need for certain LOD expression work-arounds required to manage duplicate values in the legacy approach.

Versioning Note: Any data source with Table Joins created prior to Tableau 2020.2 and upgraded to version 2020.2 or later will have all table joins merged into a single migrated object on the data connection page.

Migrated Data

With either approach, Tableau can combine tables within a single data connector or across multiple data environments. The example below demonstrates the basics of these variations via a Table Join between two tables in a single Excel file, then repeats the process with the new Relationship approach. The section following it explains the process for merging tables across data environments.

35

Table Join Exercise

The Legacy Approach: Joining Tables in Tableau within a Single Data Connector

In order to take advantage of the performance and simplicity benefits discussed above when creating a new data source, it is best to use the new Relationship Model whenever possible. There are still times, however, where physically joining the data is advantageous or necessary. It is also possible to join multiple tables together and then set up a relationship between collections of joined tables in a single data source. It is therefore important to understand the mechanics of table joining as well.

This walk-through explains how to join two tables from a single Excel workbook. The process is similar to that for joining multiple tables from a single database such as MS SQL Server.

» Open Tableau Desktop.

» On the Start page, in the Connect section, click "Microsoft Excel." (If the new workbook opens at the worksheet view, click the "Connect to Data" hyperlink in the top left of the screen to navigate to the Connect pane.)

» Navigate to the folder containing the downloaded Excel file, titled "Data Connection – MA MVA & Trauma Hospitals." (Instructions to download the training files accompanying this book are on page 5).

» Double-click "Data Connection – MA MVA & Trauma Hospitals.xlsx".

» In the left pane, click "2018 MA MVA by County" table and drag and drop onto the canvas (double-clicking the table also performs the same action).

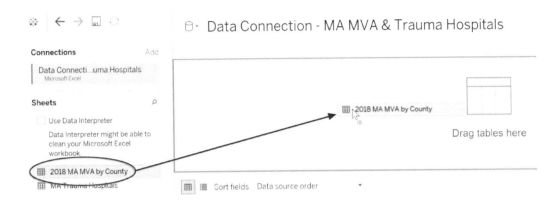

The "2018 MA MVA by County" table has been placed on the canvas. The data is displayed in the data grid, allowing the user to view the contents of that data source. In versions prior to Tableau 2020.2, dragging and dropping a new table onto the canvas prompted a Table Join. In Tableau 2020.2 or later, to enter the Table Join area, the user must double-click (or right-click and select "Open") the table present on the canvas.

» Double-click the "2018 MA MVA by County" table on the canvas, opening the Table Join area.

Next, join "2018 MA MVA by County" with the "MA Trauma Hospitals" table:

» Click the "MA Trauma Hospitals" table and drag and drop it next to "2018 MA MVA by County."

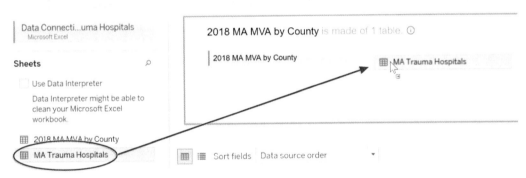

When this table is added to the canvas, Tableau automatically performs an inner table join on the common field between the two tables, "County." The joined dataset preview is visible in the lower half of the screen.

County	Motor Vehicle Acc...	Trauma Hospital	Trauma Level	Location	County (MA Trau...	Latitude	Longitude
Hampden	12,165	Baystate Medical cen...	1	759 Chestnut Street, ...	Hampden	42.121522	-72.60301
Berkshire	1,408	Berkshire Medical Ce...	3	725 North Street, Pitt...	Berkshire	42.460075	-73.24928
Worcester	11,970	Umass Memorial Med...	1	55 Lake Avenue North...	Worcester	42.277480	-71.76167
Essex	10,928	Anna Jaques Hospital	3	25 Highland Avenue, ...	Essex	42.813693	-70.89092
Essex	10,928	Lawrence General Ho...	3	35 Prospect Street, L...	Essex	42.708148	-71.14724
Essex	10,928	Beverly Hospital	3	85 Herrick Street, Bev...	Essex	42.564151	-70.87514
Middlesex	16,877	Lowell General Hospital	3	295 Varnum Avenue, ...	Middlesex	42.647803	-71.34223
Essex	10,928	North Shore Medical ...	3	81 Highland Avenue, ...	Essex	42.511211	-70.90516

▲ Defining Table Joins

When a second table is added to the canvas, Tableau makes a guess as to how the tables should be joined by identifying fields with the same name. If Tableau chooses incorrectly or no shared field names exist, the join clause can be manually defined. Tableau also updates the preview in the data grid below to reflect the new data source being created by the Table Join.

» Click the Join icon to view the options.

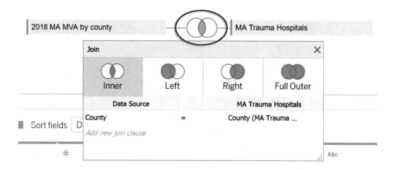

Tableau recognized that both tables have a common data field—County—and has joined the tables via an inner join. If this choice is incorrect, select other join options.

Table Joins

The type of Table Join used will determine how two tables are combined to form a new table with fields from both.

An in-depth analysis of Table Joins is beyond the scope of this book, but below is a quick overview of the four Joins that Tableau allows:

Inner Join: A row is returned only when the value is matched in both tables.

Left Join: All rows are returned from the left table; matching records only are returned from the right table. If no matching records exist, the fields from the right table return NULL.

Right Join: All rows are returned from the right table; matching records only are returned from the left table. If no matching records exist, the fields from the left table return NULL.

Full Outer Join: A row is returned when a value is present in either table. If no matching records exist, the fields from the other table will return NULL.

Tableau correctly selected the fields to join (County) in this example. However, it is possible to change the field on which the Join is performed. To view available fields for a possible join:

» Click either field name in the Join box to view a drop-down menu of available fields to join.

» For this example, leave the join on "County."

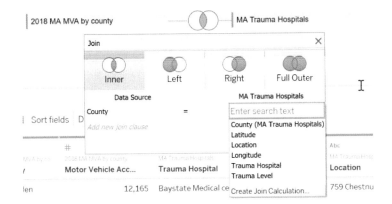

◄ Join Calculations

It is possible to make calculations part of Join criteria. Select "Create Join Calculation" to achieve more complex joins or to resolve data type mismatches between tables.

» Click the title bar to highlight the title.

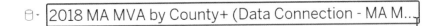

2018 MA MVA by County+ (Data Connection - MA M...

» Change the title to: "Ch. 03 – 2018 MA MVA and Trauma Hospitals by County (Inner Join)."

» Edit the Connection to "Extract."

» Click the worksheet tab at the bottom left of the screen to go to the worksheet.

» Save the file as a Tableau Data Extract (*.hyper) in the My Tableau Repository \ Datasources folder.

The tables are now joined. The Dimensions of each table are displayed in the upper section of the Data pane; the Measures are displayed in the lower section. There is one Tableau-generated Count field for both tables—2018 MA MVA by county (Count).

Data-Pane Organization ▷

When multiple tables are joined in a single data source, Tableau automatically groups the fields by table name (as displayed here, at right) to keep them organized. To use Folders as an organizing device instead, right-click the white space of the Data pane, select Group by, then Folder. Right-click again to choose Create Folder. Drag and drop selected fields into this new Folder.

One dataset **Count** for the joined data source

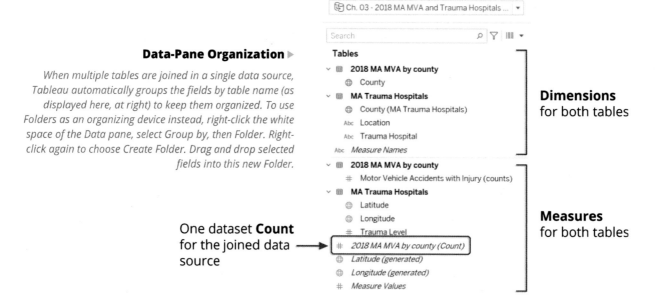

To evaluate the behavior of the inner join, the dataset's Count field will be utilized. This field counts the number of rows in the data source. Tableau generates this field for every data source connection.

» Click and drag "2018 MA MVA by County (Count)" to Text on the Marks card. The total number of rows in this inner join is 17.

40

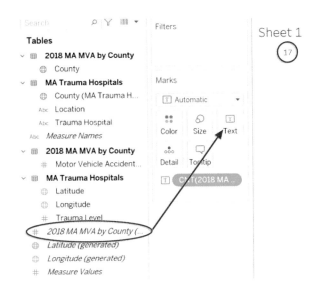

» Click and drag "County" from the 2018 MA MVA by County section and place on the Rows shelf.

In this inner join, the number of listed counties has been reduced to those present in both the "2018 MA MVA by County" table and the "MA Trauma Hospitals" table: Eight (8) from the original 14 counties listed for the 2018 MA MVA by County table. Notice three counties (Essex, Middlesex, and Suffolk) display numbers greater than one. Those counties have more than one trauma hospital per county.

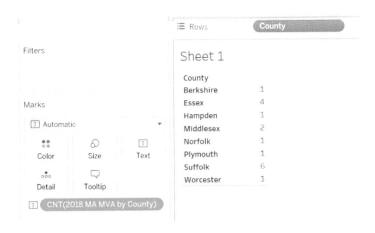

» Double-click the worksheet tab at the bottom of the screen and rename to "MA MVA – Inner Join."

» Click "File" on the Menu bar then click "Save As."

» Rename the workbook "Data Connections" then click "Save."

Relationships Exercise

The Relationship Data Model: Relating Tables in Tableau within a Single Data Connector

Here, the same two tables, "2018 MA MVA by County" and "MA Trauma Hospitals" will be used to create a relationship.

> » Open a new worksheet by clicking "Worksheet" on the Menu bar, then "New Worksheet."

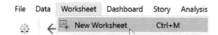

> » Click "Data" on the Menu bar then select "New Data Source."

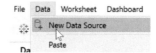

> » In the Connect pane, click "Microsoft Excel."

> » Locate and select the Excel file "Data Connection – MA MVA & Trauma Hospitals. xlsx."

> » Click "Open."

> » In the left pane, click "2018 MA MVA by County" table and drag and drop onto the canvas.

> » Then click "MA Trauma Hospitals" in the left pane and drag and drop onto the canvas.

Tableau automatically performs a relationship. Instead of a Venn diagram (used to display a table join), Tableau displays a single orange line between the two tables—Tableau calls this a "noodle"—indicating the tables have a relationship.

Tableau recognizes that both tables have a common data field—County—and has related the tables via that field. If this choice is incorrect, other fields can be selected in the Edit Relationship dialog box. This dialog box appears automatically when the relationship is created or can be viewed by clicking the orange Noodle.

Click each table's field name for a list of corresponding fields.

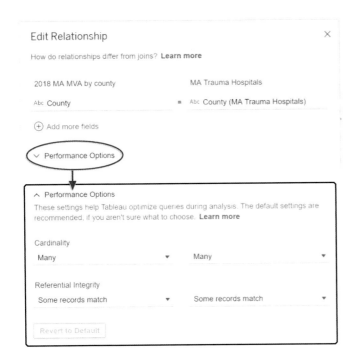

Performance Options

These settings help optimize queries during analysis. If the shape of the data is known, these settings can be edited to reflect the uniqueness and matching between records. If not known, use Tableau's recommended default settings.

Cardinality: *is the numeric relationship between rows in one table and rows in another. Selecting "many" tells Tableau that the values for the joined field(s) are not unique. Selecting "one" tells Tableau the field values are unique (i.e., one row per value).*

Referential Integrity: *ensures relationships between tables stay consistent. Selecting "Some Records Match" tells Tableau that not every record has a corresponding record in the joined tables. Selecting "All Records Match" tells Tableau all values for the joined field will have a corresponding record in the joined tables.*

» Click the title bar to highlight the title.

» Change the title to: "Ch. 03 – 2018 MA MVA and Trauma Hospitals by County (Relationship)."

» Edit the Connection to "Extract."

» Click the worksheet tab to go to the worksheet.

The tables are now related. The dimensions and measures are listed with their corresponding table name, separated by a horizontal line. Each table contains a dataset count field (e.g., 2018 MA MVA by county (Count)); recall a table join contains only one count field for the joined table.

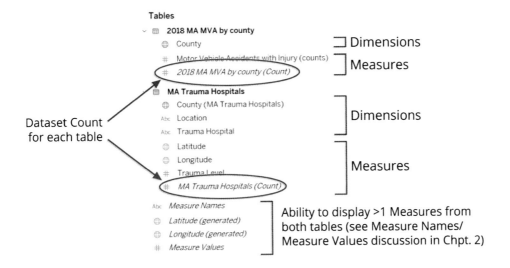

To evaluate the behavior of the Relationship, each dataset's Count field will be utilized.

» Drag and drop "2018 MA MVA by County (Count)" to Text on the Marks card. The total number of rows in the "2018 MA MVA by County" data source is 14.

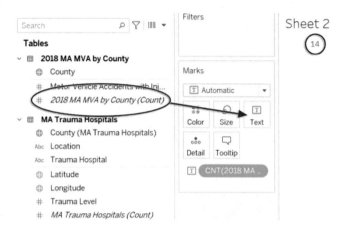

» Drag and drop "County" from the 2018 MA MVA by County section to the Rows shelf.

The "County" dimension disaggregates the Count to the dataset's lowest level of detail: one row of data per County. All 14 counties with reported motor vehicle accidents with injury data are displayed.

Perform the same evaluation for the MA Trauma Hospitals Count and County.

» Create a new worksheet by clicking "Worksheet" on the Menu bar, then "New Worksheet."

» Drag and drop "MA Trauma Hospitals (Count)" to Text on the Marks card. The total number of rows in the "MA Trauma Hospitals" data source is 17.

» Drag and drop "County (MA Trauma Hospitals)" to the Rows shelf.

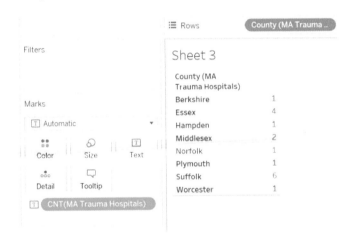

The "County (MA Trauma Hospital)" dimensions disaggregates the Count, but notice the fewer Counties and three of those Counties (Essex, Middlesex, and Suffolk) have numbers greater that one, indicating more than one trauma hospital in those counties. This text table appears exactly like the Inner Join.

How the relationship versus the table join handles the aggregation of the measures is distinctive. Below are the MA MVA by County text tables built with an inner join and a relationship—with the additional field "Motor Vehicle Accidents with Injury (counts)" incorporated in both tables. The row-level counts are the same for both examples, however, the "Motor Vehicle Accidents with Injury (counts)" aggregations are different.

With the Trauma Hospital dimension omitted in this view, the inner joined "Motor Vehicle Accidents with Injury (counts)" value is over-inflated— the result is multiplied by the number of trauma hospitals per county (e.g. MVA for Suffolk is over-inflated six times).

Compare this to the relationship example where the values for Motor Vehicle Accidents with Injury (count) are displayed accurately despite those three counties having more than one trauma hospital.

(Note: The Inner Join displays fewer counties as it retained only those counties that matched in both tables; the Relationship however retained all counties and displays them when using measures from the MA MVA with Injury 2018 table.)

Inner Join Example

County	Count of MA MVA with Injury 2018	Motor Vehicle Accidents with Injury (counts)
Berkshire	1	1,408
Essex	4	43,712
Hampden	1	12,165
Middlesex	2	33,754
Norfolk	1	9,567
Plymouth	1	9,516
Suffolk	6	33,600
Worcester	1	11,970

Relationship Example

County	Count of MA Trauma Hospitals	Motor Vehicle Accidents with Injury (counts)
Barnstable	0	3,386
Berkshire	1	1,408
Bristol	0	12,010
Dukes	0	271
Essex	4	10,928
Franklin	0	656
Hampden	1	12,165
Hampshire	0	1,453
Middlesex	2	16,877
Nantucket	0	59
Norfolk	1	9,567
Plymouth	1	9,516
Suffolk	6	5,600
Worcester	1	11,970

Unions vs. Relationships and/or Table Joins

Relationships and Table Joins in their simplest form place one table next to another, lining them up row by row based on the data values of key field(s) to create a wider final dataset. Table Joins can also increase or decrease the number of rows in the resulting data source based on the type of join and whether any matches are found for the key field. Unions align two tables column by column, essentially appending the rows of data to make a longer final dataset. Another way to think of this difference; relating or joining tables is a way to append new columns to a dataset; creating a Union is a way to append new rows to existing columns in the dataset.

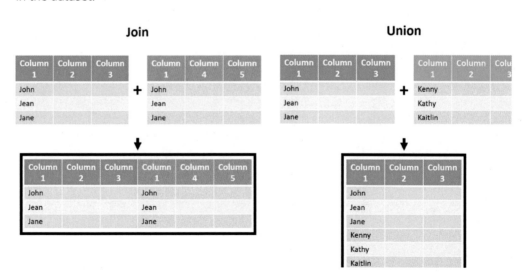

Unions

Unions are useful in any situation in which data tables are generated at regular intervals with identical columns, but with new data values, and where a compilation of data across those intervals is needed for analysis. For example, monthly financial reports are sometimes stored as individual tabs in an Excel workbook. Unions are a fast way to merge these tabs for analysis in Tableau. Unions can occur only between tables in the same data source. Not all data sources support Unions; when they are supported, the bottom of the left pane of the Data Source Page displays a "New Union" option.

Here are the conceptual steps to create a manual Union:

» Double-click the "New Union" option at the bottom of the left pane of the Data Source Page to open the Union dialog box.

 New Union

» Drag and drop the desired tables from the left pane into the Union dialog box.

» Select "Apply."

Where possible, tables should have the same structure, column headers, and data types. If this is not possible, mismatched columns can nevertheless be merged.

» Select the columns to merge.

» Click the drop-down arrow; select "Merge mismatched fields."

Additional notes on Unions:

• Unmatched columns (one exists in the first table, but not in the second) are retained; missing data are treated as NULL.

• Tableau generates meta-data fields about the Union and adds them to the data, including Sheet and Table names.

• A wildcard search from the Union dialog box can find all matching tables, so they can automatically be included in the Union.

Joining or Relating Tables in Tableau: across Data Sources ("Cross-Database Join or Relationship")

Tableau has the ability to join or relate tables across different databases and data environments. The conceptual walk-through below uses screen shots to show how to join an Access and an Excel table; many different cross-database combinations are possible. Much of what has been said so far about Table Joins and Relationships in a single data source applies to Cross-Database Joins or Relationships as well; note however, the important difference highlighted below. This example will show a Cross-Database Join but the principles apply to Relationships as well.

47

To create a Cross-Database Join, start in the Data Connection page view.

» Select the first table for the join by dragging it to the Canvas.

» Next, Click the "Add" button to the right of the Connections header.

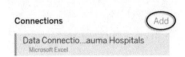

» Select the desired File or Server connection from the Connection List menu that appears. The list displays only the databases for which Cross-Database Joins are supported. Once the multi-connection data source is established, joins can be created as usual.

» Drag and drop the desired table/sheet onto the Canvas, then set the Join criteria using the steps described for Table Joins, above.

Once you have a multi-connection data source, Tableau color-codes each table and its corresponding columns as an added visual cue.

Cross-Database Join or Relationship Notes:

Any grayed-out connection types are not supported for Cross-Database Joins or Relationships.

When using an Extract as part of a multi-connection data source, designate it the primary connection to retain any metadata customizations (default property settings, calculated fields, groups, and aliases). Should a multi-connection data source require multiple Extracts, only the customizations in the primary connection Extract will remain.

To troubleshoot multi-connection data sources, verify that the data types of the key fields match. It is often possible to create a calculated field to fix column mismatches as long as calculations are supported by all active connections.

3.1 Reshaping Data Files: Using Data Interpreter, Pivot, and Column-Splitting

EXAMPLE: MICROSOFT EXCEL FORMATTED AS A REPORT

Excel data files are often formatted as reports that include titles, row spacing, merged cells, and other features, making them hard to work with in Tableau. Tableau´s data-connection process provides tools to mitigate this difficulty: Data Interpreter, Pivoting, and Column-Splitting.

For Tableau to correctly use imported data, data table(s) must be in a "raw" format, with variables in columns and values in rows. The table must be free of all processing; even common, easily read formatting seen in spreadsheets or pivot tables, such as totals and line breaks, must be omitted. (The first row in the file can contain field headers or column names.) Everything else, including empty columns and/or rows, should be deleted.

Comparing the tables below further illustrates this point.

Incorrect Data-Table Formatting

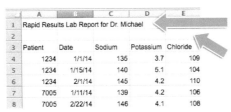

Title should **NOT** be at the top of the table.

There should **NOT** be any line breaks.

Correct Data-Table Formatting

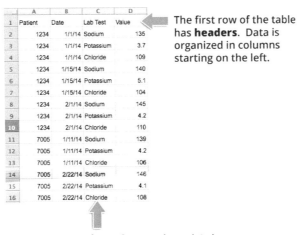

The first row of the table has **headers**. Data is organized in columns starting on the left.

Data has been "**pivoted**," or reshaped. Lab tests appear as a single column; test results appear in a second column named Value. This arrangement changes lab results from three Measures into a Dimension (Lab Test) and a Measure (Value).

The pair of images above shows "before" and "after" versions of an Excel file whose data has been modified to work more smoothly in Tableau. (The original Excel file is not affected.) Tableau data-preparation tools can be launched from the Data Connection Page:

- **Tableau Data Interpreter** detects the data, including sub-tables, and removes extra formatting such as titles and blank space from Excel data sources.

- **Pivot** converts Excel or text table data to a narrower table structure. Multiple, adjacent columns are transformed into a column with the field names and a separate column containing the field values.

- **Split** and **Custom Split** generate new fields according to user-defined requirements.

49

EXERCISE: USING TABLEAU'S DATA-PREPARATION TOOLS

This exercise lists the steps to connect to the Excel worksheet displayed below. Follow them using the "Data Interpreter Example - WHO Death Projections.xls" file in the download dataset for this book.

This spreadsheet has been created in a typical report format; title on the first row, followed by several empty rows, then column headers (separate from the first row of data and spread across multiple rows), and data values divided across several columns.

Projection of deaths per 100,000 Population

| | 2030 | | | | | | | | | | | | 2015 | | | | | | | | | | | |
| | Male | | | | | | Female | | | | | | Male | | | | | | Female | | | | | |
	0-4 years	5-14 years	15-29 years	30-49 years	50-69 years	70+ years	0-4 years	5-14 years	15-29 years	30-49 years	50-69 years	70+ years	0-4 years	5-14 years	15-29 years	30-49 years	50-69 years	70+ years	0-4 years	5-14 years	15-29 years	30-49 years	50-69 years	70+ years
All Causes	201	30	165	264	1010	5483	164	23	53	137	652	4676	304	35	184	306	1141	6192	244	27	60	157	728	5461
Communicable & other Group I	88	3	9	27	61	447	69	3	8	20	41	420	178	6	11	37	79	490	139	5	11	23	48	459
Infectious and parasitic diseases	13	2	6	20	33	134	11	2	4	14	21	123	33	4	8	29	47	145	28	3	5	15	26	132
Tuberculosis	0	0	0	1	2	5	0	0	0	0	1	2	1	0	1	2	6	13	0	0	0	1	2	5
STDs excluding HIV	0	0	0	0	0	0	0	0	0	0	0	1	1	0	0	0	0	0	1	0	0	0	0	1
Syphilis	0	0	0	0	0	0	0	0	0	0	0	0	1	0	0	0	0	0	1	0	0	0	0	0
Chlamydia	0	0	0	0	0	0	0	0	0	0	0	0	0	0	0	0	0	0	0	0	0	0	0	0
Gonorrhoea	0	0	0	0	0	0	0	0	0	0	0	0	0	0	0	0	0	0	0	0	0	0	0	0
Trichomoniasis	0	0	0	0	0	0	0	0	0	0	0	0	0	0	0	0	0	0	0	0	0	0	0	0
Other STDs	0	0	0	0	0	0	0	0	0	0	0	0	0	0	0	0	0	0	0	0	0	0	0	1
HIV/AIDS	1	1	4	16	10	14	1	1	3	10	6	10	1	1	4	20	14	6	1	1	3	10	5	3
Diarrhoeal diseases	3	0	0	0	2	33	3	0	0	0	0	36	11	1	1	1	3	34	9	1	0	1	3	39
Childhood-cluster diseases	1	0	0	0	0	0	1	0	0	0	0	0	2	0	0	0	0	0	2	0	0	0	0	0
Whooping cough	0	0	0	0	0	0	0	0	0	0	0	0	1	0	0	0	0	0	1	0	0	0	0	0

» On the Tableau Start page, under the Connect header, click "Excel."

» Select the "Data Interpreter Example - WHO Death Projection" file, then click "Open."

Sheets in Excel are treated just like tables in a database. Since there is only one file displayed in the Data Source section, the data automatically appears on the Canvas.

» Preview the data. Since this is an Excel data source, Tableau recognizes that the data is eligible for Data Interpreter.

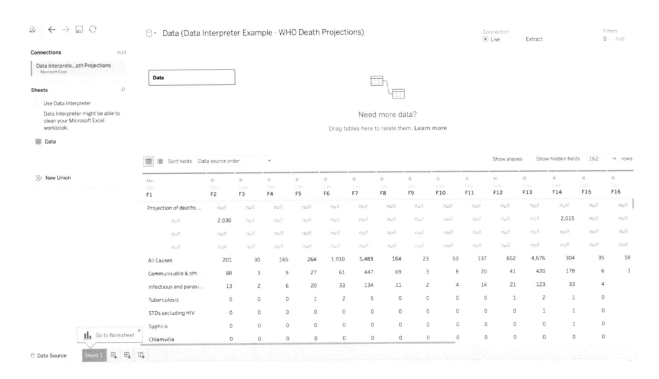

Data Interpreter scans all data to find Excel sheet areas convertible to well-structured tables, automatically discarding header/footer text and flattening multi-level table headers. If the sheet is already structured properly, these actions do not occur.

» Click the "Use Data Interpreter" box.

Data Interpreter looks for patterns of well-structured tables in the Excel data source. It re-structures only the Tableau data source, never modifying the underlying data file.

▲ Data Interpreter

When Data Interpreter is turned on, Tableau does its best to clean up titles, blank rows, multiple header rows, and other formatting anomalies. It will not, however, pivot or split fields automatically.

Data Interpreter works only on Excel workbooks.

To ensure quality control, look over Data Interpreter's modifications.

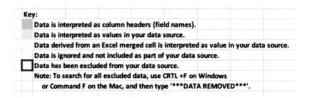

» Click "Review the results"; this opens a separate Tableau-generated Excel file.

The first spreadsheet tab is a color key that assists in clarifying Data Interpreter´s results.

Key:
- Data is interpreted as column headers (field names).
- Data is interpreted as values in your data source.
- Data derived from an Excel merged cell is interpreted as value in your data source.
- Data is ignored and not included as part of your data source.
- Data has been excluded from your data source.
- Note: To search for all excluded data, use CRTL +F on Windows or Command F on the Mac, and then type '***DATA REMOVED***'.

The next tab displays the underlying details of the changes Data Interpreter has made to the mirror file it created.

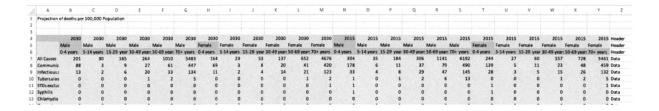

» Unless the viewer wishes to dismiss the changes, "Review the results" can be closed.

Pivot Tool

Data Interpreter correctly identifies data values and flattens multi-line column headers. This does not guarantee, however, that data is optimally structured. The table layout is in a cross-tab format—useful for report consumption, but not for data analysis. Year, Gender, and Age Range variables are spread across multiple columns, making it necessary to reduce columns to one per field. This can be done using the Pivot Tool. The number of rows then increases, providing a narrower data structure better suited for report creation in Tableau.

» Select the columns to be pivoted. Click the first column header "2030 Male 0-4 years."

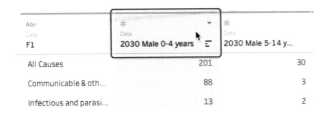

» Scroll all the way to the right and, while holding down the Shift key, click the last column header. This will highlight all columns from the first through the last selected one.

» Hover the cursor over the last selected column header to make its caret visible.

» Click the caret to display a dropdown menu, then select "Pivot."

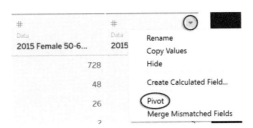

Pivoting displays multiple column headers in one column labeled "Pivot Field Names" and numeric values in a second column labeled "Pivot Field Values."

Abc Data F1	Abc Pivot Pivot Field Names	# Pivot Pivot Field Values
All Causes	2015 Female 0-4 years	244
All Causes	2015 Female 15-29 years	60
All Causes	2015 Female 30-49 years	157
All Causes	2015 Female 5-14 years	27
All Causes	2015 Female 50-69 years	728
All Causes	2015 Female 70+ years	5,461

Column-Splitting

"Pivot Field Names" contains multiple categorizations in one column. The column can be split into three columns; Year, Gender, and Age Range. Tableau´s Split and Custom Split text field functions identify patterns that use separator-characters such as hyphens, symbols, spaces, or a repeated pattern of values present in each row of the field. Splitting uses the separator to organize the values into individual columns. Our example will demonstrate a Custom Split, relying on a blank space as a separator.

» Right-click the "Pivot Field Names" header; select "Custom Split."

» Place the cursor in the "Use the separator" text box and enter one space by pressing the space bar. This action removes all greyed-out separators and replaces them with a single blank space to use as a separator.

» For "Split off"," select "First" and "3" columns, then click "OK."

» Right-click the "F1" column header, then select "Rename" from the menu.

» Rename it "Cause of Death."

» Right-click the "Pivot Field Names" column header, then select "Hide."

» Name the resulting three new columns "Year," "Gender," and "Age Range (years)."

» Rename "Pivot Field Values" "Projected Deaths per 100,000."

» Connect via "Extract"; do not select any filters.

» Click the data connection title, then rename it "WHO Deaths Projection per 100,000."

» Click "Go to Worksheet" (or New Worksheet icon to its right) to begin analysis.

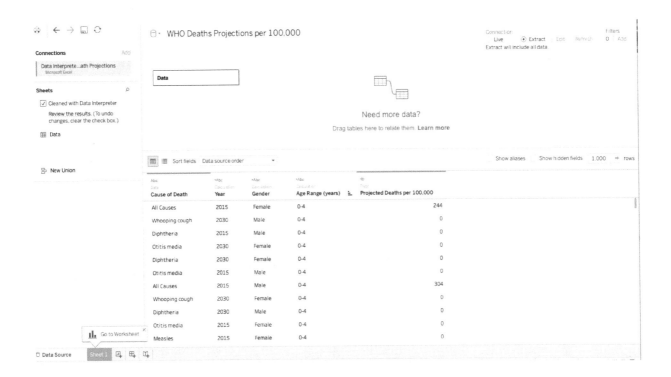

Basic Charts and Skills

CHAPTER 4

Text Tables

Text Table encodes words and numbers and arranges them in columns and rows. Also called "crosstabs" or "pivot tables," Text Tables are used to display simple relationships between quantitative values and corresponding categorical subdivisions. This structure makes tables ideal for looking up and comparing individual values. When deciding between building a Text Table and a chart, always think about how the information will be used. Choose a Text Table when your audience will need to either look up individual values or compare those values with precision.

How To: Build a Text Table to look up hospital annual discharges and case mix index by hospital service line.

Hospital Annual Discharges and Case Mix Index (CMI)
By Hospital Service Line

	Discharges ⤳	Case Mix Index (CMI)
General Medicine	15,475	1.9
Obstetrics	12,430	0.7
General Surgery	11,275	2.7
Cardiology	10,757	2.3
Cardiac/Vascular/Thoracic Surgery	9,256	2.9
Orthopedics	8,880	1.5
Pulmonary	8,775	1.5
Nephrology/Urology	6,550	1.1
Oncology	6,485	2.4
Neonatology	4,678	1.9
Neurology/NeuroSurgery	3,575	1.9
Gynecology	3,475	1.6
Otolaryngology	1,850	0.9
Psychiatry	975	0.8

Data Source: Mock hospital service line annual discharge counts and case mix index (CMI).

About the Data: Common hospital service lines were selected with mock counts of the annual number of hospital discharges. Case mix index (CMI) represents patient complexity and hospital resource needs. A higher CMI reflects a more complex and resource-intensive case load.

1 Connect to the data

» Open the file "Tableau for Healthcare – Charts Starter Workbook.twbx " downloaded from the HealthDataViz website.

» In the Data pane, click the caret to open the drop-down menu. Click on "Ch. 04 – Hospital Annual Discharges & Case Mix Index (CMI)" to select the dataset.

◄ **Data Source Navigation Layout**

When multiple datasets are present in a workbook, dragging the border between the Data window and the Tables window up will compress the dataset list into a drop down menu..

2 Create the chart

» Double-click the following three fields in the Data pane in this order:

- "Hospital Service Line"
- "Case Mix Index (CMI)"
- "Discharges"

Populating Fields Via Double-Click

There are several ways to populate a worksheet with data: double-clicking fields; dragging and dropping; typing directly onto a shelf; or using the Show Me button. When a field from the Data pane is double-clicked, Tableau makes its best guess as to where that field should go based on what is already populated in the active worksheet. The order of double-clicking will affect the data display, but fields can always be rearranged once they are on the worksheet.

The table initially looks like this:

Refresher ▶

Measure Names and Measure Values fields are Tableau's way of letting more than one measure appear in the same place. Tableau automatically adds these two fields to every data set, placing the Measure Names field beneath the dimensions, and the Measure Values field beneath the measures in the Data pane. For certain chart types, when multiple measures are used in the same location, Tableau automatically adds the Measure Names and Measure Values fields to the worksheet, and a Measures Values shelf appears showing the Measure fields present in the view.

3 Format the data

The next step is to format the data; Case Mix Index should be displayed with one decimal place.

» Right-click the "SUM(Case Mix Index (CMI))" field on the Measure Values shelf.

» Select "Format..."

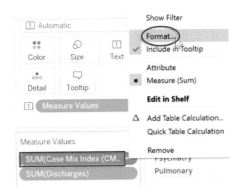

Selecting "Format" opens the Format pane, replacing the Data pane at the left of the screen.

>> Ensure the "Pane" tab is selected.

>> Click the caret to the right of the "Numbers" field to open the drop-down menu.

>> Select "Number (Custom)."

>> Change "Decimal places" to "1."

>> Click the "X" in the upper right corner of the Format pane to close it.

◄ Measure Formatting

By default, Tableau will typically display Measures in the same data format as the underlying data source. Adjusting formatting not only permits great precision (i.e., how many decimal places to include), but also allows correct formatting of elements such as percentages, monetary amounts, and numerical prefixes/suffixes.

Format Measures in one of two ways:

1. Default format change: *Change the default formatting from the Data pane, so all future uses of the Measure will display the new format. Selected formatting will then persist when the field appears in other worksheets.*

2. Single-use format change: *Change only the formatting of a Measure field already in the worksheet.*

To change the default format: *Right-click the field in the Data pane. Select Default Properties, then choose a new formatting option.*

To make a single-use format change: *Right-click the field already in the worksheet. Select Format; select Number drop-down; change to an appropriate format.*

4 Format the columns

The data columns need to be switched so that the "Discharges" data is displayed to the left of the "Case Mix Index (CMI)" data.

To transpose the columns:

» Drag and drop the "SUM(Case Mix Index (CMI))" field below the "SUM(Discharges)" field on the Measure Values shelf.

To ensure clear, readable column and row width formatting, adjust the width as follows:

» Hover the cursor between the first two columns until it changes to a horizontal, bi-directional arrow.

» Click and drag the divider to the right to completely display all text.

Column Sizing ▶

Column widths containing text can be customized as described above. Columns containing figures will remain proportional.

Row Sizing ▶

Rows will remain proportional and evenly spaced in a text table. Adjusting the height of one row by hovering and dragging will change all rows to maintain proportions.

Hospital Service Line	Dischar..	Case Mix Index (C..
Cardiac/Vascular/Thoraci..	9,256	2.9
Cardiology	10,757	2.3
General Medicine	15,475	1.9
General Surgery	11,275	2.7
Gynecology	3,475	1.6
Neonatology	4,678	1.9
Nephrology/Urology	6,550	1.1
Neurology/NeuroSurgery	3,575	1.9
Obstetrics	12,430	0.7
Oncology	6,485	2.4
Orthopedics	8,880	1.5
Otolaryngology	1,850	0.9
Psychiatry	975	0.8
Pulmonary	8,775	1.5

» Hover the cursor on the right edge of the "Case Mix Index (CMI)" column until it changes to a horizontal bi-directional arrow.

» Click and drag the width to completely display the column headers.

5 Sort the chart

The default Sort order is alphabetical by the single Dimension on the Row shelf—here, "Hospital Service Line." The desired order, however, is from highest to lowest, according to the number of Discharges. To sort in descending order:

» Click the Sort icon on the Toolbar for descending order.

Best Practice

Sorting is an important and powerful tool to direct an audience's attention.

62

6 Add a title

Add a title to the Text Table.

» Double-click the title row "Sheet 1" at the top left of the Work Area. A dialog box will appear.

◄ **Hide/Show Title Row**

The Title Row defaults to display on the worksheet. It can be hidden, if desired, by navigating to the Menu Bar, selecting the Worksheet option, and clicking Show Title to uncheck it. To redisplay the Title Row, click Show Title again.

» The Title text defaults to the generic Tableau worksheet number. Highlight and delete the current title, "<Sheet Name>".

» Enter the new title:

"Hospital Annual Discharges and Case Mix Index (CMI) By Hospital Service Line"

» Click "OK."

◄ **Title Formatting**

Titles provide a powerful tool for conveying metadata about a worksheet. In addition to including and formatting normal text, the Insert option at the top right of the Title menu screen can be used to add fields, data-connection information, and/or captions.

With "Hospital Service Line" incorporated in the chart title, the Dimension field label can be hidden.

» Right-click the Y-axis header label "Hospital Service Line."

» Click "Hide Field Labels for Rows."

Best Practice

Field headers are sometimes needed to clarify the Dimension being viewed. If, however, field members are well-defined (as with Hospital Service Line categories in this example), remove the headers to reduce clutter.

The final table looks like this:

63

Hospital Annual Discharges and Case Mix Index (CMI) By Hospital Service Line

	Discharges ⩯	Case Mix Index (CMI)
General Medicine	15,475	1.9
Obstetrics	12,430	0.7
General Surgery	11,275	2.7
Cardiology	10,757	2.3
Cardiac/Vascular/Thoracic Surgery	9,256	2.9
Orthopedics	8,880	1.5
Pulmonary	8,775	1.5
Nephrology/Urology	6,550	1.1
Oncology	6,485	2.4
Neonatology	4,678	1.9
Neurology/NeuroSurgery	3,575	1.9
Gynecology	3,475	1.6
Otolaryngology	1,850	0.9
Psychiatry	975	0.8

Insight: Presenting Hospital Service Lines in a text table allows the audience to see exact numbers in a clearly presented format. In this example, it is easy to tell that General Medicine has the highest number of discharges (15,475). Scanning the second column reveals that Cardiac/Vascular/Thoracic Surgery has the highest Case Mix Index (2.9).

7 **Rename the worksheet tab and save the worksheet**

» Right-click the "Sheet 1" tab at the bottom of the screen.

» Click "Rename Sheet."

» Enter a new title—"Text: Discharges & CMI"—then press Enter.

» Click the Save icon on the Toolbar.

Best Practice

Always use intuitive names for worksheets to keep them organized and easier to find.

Best Practice

Save, save, and then save again! Tableau has an auto-recovery feature, however saving during and after each chart is constructed is a sensible habit.

CHAPTER 5

Bar Charts

Bar Charts are the most effective way to compare values across Dimensions or Measures, where the value of the Measure is represented by the length of the bar, revealing high and low values at a glance. One axis of the chart shows the specific categories being compared; the other represents the value. Sorting (ranking) data in descending order highlights high values; ascending order highlights low values. Because Bar Charts encode data values according to the length of the bar, they should begin at the value zero. (Tableau´s default value for Bar Charts is therefore zero.)

5.1 Horizontal and Vertical Bar Charts

How To: Build a Bar Chart to compare rates of patient falls per 1,000 patient days across types of care for a single hospital.

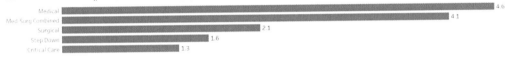

Rate of Patient Falls (per 1,000 Patient Days) by Type of Adult Care Unit for FY2019

Data Source: *Mock patient-fall data*

About the Data: *The American Nurses Association (ANA) National Database of Nursing Quality Indicators (NDNQI®) is a repository for nursing-sensitive indicators, reported at the nursing-unit level, designed to provide comparative information to hospitals for use in quality improvement activities. For this exercise, we created mock patient-fall data, similar to that captured by the NDNQI and other groups such as the Centers for Medicare & Medicaid (CMS), to compare patient-fall rates per 1,000 patient days across types of care for a single hospital.*

1 **Create a New Worksheet and Connect to the Data**

》 A new worksheet can be created in one of three ways:

Option 1: Select "Worksheet" on the Menu Bar and then select "New Worksheet."

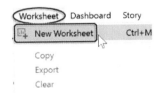

Option 2: Click the "New Worksheet" tab at the very bottom of the workbook.

Option 3: Click the "New Worksheet" icon on the toolbar.

» To select the dataset, click the caret in the dataset menu of the Data pane then click "Ch. 05 – Hospital Patient Falls (2019)."

2 Create the Chart

From the Data pane,

» Drag and drop "Type of Adult Care Unit" onto the Rows shelf.

» Drag and drop "Total Falls Rate" onto the Columns shelf.

Drag and Drop

Tableau's Drag and Drop interface makes it easy to explore data and test different visualizations quickly. Tableau also permits dragging a field already in the worksheet to another place on the worksheet to change the visualization.

Primary Data Source ▶

Notice that once a field is added to the sheet, the data source for that field is marked with a blue check mark icon. This indicates the primary data source for this worksheet. Data from other sources can be combined with this primary data source only by using a technique called "Data Blending," which will be covered in the Data Blending chapter.

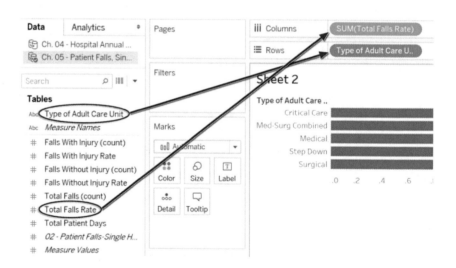

Aggregation

Note: *In this example, each Type of Adult Care Unit represents one row in the dataset. Therefore, Sum, Average, Median, Minimum, and Maximum of Total Falls Rate will return the same result. Count and Count (Distinct), however, will not. It is important to notice how a measure is being aggregated in a report. A Sum will provide a different result from that of a Count.*

Change the aggregation in one of two ways:

Aggregation of the worksheet Field: *this is a one-time change to the aggregation of a field already present in the worksheet. Right-click the field, click Measure, then select the desired aggregation.*

Aggregation of the data source Measure: *this will change the default aggregation so the change will persist when the field is used in other worksheets. Right-click the field in the Data pane, click Default Properties > Aggregation, then select the desired aggregation.*

3 Sort and Format the Chart

The default Sort order is alphabetical by the single Dimension on the Row shelf—here, "Type of Adult Care Unit." The desired order, however, is from highest to lowest, according to the Measure "SUM(Total Falls Rate)." To make the necessary change, access the quick Sort icon in one of the following two ways:

Option 1: Click the Sort icon on the Toolbar for ascending or descending order.

Option 2: Hover over the top of the chart to display the Sort icon, then click to select the desired ranking order—once to sort descending, twice to sort ascending, and a third time to return to the default order.

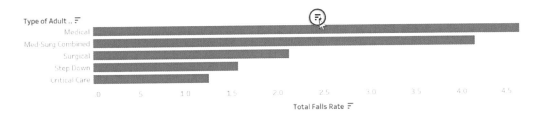

▲ End-User Sorting

The Sort icon in the Measure header and Measure axis are visible to the end-user as well as to the report-builder. Hovering over the Measure header or axis makes the icon appear, allowing viewers to sort with one click. This option can be disabled, if desired, by clicking on Worksheet on the Menu Bar and unchecking Show Sort Controls.

The Dimension, Type of Adult Care Unit, is now sorted by the Measure, Total Falls Rate, from the highest rate to the lowest.

To label each bar with the Total Falls Rate:

» In the Toolbar, click the framed "[T]" icon. The label will appear automatically.

Labeling ▶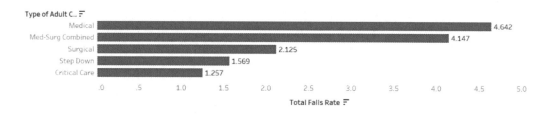

Alternatively, click Label on the Marks card, then click the box "Show mark labels." There are additional formatting options under Label.

The chart now looks like this:

Type of Adult C.. ⊤
Medical	4.642
Med-Surg Combined	4.147
Surgical	2.125
Step Down	1.569
Critical Care	1.257

.0   .5   1.0   1.5   2.0   2.5   3.0   3.5   4.0   4.5   5.0

Total Falls Rate ⊤

Best Practice

By default, Tableau bar and line graphs start at zero so as not to obscure bar or line length or distort the message in the data.

In the above image, the bar labels are carried out to the third decimal. This is unnecessary and creates clutter. To limit the label to one decimal place:

» Right-click "SUM(Total Falls Rate)" on the Columns shelf.

» In the appearing menu, select "Format…"

» In the Format pane at the left of the screen, select the "Pane" tab.

» Under "Default," click the "Numbers" caret to open the drop-down menu.

» Select "Number (Custom)."

» Change "Decimal places" to 1.

» Click the X at the top right of the Format pane to close it and return to the Data pane.

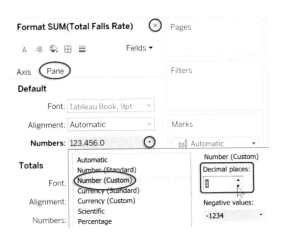

To hide the X axis:

» Right-click the X axis.

» Select "Show Header" to remove the checkmark and hide the X axis.

Best Practice

Since the labels in this report are visible on each bar, the X axis can be hidden to reduce visual clutter. The decision to do this depends on the level of precision needed.

To remove the field label:

» Right-click the header label ("Type of Adult Care Unit").

» Click "Hide Field Labels for Rows."

4 **Add a title**

» Double-click the Title Row at the top of the Work Area. A dialog box will appear.

» Highlight and delete the current title "<Sheet Name>."

» Enter the new title: "Rate of Patient Falls (per 1,000 Patient Days) by Type of Adult Care Unit for FY2019"

69

» Click "OK."

5 Rename the worksheet tab and save the worksheet

» Double-click the "Sheet 2" tab at the bottom of the screen.

» In the highlighted text, enter the new title, "Bar: Patient Falls" then click "Enter."

» Select "Save" to save the file.

The final bar chart looks like this:

Insight: The chart now makes it clear that in this example hospital for FY2019, Medical has the highest rate of patient falls per 1,000 patient days (4.6), while Critical Care has the lowest rate (1.3).

5.2 Bar Chart Variants: Side-by-Side Charts and Stacked Bar Charts

Side-by-Side and Stacked Bar Charts are variations of simple bar charts. Placing bars side by side to compare several variables enables use of both color and placement for enhanced data interpretation.

Stacked Bar Charts can be useful for the display of some part-to-whole data, but it is important to note that in the presence of numerous variables, a viewer's ability to quantify them is severely compromised. It is better to limit use of Stacked Bar Charts to the display of only two to three different variables. Use other types of charts, such as Small Multiples, to enhance display and interpretation of this type of data.

How To: Build a Side-by-Side Bar Chart and a Stacked Bar Chart as options to compare patient-falls rates per 1,000 patient days with and without injury across a range of types of adult care units.

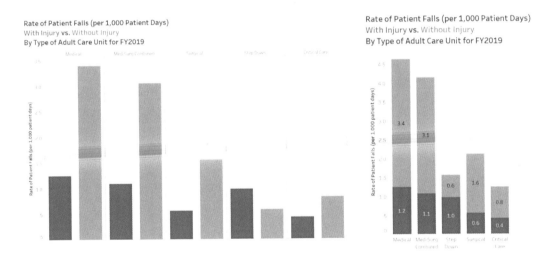

Data Source: Mock patient-fall data for a single hospital for FY2019

About the Data: The American Nurses Association (ANA) National Database of Nursing Quality Indicators (NDNQI®) is a repository for nursing-sensitive indicators, reported at the nursing-unit level, designed to provide comparative information to hospitals for use in quality-improvement activities. For this exercise, we created mock patient-fall data, similar to that captured by the NDNQI and other groups, such as the Centers for Medicare & Medicaid (CMS), to compare patient-fall and falls-with-injury rates per 1,000 patient days across types of care for a single hospital.

1 **Create a new worksheet and connect to the data**

   » At the bottom of the Tableau workspace, click the icon for a new worksheet.

   » In the Data pane, select the "Ch. 05 – Hospital Patient Falls (2019)."

2 **Create the chart**

   » Holding down the Control key, click the following fields in the Data pane:

- "Type of Adult Care Unit"
- " Falls With Injury Rate"
- "Falls Without Injury Rate"

》 Click the "Show Me" tab.

》 Select the "side-by-side bars" image.

Show Me ▶

When several fields are either selected in the Data pane or present in the active worksheet, the Show Me menu highlights the most likely visualizations to fit the specific combination of Dimensions and Measures present. Choosing one of these options rearranges the fields onto the appropriate cards and shelves to create the chosen chart type. (Note: Tableau can only make its best guess; adjustments are often necessary.)

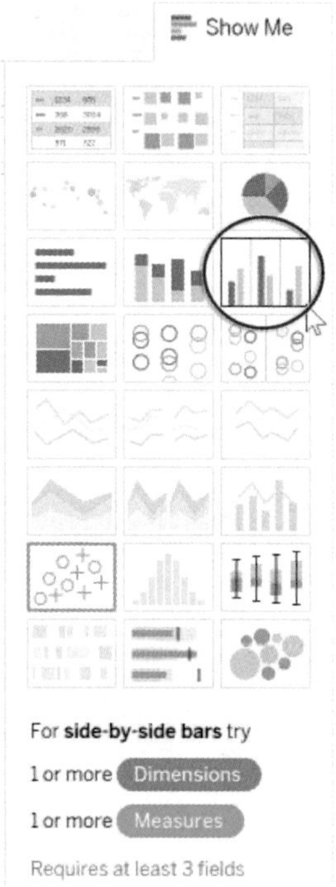

◀ **Show Me Recommendations**

At the bottom of the Show Me menu, Tableau lists the number of Dimensions, Measures, and date fields necessary to create a particular visualization. Hovering over a grayed-out chart type reveals how many and what types of fields are needed to create that chart.

》 Click the "Show Me" tab again to close the tab.

Tableau's Show Me feature has automatically added a field called "Measure Names" to Color on the Marks card. A different color is assigned to each field on the Measure Values shelf.

The chart now looks like this:

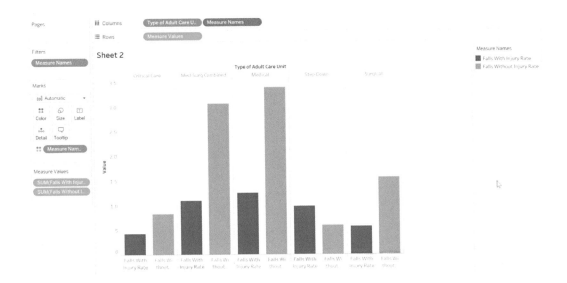

3 Format the chart

When two or more Measures display on the same axis, Tableau labels the axis "Value" by default. To edit the axis title:

» Right-click the Y axis.

» Select "Edit Axis..."

» Under the Axis Titles section, change the title to "Rate of Patient Falls (per 1,000 patient days)."

» Click the "X" at the top right of the Edit Axis dialog box to close it.

◄ **Edit Axis**

Tableau automatically populates a chart axis with a header, number range, and tick marks. Right-clicking an axis and selecting "Edit Axis..." will present a menu of customizable axis options. On the General tab, Tableau automatically sets the axis range to account for the minimum and maximum values in the visualization. A fixed range with a static start and end may be selected, or alternative range settings may be considered. The title may be edited or removed; the axis scale may be Reversed or Logarithmic. Modify tick marks by using the Tick Marks tab.

Widen the columns so that labels are fully visible:

» Hover the cursor over the far-right column divider until it changes to a horizontal, bi-directional arrow.Drag the column indicator to the appropriate width.

Remove the unneeded header "Type of Adult Care Unit":

» Right-click the column header "Type of Adult Care Unit" at the top of the chart.

» Select "Hide Field Labels for Columns."

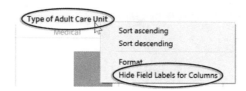

Edit the chart colors.

» Hover over the "Measure Names" color legend header to the right of the chart.

» Click the appearing drop-down caret in the right corner of the legend.

» From the appearing menu, select "Edit colors..."

» Click the caret for the Color Palette drop-down and select "Color Blind."

» Click the "Falls With Injury Rate" data item in the left column to highlight it, then click a blue color in the Color Blind color palette.

» Click the "Falls Without Injury Rate" data item, then click a light gray color in the color palette.

» Click "OK."

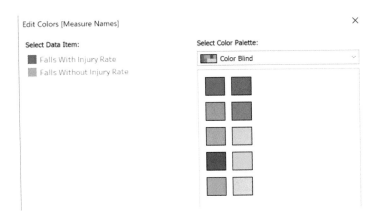

◄ Advanced Color Editing

Double-clicking a color on the Select Data Item column opens an advanced color selection menu, enabling the user to select any color across the spectrum, pick a color visible on the screen, or input an RGB or hex code for more precise color selection.

Sort the bars from highest to lowest. Note that with two fields on the Column shelf, clicking the quick Sort icon will default the sort to the most nested field (that is, the field farthest to the right on the shelf—in this case, the Measure Names field). If applying the Sort to the "Type of Adult Care Unit" dimension is desired, the corresponding field must be highlighted before the quick sort is selected.

» Click the "Type of Adult Care Unit" field on the Columns shelf to highlight it.

» Click the Descending Sort icon on the Toolbar.

The chart now looks like this:

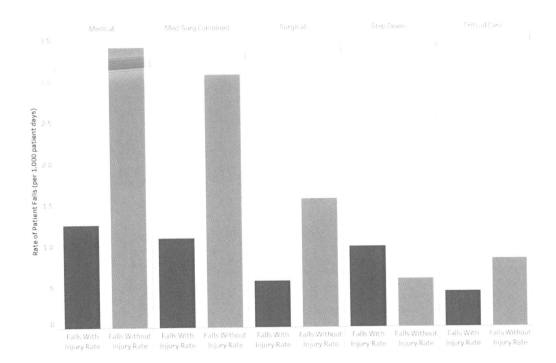

▲ Sorting Measure Values

When more than one Measure is present in the Sort (as in this Side-by-Side chart), Tableau will, by default, sort on the aggregation of the Measures.

4 Add a title

» Double-click on the Title Row at the top of the workspace to open the Edit Title dialog box.

» Highlight and delete the default title, "<Sheet Name>."

» Enter the title:

"Rate of Patient Falls (per 1,000 Patient Days)
With Injury vs. Without Injury
By Type of Adult Care Unit for FY2019"

» The bars and their labels in the title should be color-coordinated for clarity. Highlight "With Injury" and click the Color icon. Change the color to blue.

» Perform the same steps for "Without Injury," changing the color to light gray.

With the bar categories identified by color in the title, the Measure Names headers may now be hidden.

» Right-click any header below the bars.

» Click "Show Header" to remove the checkmark.

The final Side-by-Side Bar Chart looks like this:

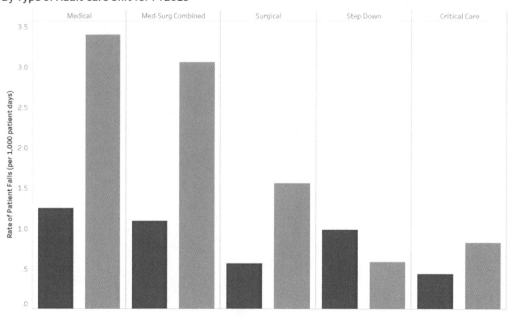

Rate of Patient Falls (per 1,000 Patient Days)
With Injury vs. Without Injury
By Type of Adult Care Unit for FY2019

5 **Rename the worksheet tab and duplicate the worksheet**

>> Double-click the Sheet Tab at the bottom of the workspace.

>> Enter a new name, "Side-by-Side Bar: Patient Falls."

>> Right-click the renamed Sheet Tab, then select "Duplicate Sheet."

▲ **Duplicate Worksheets**

Duplicating an existing worksheet to create a new report is a common time-saver in Tableau. Duplicated sheets retain all filters, titles, and formatting customizations of the original sheet. Duplicating sheets is also a great way to test different chart variations without altering the original view.

6 **Stack the bars**

To change each pair of side-by-side bars to a stacked bar:

>> Drag the "Measure Names" field off the Columns shelf and drop it onto any gray non-workspace area to delete it.

◀ **Removing Fields**

As the field is being dragged to the gray area, a small red X should appear just under the cursor. This X indicates that once the mouse is released, the field will disappear. If the red X is not visible, the field will not be removed.

Why Not Select "Stacked Bar" in Show Me?

The stacked bar option in Show Me plots a single Measure on the worksheet as a bar and breaks out the color of this bar based on the categories from a single, selected Dimension. However, the visualization in this chapter requires two chart Measures to be stacked one atop the other. This display is best accomplished by selecting the side-by-side option, then dragging the Measure Names field off the shelf and into the gray non-workspace area.

The Measures are now stacked for each Type of Adult Care Unit. The Sort previously performed on the aggregation of the two Measures is easy to see in this chart. The Falls With Injury Rate values are visible at the top of the bars; for better comparison of these smaller values, reorient the Falls With Injury Rate values to the bottom of the bars, aligning the measures at the same point on the axis (i.e. at 0).

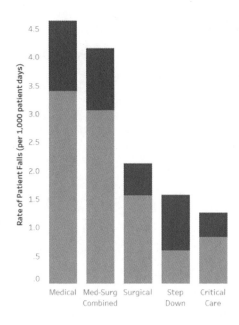

To transpose the bars in each pane:

» On the Measure Values shelf, drag and drop the "SUM (Falls With Injury Rate)" field below the "SUM(Falls Without Injury Rate)."

The chart now looks like this:

Best Practice

In stacked bar chart, orient the most important measure at the bottom so the comparison begins at the same spot (i.e. at 0) on the axis.

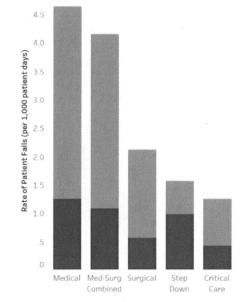

7 Format the chart

In the Side-by-Side Bar chart exercise, the Sort was performed on the selected field using the "quick" Sort icon. Because there were two Measures represented by the Measure Values field on the Rows shelf, Tableau sorted on the aggregation of the two Measures. To sort on a single Measure (for example, Falls With Injury Rate), use the Sort dialog box.

» Right-click the "Type of Adult Care Unit" field on the Columns shelf.

» Select the "Sort..." option.

» In the "Sort By" section, click the drop-down caret and select "Field."

» In the "Sort Order" section, select "Descending."

» In the "Field Name" section, click the caret and select the field "Falls With Injury Rate."

◀ Sort by Field

The Sort menu provides additional flexibility and precision for ordering data. This feature permits sorting based on data-source order, alphabetical order, or any valid aggregation of a Dimension or Measure within the selected dataset. (The field being sorted does not need to be on a shelf in the worksheet.) It is important to specify ascending (from smallest to largest) or descending (from largest to smallest) sort order.

» Click the X in the top right corner to close the dialog box.

The blue bars, representing Falls With Injury Rate, are now sorted from highest to lowest.

79

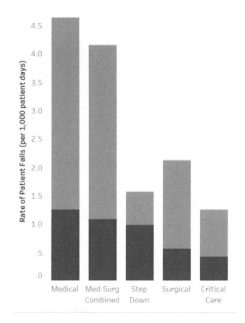

For clarity, add labels to the newly created stacked bars.

>> Click the "[T]" icon on the Toolbar.

Reduce the label values to one decimal place:

>> Right-click the "Measure Values" field on the Rows shelf.

>> Select "Format..."

>> Select the "Pane" tab.

>> Under "Default," click the "Numbers" caret to open the drop-down menu.

>> Select "Number (Custom)."

>> Change "Decimal places" to 1.

>> Click the X in the top right of the Format pane to close.

8 Rename the worksheet tab and save the worksheet

>> Double-click the worksheet tab at the bottom of the screen.

>> In the highlighted text, enter the new title, "Stacked Bar: Patient Falls," then click "Enter."

>> Click the "Save" icon on the Toolbar.

The final Stacked Bar Chart looks like this:

Rate of Patient Falls (per 1,000 Patient Days)
With Injury vs. Without Injury
By Type of Adult Care Unit for FY2019

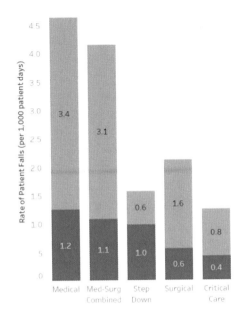

Insight: Medical has both the highest rate of falls (4.6) and the highest rate of falls with injury (1.2) per 1,000 patient days.

CHAPTER 6

Formatting

Formatting requires skill, patience, and meticulous attention to detail. Some people find it tedious; but good formatting reveals the story in your healthcare data with clarity and simplicity. If on the other hand, you burden your text with inconsistent fonts (mismatched in type, size, or color), odd alignments, or distracting lines, your audience must wade through the visual "noise" to find that story. Drawing on the best practices of data visualization to effectively format your charts will help move your reports and dashboards (and all your hard work) from good to great.

Tableau incorporates many visualization best practices into the default designs of its tables and graphs; however, additional formatting may be required, depending on the data in the view, the available space, and the message to be conveyed by the chart. Tableau's formatting options (specifically, Fonts, Alignment, Shading, Borders, and Lines) allow the report-creator to customize the visualization's appearance and to focus the message.

Consider the following best practices for these formatting options:

Shading/Borders/Lines

- Keep in mind a fundamental principal: maximize the "data-ink to non-data-ink ratio" (Tufte, 93). The "data ink" should be showcased on the page, while the "non-data ink" should play a supporting role to the chart, helping to convey, and not distract from, the message of the data.

- Ask this question about each component of a chart: "Would the data suffer any loss of meaning or impact if this element were not present?" If the answer is "no," then remove it. (Few, 142). Any non-data ink that makes the cut should be muted so that it doesn't compete with the data ink.

In the "Don't do this" example below, the non-data ink—gridlines, column shading, font bolding, unnecessary labels ("Sex" and "Age Range/Date"), decimals out to two places, redundancy in Y axis and line labeling—is overwhelming the data ink.

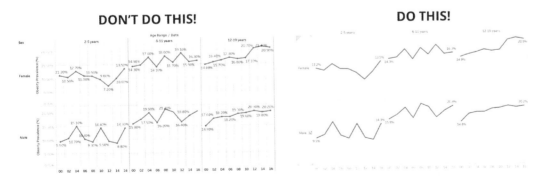

Remember, non-data ink needs to play a supporting role to strengthen the message in the data, not distract from it.

Fonts

- Should be as legible as possible

- Should be consistent throughout reports

- Should have a number set that lines up properly and is clear and easy to read

Fortunately, Tableau has default font selections suited for data visualization, but font style still requires consideration.

Choose Sans-Serif Fonts for Visualizations

A serif font has embellishments that look like little feet attached at a 45- or 90-degree angle to the upright lines of the font, linking the letters one to the next so they appear connected and flow across the page. For example: this text is printed in a serif font. Fonts with serifs are intended for a long sequence of words that exceeds one line. Though research is inconclusive, such fonts are considered by many to be easier to read for printed text, but can make reading on screens difficult, depending on resolution.

Serif font   Sans-Serif font

Conversely, sans-serif fonts (sans = "without") do not have the little feet. They are simpler and easier to take in at a glance—a good choice for labels and titles on graphs and charts, or for data displayed in a table. As this discussion makes clear, sans-serif fonts are the best choice for visualizations.

Alignment

- Quantitative values should be right-justified so that the numbers line up: the ones, tens, hundreds, and so on fall correctly into columns.

- Text usually works best when it's left-justified, because readers in Western cultures read left to right (the opposite would apply for audiences who read right to left).

The example below compares two text tables: one containing left-justified text and right-justified numbers; the other with centered text and numbers. The centered text is difficult to read because our focus must adjust to the place where the text begins and that point shifts on each line. Further, centered numbers are difficult to read, understand, and compare because their digits do not line up evenly.

Left-Justified Text and Right-Justified Numbers

	Discharges ⯾	Case Mix Index (CMI)
General Medicine	15,475	1.9
Obstetrics	12,430	0.7
General Surgery	11,275	2.7
Cardiology	10,757	2.3
Cardiac/Vascular/Thoracic Surgery	9,256	2.9
Orthopedics	8,880	1.5
Pulmonary	8,775	1.5
Nephrology/Urology	6,550	1.1
Oncology	6,485	2.4
Neonatology	4,678	1.9
Neurology/NeuroSurgery	3,575	1.9
Gynecology	3,475	1.6
Otolaryngology	1,850	0.9
Psychiatry	975	0.8

Centered Text and Numbers

	Discharges ⯾	Case Mix Index (CMI)
General Medicine	15,475	1.9
Obstetrics	12,430	0.7
General Surgery	11,275	2.7
Cardiology	10,757	2.3
Cardiac/Vascular/Thoracic Surgery	9,256	2.9
Orthopedics	8,880	1.5
Pulmonary	8,775	1.5
Nephrology/Urology	6,550	1.1
Oncology	6,485	2.4
Neonatology	4,678	1.9
Neurology/NeuroSurgery	3,575	1.9
Gynecology	3,475	1.6
Otolaryngology	1,850	0.9
Psychiatry	975	0.8

Formatting Hierarchy in Tableau

Formatting defaults and customization can be applied at different levels, from the overall Workbook level, to individual Worksheets, and down to individual parts of a view. Understanding the levels will help guide formatting-option selection.

1) **Workbook** - Formatting at the Workbook level affects all Worksheets, Dashboards, and Stories in any single workbook. Workbook Themes, Fonts, and Lines are formatting options at this level.

2) **Worksheet** - Formatting at the Worksheet level affects either the entire active Sheet or its Rows or Columns only. Worksheet-level formatting choices are Font, Alignment, Shading, Borders, and Lines.

3) **Individual Components** - The individual components of a chart include Headers, Axes, Panes, Labels, Lines, and Title. The available formatting options are component-specific.

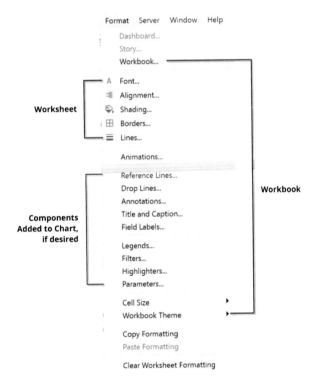

◄ **Format Menu**

Selecting "Format" from the Menu bar accesses formatting options at Workbook and Worksheet levels.

Default (intrinsic) chart components can most efficiently be modified by right-clicking them directly in the chart. (That is, features built into charts are best managed by right-clicking.) Optional features can be formatted from the menu shown at left. If you cannot find a feature you wish to modify on the menu, try right-clicking that feature in the chart.

Formatting at the Workbook Level

Two main components can be formatted at the Workbook level: Workbook Theme and Workbook Fonts & Lines.

Workbook Theme

Each of the four available Workbook Themes corresponds to a version of Tableau Desktop.

1) **Default:** Version 10.0 and higher

2) **Previous:** Versions 8 and 9.3

3) **Modern:** Versions 3.5 to 7.0

4) **Classic:** Versions 1.0 to 3.2

To view these themes:

» Click "Format" on the Menu Bar.

» Select the "Workbook Themes" option.

Workbooks retain the themes originally selected for them even when Tableau versions change.

In our training workbooks, the Workbook Theme is set to "Default."

Workbook - Fonts & Lines

Fonts in Tableau Desktop can be set at the Workbook level to ensure consistency across Worksheets, Dashboards, and Stories. To do this:

» Click "Format" on the Menu Bar.

» Select "Workbook..."

The Format pane on the left of the screen displays editing options for Fonts and Lines. Fonts for several high-level components of the workbook can be controlled here. Choose All (all fonts across all Worksheets, Dashboards, and Stories), or specific components (Worksheets, Tooltips, and Titles for Worksheet, Dashboard, and/or Story).

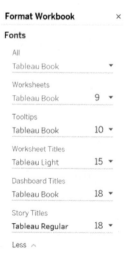

The default font is "Tableau," a custom font created to meet best practice criteria. It is available in six styles:

Tableau Light
Tableau Book
Tableau Regular
Tableau Medium
Tableau Semibold
Tableau Bold

The Worksheet Titles in this training workbook have been changed from Tableau Light to Tableau Medium and the font size has been reduced to 14. This change both demonstrates how to change a font and highlights titles more effectively.

◀ **Edited Settings**

When a default setting is changed, a dot appears to the left of the selected option. This visual cue is a helpful guide in future editing. Clicking the "Reset to Defaults" button at the bottom of the pane clears all edits.

Formatting Lines—Grid, Zero, Trend, Reference, and Drop, as well as Axis Rulers and Ticks—ensures a consistent look across the Workbook. Editing options include Line type, weight, color, and opacity, as well as an option to turn them all "Off".

Gridlines can serve to orient the viewer; however, since they are non-data ink, removing them often results in a cleaner look. The Gridlines in this training workbook have been set to "Off."

Formatting changes can be made at any point and will apply globally to both existing and new Worksheets, Dashboards, and Stories.

Formatting at the Worksheet Level

Worksheets can be individually formatted; use the Format menu on the Menu bar of the currently active worksheet. Font, Alignment, Shading, Borders, and Lines display editing options for the Sheet, Rows, or Columns.

Selecting any format option from the menu opens a Format pane on the left of the screen, replacing the Data pane. In the screenshot below, the Font option icon has been selected. The Format Pane Header indicates the selection; the corresponding icon is outlined with a square. Icons in the Format pane enable easy navigation among Worksheet formatting options. (The Field Selector will be discussed in the next section.)

Format Pane Header

Three tabs—Sheet, Rows, and Columns—offer access to formatting options at the Worksheet level.

- **Sheet** means the currently active worksheet. Any editing under the Sheet tab affects the entire Worksheet (exclusive of Title and Tooltip).

- **Rows** run horizontally across the active Worksheet and are represented by discrete or continuous fields. If a discrete field is on the Rows shelf, the rows are easy to distinguish; a continuous field, however, with its axis, looks like one big row. Editing under the Rows tab affects all rows in the chart.

- **Columns** run vertically through the active Worksheet and can also be represented by discrete or continuous fields. If a discrete field is on the Columns shelf, the columns are easy to distinguish; a continuous field, however, with its axis, looks like one big column. Editing under the Columns tab affects all columns in the chart.

Two commonly used Worksheet format options are Row/Column Dividers (using the Borders option) and Row/Column Shading (using the Shading option). Both help the viewer to keep track of figure alignment while reading the chart.

Steps to Format the Row/Column Dividers

If the Format pane is open, click the "Borders" icon in the top row of icons; otherwise, click "Format" in the Menu Bar, then select "Borders."

The Sheet tab displays options for both the Row and Column Dividers. Each Divider section displays Pane, Header, and Level formatting options.

- **Pane** displays data marks.

- **Header** shows Dimension members labeling the view.

- **Level** controls where formatting occurs, depending on the number of fields on the Row/Column shelf.

In the example below, a text table will be formatted with Row dividers. (Column dividers are formatted in the same way.) The Row Divider Pane and Header each displays the selection of a thin, light-gray line. The Level slider, however, is at the far left, essentially showing "no level" of divider; the resulting chart has no Row Divider lines.

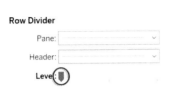

Age Range	Sex	Obesity Prevalence (%)
2-5 years	Female	13.5%
	Male	14.3%
6-11 years	Female	16.3%
	Male	20.4%
12-19 years	Female	20.9%
	Male	20.2%

Slide the Row Divider Level to the right; Row Divider lines appear. The number of Dimensions on the corresponding Row shelf (in this case, two Dimensions, Age Range and Sex) determines the number of available levels.

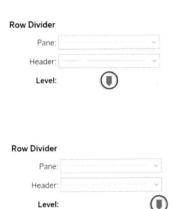

Age Range	Sex	Obesity Prevalence (%)
2-5 years	Female	13.5%
	Male	14.3%
6-11 years	Female	16.3%
	Male	20.4%
12-19 years	Female	20.9%
	Male	20.2%

Age Range	Sex	Obesity Prevalence (%)
2-5 years	Female	13.5%
	Male	14.3%
6-11 years	Female	16.3%
	Male	20.4%
12-19 years	Female	20.9%
	Male	20.2%

Steps to Format the Row/Column Shading

Shading can be applied to Rows or Columns in bands of color to make data easier to differentiate. Click the paint-bucket icon to access Shading options.

Row and Column Banding options here (under the Sheet tab) are the same as for Dividers described above. In each Banding section, Pane, Header, and Banding Size options are available. If more than one Dimension shares a Row or Column shelf, the Level option also appears. The Banding Size slider permits banding every other row/column or every two, three, four, or more rows/columns.

The examples below display two of the options for the Row Band Size slider. (The banding color has been darkened for better visibility here.)

Hospital Service Line	Discharges	Case Mix Index (CMI)
General Medicine	15,475	1.9
Obstetrics	12,430	0.7
General Surgery	11,275	2.7
Cardiology	10,757	2.3
Cardiac/Vascular/Thoracic Surgery	9,256	2.9
Orthopedics	8,880	1.5
Pulmonary	8,775	1.5
Nephrology/Urology	6,550	1.1
Oncology	6,485	2.4
Neonatology	4,678	1.9
Neurology/NeuroSurgery	3,575	1.9

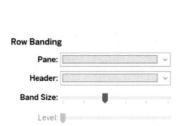

Hospital Service Line		Discharges	Case Mix Index (CMI)
General Medicine		15,475	1.9
Obstetrics		12,430	0.7
General Surgery		11,275	2.7
Cardiology		10,757	2.3
Cardiac/Vascular/Thoracic Surgery		9,256	2.9
Orthopedics		8,880	1.5
Pulmonary		8,775	1.5
Nephrology/Urology		6,550	1.1
Oncology		6,485	2.4
Neonatology		4,678	1.9

Other Worksheet Formatting

Formatting options on the Format menu bar can be applied specifically to features that have been added to the chart: Animations of chart values; Reference Lines, Drop Lines, Annotations, Title & Captions, and Field Labels in the chart; and Legends, Filters, Highlighters, and Parameters positioned at the periphery of the chart.

Animations can help to identify pattern changes in the data, highlighting how data clumps together or teases apart when filters, parameters, set actions, and/or sorting is applied.

Tableau's animation default is set to "off." When activating animations, settings include:

- **Workbook** or a **Selected Sheet**

- **Duration:** set the animation speed fast or slow or select a custom speed

- **Style:** choose Simultaneous (all values adjust at the same time) or Sequential (values adjust in a step-by-step pattern)

◄ Animations

Animations stylistically show the movement of data elements when filters, parameters, or other interactive capabilities are applied to a chart. They can either enhance or detract from a visualization's message, so be cautious and deliberate in their application, especially in dashboards with multiple worksheets. Animations can add an appealing aesthetic to help users trace the movement of data as the chart changes, but can also possibly overwhelm the visualization—and the viewer—if overutilized.

Formatting Individual Chart Components

The same formatting options—Font, Alignment, Shading, Borders, and Lines—available for Sheets, Rows, and Columns can be applied specifically to individual components of a chart. Such components include Headers, created by discrete (blue) fields; Axes, continuous (green) fields; Panes (where data marks are displayed); Axis Titles; Field Labels; Mark Labels; and Totals (if displayed). The available formatting options are determined by the selected component.

Access these components in one of two ways, with Option 1 recommended:

> **Option 1:** Right-click a relevant chart element.
> * Right-click the field or component on the chart.
> * Select "Format" from the submenu.

Pane Formatting

Right-clicking in the Pane seems like a natural approach to formatting mark labels, but it does not open the necessary formatting controls; instead, the global Format Font controls for the worksheet appear. For a precise and targeted path to formatting in the pane, right-click the Header, the Axis, or the field itself. Additional formatting options for labels in the Pane are located under Label on the Marks card.

Option 2: Format using the Menu bar.

- Click "Format" on the Menu bar.
- Select the desired Formatting option: Font, Alignment, Shading, Borders, or Lines.
- Click the "Fields" caret.
- Select the field corresponding to the component to be formatted.

The Format pane will remain open until manually closed (click the "X" in the top right corner).

Header, Axis, Pane Formatting

The most commonly formatted sections of a chart are the Header, Axis, and/or Pane. It is important to identify which field on the Rows or Columns shelf generates the specific component to be formatted. Discrete (blue) fields create Header labels; continuous (green) fields create Axes. The Pane displays the Measure figures as "marks" (in the example below, the marks are bars).

The Bar chart created in a previous chapter (with the axis re-displayed), highlights these components.

- **Header** represents the Dimension "Type of Adult Care Unit" field on the Rows shelf.

- **Axis** represents the Measure "SUM(Total Falls Rate)" field on the Columns shelf.

- **Pane** displays the marks for the Measure "SUM (Total Falls Rate)."

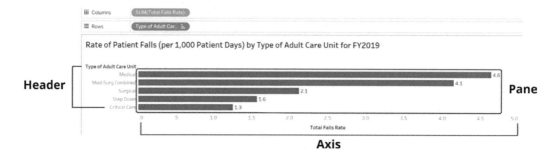

Availability of formatting options is determined by individual chart components:

- **Header:** any Font (type, size, style), Alignment, Shading, and Totals label used can be formatted.

- **Axis:** any Font, Shading, Scale layout along the axis, and Title font can be formatted.

- **Pane:** any Font, Alignment, Numbers, and Totals used can be formatted.

Because numbers need to be presented in a variety of ways, it is helpful to have multiple formatting options. Fortunately, Tableau offers several: Number (Custom) and Percentage (with Decimal place adjustment) are most commonly used in this manual.

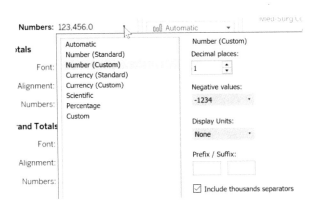

Dates

Right-clicking a Date field presents additional Default Date formatting options. Available options are determined by the field type—Discrete or Continuous.

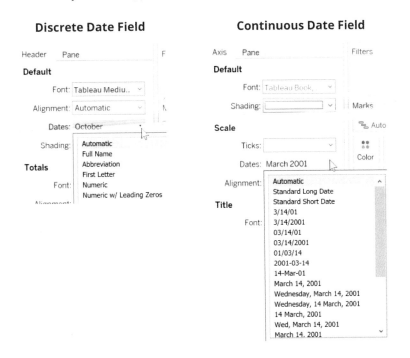

Titles

Worksheet title formatting can be a bit confusing because formatting tools are in two locations. The Edit Title dialog box (which appears when the Title Row is double-clicked) allows the creation and alignment of a title and font formatting (type, color, size, style). The Format Title control that appears in the Format pane affects only background shading and borders. Right-click the title to access this option.

Mark Labels

Default fonts, text color, and number or date formatting can be controlled from the Pane tab of the Format menu as described above. However, it is easier to format these labels by using the Label button on the Marks card (recommended). This button offers many additional display and formatting options. A user can control font type, size, color selection, color matching, and opacity; choose which marks to label; and label display parameters within the constraints of the view. The Labels button on the Marks card provides more options to control how labels are displayed.

Reference Lines and Trend Lines

Right-click any Reference or Trend Line and select "Format" from the menu to edit that Line's type, weight, color, and opacity. Shading can be added above or below it. Any labels identifying line values can be formatted here (font, alignment, numbers, shading).

Troubleshooting Tip

If an edit made in the Format pane does not display where expected, check the following:

- Does the header on the Format pane address the correct location of the desired formatting?

- Has the correct tab been selected?

- Has the correct section been selected?

CHAPTER 7

Line Charts

Lines may be used in many ways to visualize trends or distributions of data, to forecast results, or in the case of a Scatter Plot, to display positive, negative, or loose correlations (or none at all) between variables as a trend line (also known as a Line of Best Fit). This chapter will guide the creation of a Line Chart to connect a series of data points over time in order to display the distribution and trend of the points.

How To: Build a Line Chart to compare viral surveillance results that are positive for Influenza A by month over a four-year time span.

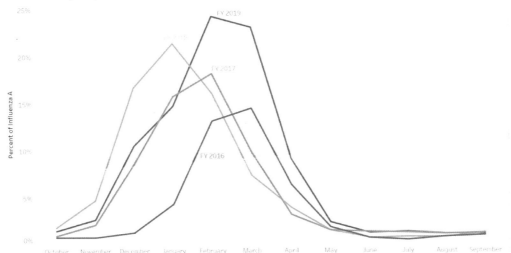

Flu Viral Surveillance
% Respiratory Specimens Positive for Influenza A
October through September for Flu Seasons 2016-2019

Data Source: Centers for Disease Control and Prevention (CDC) Seasonal Flu Activity & Surveillance.

About the Data: National influenza viral surveillance results (percentage of positive Influenza A tests for respiratory specimens received at clinical laboratories) by month for four flu seasons: Oct 2015-Sep 2016, Oct 2016-Sep 2017, Oct 2017-Sep 2018, and Oct 2018-Sep 2019. The Influenza Division at the CDC, working with state and local health departments, clinical labs, hospitals, clinics and other healthcare facilities, collects and analyzes flu data year-round and presents the data through its weekly report, FluView.

1 **Create a new worksheet and connect to the data**

» At the bottom of the Tableau workspace, click the icon for a new worksheet.

» In the Data pane, select the "Ch. 07 - US Flu Occurrences" dataset.

In the Data pane, notice the Data Type icon to the left of the "Date" field. Tableau recognizes this field as containing Date values.

 Date

◄ **Hierarchical Dates**

Dates in Tableau work in a hierarchical structure that enables the user to query reports at increasing levels of detail.

Date fields in Tableau work in a hierarchy from the highest level of aggregation, Year, through Quarter, Month, and so on, to the lowest level of granularity of that date or date/time field (as displayed below).

When a Date field is moved into the workspace, it will default to discrete (blue), set at the highest level of aggregation, YEAR. A (+) sign will appear to the left of the text on the field, indicating the presence of a hierarchy.

In the example below, clicking the (+) on the field displays a new field at the next lower level in the hierarchy. When the (+) is no longer visible on the field, the lowest level of the hierarchy has been reached. Clicking on the now (-) sign will recompress the hierarchy.

YEAR(Date)	QUARTER(Date)	MONTH(Date)	DAY(Date)
Year of Date	Quarter of Date	Month of Date	Day of Date
2015	Q4	October	25
		November	29
		December	27
2016	Q1	January	31
		February	28
		March	27

Both the Date's level of aggregation and field type (discrete or continuous) can be changed. There are two ways to modify either of these categories:

Option 1: Right-click the Date field present on the desired shelf. Within the context menu that appears are two date format sections: Date Part and Date Value.

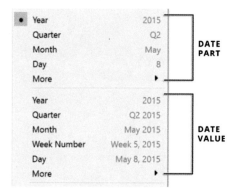

Option 2: Right-click and drag the Date field from the Data pane to the desired shelf. The Drop Field menu that appears displays the date format options Date Part and Date Value, as well as other aggregation options. This option serves as a shortcut to customizing the newly added field.

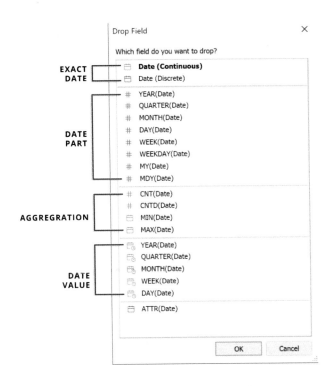

◄ Date Defaults

It is crucial to note that no matter which way dates are entered into the data source, Tableau views them all hierarchically, aggregating by Year when first placed on a worksheet. If another level of aggregation is desired, choose between options 1 or 2, above.

Date Part and Date Value will display different views of the date.

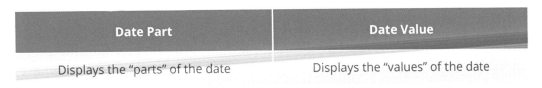

Date Part	Date Value
Displays the "parts" of the date	Displays the "values" of the date

Date Example: **January 1, 2017**

Year	2017
Month	January
Day	1

Year	2017
Month	January 2017
Day	January 1, 2017

Field defaults to discrete (blue)   Field defaults to continuous (green)

⊞ MONTH(Date)   ⊞ MONTH(Date)

Displays headers   Displays continuous axis

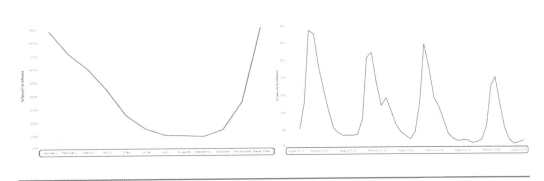

In this flu example line chart, viewing the flu occurrences trend over time is helpful; however, viewing the data by discrete months will allow for seasonal comparison across four different years. Option 1 (explained above) will be used in the creation of this chart, but feel free to experiment with Option 2 if desired.

2 Create the chart

From the Data pane:

» Drag and drop "Percent of Influenza A" onto the Rows shelf.

» Drag and drop "Date" onto the Columns shelf.

» Right-click the "YEAR(Date)" field on the Columns shelf and select "Month" from the Date Part section of the menu.

The chart now looks like this:

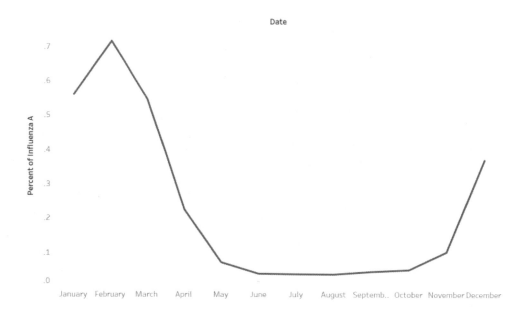

The line currently displays the sum of flu data for all four years, which is not an accurate aggregation for this percentage metric. To disaggregate the date by year, and give each of the four flu seasons a unique line color for the chart:

» » Drag and drop "Date" from the Data pane onto Color on the Marks card.

Marks Card – Color ▶

Dragging and dropping a Dimension or Measure onto Color on the Marks card creates a color key to that field's data elements.

Options for discrete field types are clearly delineated hues, while continuous field type options are progressive/gradual shades.

If there is no field on Color, default colors can still be changed by clicking "Color."

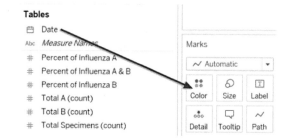

The chart now looks like this:

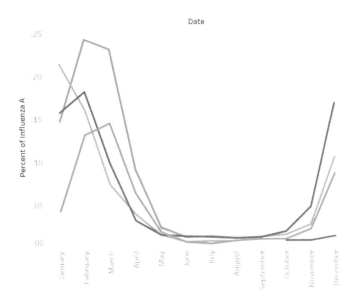

3 Format the chart

Notice that five lines are displayed on the chart. Flu season data starts in October, but the months for the current view start with January. It is more logical to display data from October through September instead of over a calendar year. To change month order:

» Right-click "Date" in the Data pane.

» Select "Default Properties."

» Select "Fiscal Year Start."   ◀ **Changing the Start of the Year**

» Select "October."   *Tableau date fields default to January. Sometimes, as with fiscal-year reporting, the start date must be changed to a different month.*

Resize the chart to view the month labels.

» On the Toolbar, click the dropdown caret to the right of "Standard" and select "Entire View."

The chart now looks like this:

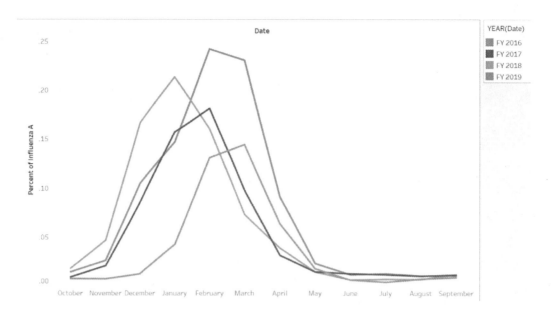

The reformatted chart makes clear that flu occurrences rise dramatically beginning in November and peak in the winter (roughly December through March).

To change the "Percent of Influenza A" field from a decimal to a percentage:

» Right-click "Percent of Influenza A" in the Data pane.

» From the context menu, select "Default Properties."

» Select "Number Format."

» In the appearing Default Number Format dialog box, select "Percentage."

» Change Decimal places to "0."

Tableau auto-generates a color for each line. To change these colors:

» Hover over the YEAR(Date) color-legend header and click the appearing caret to open the sub-menu.

» Select "Edit Colors."

» Click the caret for the Color Palette drop-down, and select "Color Blind."

» Click the "Assign Palette" button below the color palette to let Tableau assign colors to the data items. Color selection may also be manually edited by clicking the data item to highlight it, then clicking a color in the palette to assign.

To hide the "Date" field label (since months are displayed at the bottom of the chart, this label is unnecessary):

» Right-click the field label "Date."

» Select "Hide Field Labels for Columns."

Add labels to the lines:

» While holding down the "Control" key, drag and drop the "YEAR (Date)" field (on the Marks card) onto Label. This action will place a copy of the "YEAR(Date)" field that is on Color onto Label.

The data marks for September are close together, so the line labels are not fully displayed. To display all four labels:

» Click Label on the Marks card.

» When a menu appears, in the "Options" section at the bottom, click "Allow labels to overlap other marks."

The labels remain difficult to read. To move them:

» Click a label to highlight it. The cursor, when placed over the label, should change to a four-directional arrow.

◄ Automatic vs. Manual Label Placement

Clicking and dragging a label offers precision placement, but the label will remain as placed with subsequent data refreshes. To reset a label to automatic, right-click the label, select Mark Label, then Reset Position.

» Click the label and drag it to a location next to the corresponding line, which will then be auto-highlighted.

» Follow the same steps for the other line labels.

To match the label colors with the line colors:

» Click "Label" on Marks card.

» Click the caret for the Font option.

» Click the "Match Mark Color" button.

101

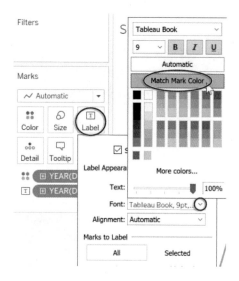

4 **Add a title**

» Double-click the Title Row at the top of the workspace to edit it.

» Add the title

"Flu Viral Surveillance
% Respiratory Specimens Positive for Influenza A
October through September for Flu Seasons 2016-2019"

Rename the worksheet tab and save the worksheet

» Double-click the worksheet tab at the bottom of the screen.

» In the highlighted text, enter the new title, "Line: Influenza A," then click "Enter."

» Click the "Save" icon on the Toolbar.

The final chart looks like this:

Flu Viral Surveillance
% Respiratory Specimens Positive for Influenza A
October through September for Flu Seasons 2016-2019

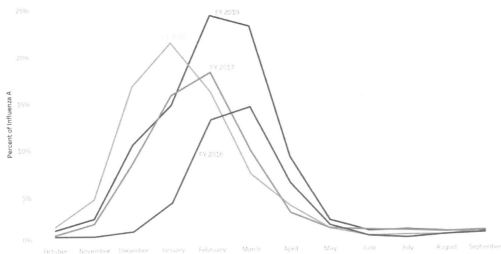

Insight: This chart enables the viewer to see that Influenza A rates peaked at different times of the winter for the four flu seasons. FY2018 peaked the earliest—21% in January—and FY2019 peaked the highest—24% in February and 23% in March. FY2016 started later and was milder than the other three seasons. What could have caused these seasonal differences in Influenza A rates? (Answer: According to the CDC, H1N1 predominated in FY2016; H3N2 predominated in FY2017 and FY2018. FY2019 saw both H1N1 and H3N2).

Highlight Tables/Heat Maps

ighlight Table/Heat Map encodes and displays quantitative values as color. One familiar example is a weather map whose colors represent varying amounts of rainfall or degrees of temperature. But Highlight Tables/Heat Maps need not be limited to geographic data; they can also be structured as a matrix of cells, as in a table or crosstab view, that uses density of color to represent varying amounts or ranges of data. This display offers the precision of a text table with the visual pattern recognition provided by the color or hue saturation.

This exercise will guide the creation of a Highlight Table/Heat Map in a crosstab view, using color in each of the cells to display and highlight the different values in the data.

How To: Build a Highlight Table/Heat Map displaying U.S. healthcare expenditures by type and by payer.

2018 U.S. Healthcare Expenditures (in billions)
By Type and by Payer

	Medicaid	Medicare	Other Health Insurance Programs	Other Third Party Payers	Out of Pocket	Private Health Insurance
Hospital Care	$196.6	$297.0	$72.2	$110.1	$34.8	$481.1
Physician and Clinical Services	$77.4	$170.2	$34.6	$70.4	$61.2	$311.8
Prescription Drugs	$33.4	$107.2	$11.3	$1.8	$47.1	$134.3
Other Health, Residential, and Personal Care	$111.1	$4.9	$2.7	$52.5	$6.8	$13.6
Nursing Care Facilities and Continuing Care Retirement Communities	$49.9	$38.1	$5.7	$12.9	$44.8	$17.1
Dental Services	$12.8	$1.2	$4.0	$0.6	$54.9	$62.2
Durable Medical Equipment	$8.1	$8.1	$0.2	$70.4	$25.5	$11.3
Other Professional Services	$7.7	$27.2	$0.4	$7.4	$26.1	$35.1
Home Health Care	$35.9	$40.3	$0.8	$2.8	$10.2	$12.2

Data Source: Centers for Medicare and Medicaid Services. https://www.cms.gov/Research-Statistics-Data-and-Systems/Statistics-Trends-and-Reports/NationalHealthExpendData/NHE-Fact-Sheet. NHE Tables download.

About the Data: National Health Expenditures evaluate annual US health spending by the type of goods or services provided and through the funding of those services or goods.

1 **Create a new worksheet and connect to the data**

» At the bottom of the Tableau workspace, click the icon for a new worksheet.

» In the Data pane, select the "Ch. 08 – 2018 U.S. Healthcare Expenditures" dataset.

2 Create the chart

From the Data pane:

》 Drag and drop "Payers" onto the Columns shelf.

》 Drag and drop "Type of Expenditure" onto the Rows shelf.

》 Drag and drop "Healthcare Expenditures (in billions)" onto Color shelf on the Marks card.

》 Click the framed [T] Label icon on the Toolbar to add the Healthcare Expenditures' labels to the chart.

The chart looks like this:

			Payers			
Type of Expenditure	Medicaid	Medicare	Other Health In..	Other Third Pa..	Out of Pocket	Private Health In..
Dental Services	12.8	1.2	4.0	0.6	54.9	62.2
Durable Medical Equipme..	8.1	8.1	0.2	70.4	25.5	11.3
Home Health Care	35.9	40.3	0.8	2.8	10.2	12.2
Hospital Care	196.6	297.0	72.2	110.1	34.8	481.1
Nursing Care Facilities an..	49.9	38.1	5.7	12.9	44.8	17.1
Other Health, Residential,..	111.1	4.9	2.7	52.5	6.8	13.6
Other Professional Servic..	7.7	27.2	0.4	7.4	26.1	35.1
Physician and Clinical Ser..	77.4	170.2	34.6	70.4	61.2	311.8
Prescription Drugs	33.4	107.2	11.3	1.8	47.1	134.3

3 Format the chart

Resize the column and row headers to view the complete dimension labels.

》 Click the caret for the Fit drop-down menu on the Toolbar and select "Entire View."

Adjusting the Chart to the Workspace ▷

Tableau's standard chart sizing may not be an optimal use of screen real estate for the displayed visualization. Use the quick fit options in the toolbar to "Fit Width," "Fit Height," or "Entire View" to dynamically expand the chart to the amount of space available on a worksheet or within a dashboard. Be careful when very small or very large amounts of data are displayed; a poor fit selection may render the chart illegible. If a quick filter is incorporated into the chart functionality, it is a good practice to test the filter with both the smallest and largest amount of possible data, adjusting chart size to ensure readability.

》 Adjust any headers as needed by hovering the cursor over the appropriate border until it changes to a bi-directional arrow, then drag to an appropriate sizing to view the complete label.

Sort the expenditures along the dimension "Type of Expenditure" from highest to lowest.

》 Click the "Type of Expenditure" field on the Rows shelf to highlight it.

》 Click the "Sort Descending" icon on the Toolbar.

To hide the column and row field labels:

» Right-click "Payers" field label.

» Click "Hide Field Labels for Columns."

» Right-click "Type of Expenditure" field label.

» Click "Hide Field Labels for Rows."

The chart looks like this:

	Medicaid	Medicare	Other Health Insurance Programs	Other Third Party Payers	Out of Pocket	Private Health Insurance
Hospital Care	196.6	297.0	72.2	110.1	34.8	481.1
Physician and Clinical Services	77.4	170.2	34.6	70.4	61.2	311.8
Prescription Drugs	33.4	107.2	11.3	1.8	47.1	134.3
Other Health, Residential, and Personal Care	111.1	4.9	2.7	52.5	6.8	13.6
Nursing Care Facilities and Continuing Care Retirement Communities	49.9	38.1	5.7	12.9	44.8	17.1
Dental Services	12.8	1.2	4.0	0.6	54.9	62.2
Durable Medical Equipment	8.1	8.1	0.2	70.4	25.5	11.3
Other Professional Services	7.7	27.2	0.4	7.4	26.1	35.1
Home Health Care	35.9	40.3	0.8	2.8	10.2	12.2

To emphasize the column and row dividers:

» Click "Format" on the Menu Bar.

» Select "Borders..." from the drop-down menu.

» In the Format window, ensure the "Sheet" tab is selected.

» Scroll down to the Row Divider section, then click and drag the "Level" slider to the right. This will display the Row dividers.

» Perform the same step in the Column Divider section.

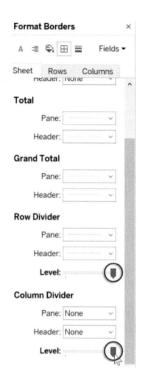

» Under the Row Divider section, click the caret for "Pane."

» Select a solid, thin line, and a white color box.

» Perform the same steps for Column Divider, Pane section.

» Then click the "X" in the top right corner of the Format window to close it.

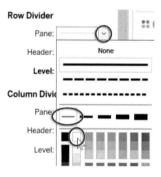

The Payers and Type of Expenditure headers can be realigned for improved legibility.

» Right-click "Type of Expenditure" on the Rows shelf.

» Select "Format..."

» In the Format window, ensure the "Header" tab is selected.

» Under "Default", "Alignment" click the caret and select the Horizontal right alignment icon.

» At the top right of the Format window, click the caret for "Fields" and select "Payers."

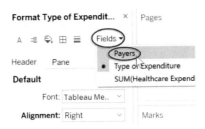

» Under "Default", "Alignment" click the caret and select the Vertical lower alignment icon.

To format the Expenditure values as currency:

» Right-click "SUM (Healthcare Expenditures)" field on the Colors shelf.

» In the Format window, select the Pane tab.

» Under Default, Numbers, click the caret and select "Currency (Custom)"

» Decrease the Decimal places to "1."

4 Add a title

» Double-click the Title Row to open the Edit Title dialog box.

» Enter the title, "2018 U.S. Healthcare Expenditures (in billions) By Type and by Payer."

5 Rename the worksheet tab and save the worksheet

» Double-click the worksheet tab at the bottom of the screen.

» In the highlighted text, enter the new title, "Heat Map: Healthcare Expenditures," then click "Enter."

» Click the "Save" icon on the Toolbar.

The final highlight table/heat map looks like this:

2018 U.S. Healthcare Expenditures (in billions)
By Type and by Payer

	Medicaid	Medicare	Other Health Insurance Programs	Other Third Party Payers	Out of Pocket	Private Health Insurance
Hospital Care	$196.6	$297.0	$72.2	$110.1	$34.8	$481.1
Physician and Clinical Services	$77.4	$170.2	$34.6	$70.4	$61.2	$311.8
Prescription Drugs	$33.4	$107.2	$11.3	$1.8	$47.1	$134.3
Other Health, Residential, and Personal Care	$111.1	$4.9	$2.7	$52.5	$6.8	$13.6
Nursing Care Facilities and Continuing Care Retirement Communities	$49.9	$38.1	$5.7	$12.9	$44.8	$17.1
Dental Services	$12.8	$1.2	$4.0	$0.6	$54.9	$62.2
Durable Medical Equipment	$8.1	$8.1	$0.2	$70.4	$25.5	$11.3
Other Professional Services	$7.7	$27.2	$0.4	$7.4	$26.1	$35.1
Home Health Care	$35.9	$40.3	$0.8	$2.8	$10.2	$12.2

Insight: The darker blue sections make it easy to see that Hospital Care and Physician & Clinical Services are the highest types of expenditures. Private Health Insurance along with Medicare and Medicaid have the highest expenditures of the Payer groups. And the highest expenditure intersection is Private Health Insurance for Hospital Care.

CHAPTER 9

Small Multiples Charts

Edward Tufte popularized Small Multiples, which he described in Envisioning Information as "Illustrations of postage-stamp size...[sorted] by category or...label, sequenced over time like the frames of a movie, or ordered by a quantitative variable not used in the single image itself"(67).

Repeating a basic chart type in a grid formation, while altering a single condition for easy data comparison, creates a Small Multiple. If the reader can understand the first chart, the others are readily understood; thanks to carefully balanced parallel construction, all the charts convey the same message. The single differing value in each subsequent chart is easily compared to its fellows by a glance up, down, or across the charts. And because the charts are close together and visible at a single glance, the structure and patterns in complex data are clear and comprehensible.

As with any data display, a Small Multiple may be built using bars, lines, box plots, area charts, or even multiple maps, depending on the type of data to be communicated. The simplicity of the chart is paramount; therefore, keep measures, scales, sizes, and shapes consistent and proportionate to assure that the real story in the data is communicated.

How To: Build a Small Multiple Line Chart to compare child/adolescent obesity by gender and age range over time.

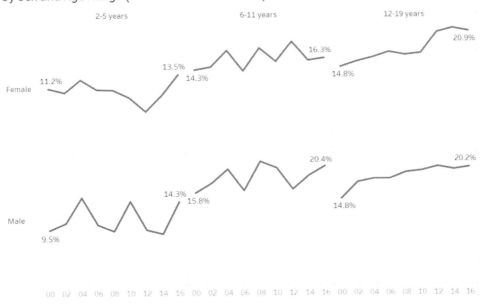

Prevalence (%) of Obesity (BMI >= 30) by Sex and Age Range (Children to Adolescents) from 2000 to 2016

Data Source: Centers for Disease Control and Prevention (CDC), National Center for Health Statistics (NCHS), 2000-2016 National Health and Nutrition Examination Survey (www.cdc.gov/nchs).

About the Data: *TThe NCHS is a health statistics agency providing accurate and timely data to drive improvements in the health of adults and children in the US. The National Health and Nutrition Examination Survey (NHANES) captures data about the health and nutrition status of adults and children in the U.S. through interviews and physical examinations. This example uses the agency's survey data on the prevalence of obesity [body mass index (BMI) equal to or greater than 30] from 2000 to 2016 by gender and age range.*

1 Create a new worksheet and connect to the data

» At the bottom of the Tableau workspace, click the icon for a New Worksheet.

» In the Data pane, select the "Ch. 09 - Obesity Prevalence" dataset.

2 Create the chart

From the Data pane:

» Drag and drop "Sex" onto the Rows shelf.

» Drag and drop "Age Range" then "Date" onto the Columns shelf. Leave the Date aggregation at the discrete Year level.

» Drag and drop "Obesity Prevalence (%)"onto the Rows shelf.

Best Practice

To accurately compare Small Multiple charts, the axis scales must be consistent for all axes.

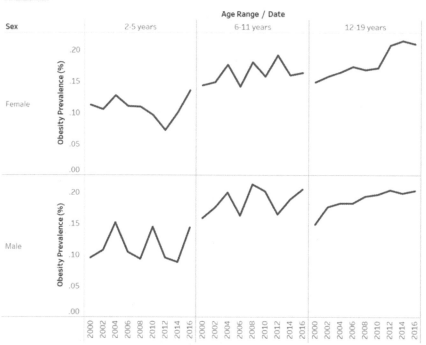

▲ **Dimension Order**

The order of multiple Dimensions on a row or column shelf affects how Measure data is divided. In the example above, the visualization would be markedly different if Date were positioned before Age Range. Experiment with Dimension order to find the best visualization.

3 Format the chart

Labeling every data point can sometimes clutter a view; labeling the first and last data points on a line can provide the necessary clarity. To add labels to the ends of the lines:

» Click "Label" on the Marks card.

» Click the box for "Show mark labels."

» In the Marks to Label section, select "Line Ends."

» Click outside of the Label dialog box to close it.

The Obesity Prevalence values are displayed as integers. To change them to percentage:

» Right-click "SUM(Obesity Prevalence(%))" field on the Rows shelf.

» Click "Format."

» In the Format window, select the Pane tab.

» Under the Default section, click the caret for Numbers.

» Select "Percentages" and change decimals to 1.

With the lines labeled, the y-axis is unnecessary. To hide it:

» Right-click a Y axis.

» Click "Show Header" to remove its checkmark.

Hide the Field Labels:

» Right-click "Age Range/Date."

» Click "Hide Field Labels for Columns."

» Right-click "Sex."

» Click "Hide Field Labels for Rows."

The four digits of the year labels appear crowded. To format them for easier viewing:

» Right-click "YEAR (Date)" on the Columns shelf.

» Select "Format."

» Ensure the Header tab is selected.

» In the Default section, click the drop-down caret for "Dates" and change to "Two-digit."

» Hover over the chart's right border and drag to the desired width to clearly view the year labels.

To make the dimension headers slightly more prominent:

» Right-click a column header and select "Format."

» In the Default section, click the drop-down caret for Font.

» Change the font to Bold.

» Perform the same steps for the row headers.

4 Add a title

» Double-click the Title Row at the top of the workspace.

» Add title:

"Prevalence (%) of Obesity (BMI >= 30)
By Sex and Age Range (Children to Adolescents) from 2000 to 2016"

5 Rename the worksheet tab and save the worksheet

» Double-click the worksheet tab at the bottom of the screen.

» In the highlighted text, enter the new title, "Small Multiples: Obesity Prevalence," then click "Enter."

» Click the "Save" icon on the Toolbar.

The final chart looks like this:

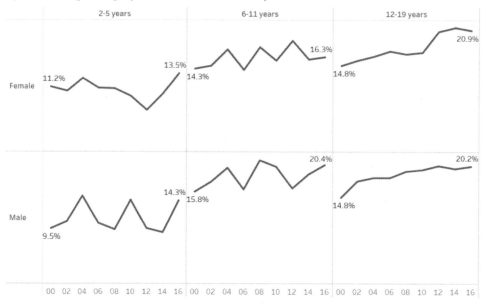

Prevalence (%) of Obesity (BMI >= 30)
by Sex and Age Range (Children to Adolescents) from 2000 to 2016

Insight: This Small Multiple Line Chart makes it possible to identify several interesting trends. It is evident, for example, that the obesity prevalence skews lower for the 2-5 year-old group than either of the other age ranges. Obesity has trended up from 2000 to 2016 for both sexes in all three age groups, however, the trend for individual years diverged by gender. Obesity went down for 2-5 year-old females in 2010, but spiked up for Males, while the opposite was true for 6-11 year old Males and Females in 2012.

Deviation Charts

A Deviation Chart displays the way sets of quantitative values differ from reference or primary sets of values. Examples are the differences between actual expenses compared to budgeted ones, or between state childhood immunization rates compared to national rates. A Deviation Chart can show the reference (for example, an expense budget) as the anchor or constant over time (regardless of how it may change), while showing how the other value (for example, actual expenses) differs from it. This flexibility allows the easy monitoring of such information as; "Are we over or under budget, and by how much?" or "Are we meeting or missing target, and by how much?" Deviation Charts answer directly and simply the basic but crucial question, "Is one measure more or less than another measure?"

The following exercise displays the difference between budgeted and actual full-time employees across five city centers. This could be presented with a side-by-side bar chart plotting actual and budgeted FTEs counts next to one another, or a bar showing actual FTEs with a reference line overlaying budgeted FTEs. These provide more context to the user concerning the raw FTE counts; however it is more cognitive work for the audience to see and interpret the difference between the two values. A deviation chart solves this problem by performing the math for the end-user and displaying just the difference under or over the budgeted amounts.

10.1 Deviation Bar Charts

How To: Build a Deviation Bar Chart to compare budgeted and actual full-time employees (FTE) in five city health centers.

Deviation of Actual FTE to Budgeted FTE
By City Health Center

Data Source: *Mock city health center data*

About the Data: *We created mock data on the difference between the budgeted and actual numbers of full-time equivalents (FTE) for five city health centers.*

1 **Create a new worksheet and connect to the data**

» At the bottom of the Tableau workspace, click the icon for a new worksheet.

» In the Data pane, select the "Ch. 10 - City Health Center Full-Time Equivalent (FTE) Counts" dataset.

2 **Create a calculated field**

The dataset includes budgeted FTEs and actual FTEs as separate Measures. For a Deviation Chart, the difference between budgeted and actual FTEs is required and must be calculated.

» Click the drop-down caret to the right of the Search window in the Data pane.

» Select "Create Calculated Field..." from the menu that appears.

Calculated Fields ▶

Calculated Fields can be used to create simple aggregations such as MIN, MAX, and AVG; construct IF / THEN and CASE / WHEN statements; perform date-field and string manipulation; and a host of other functions. This book covers some basic, common Calculated Fields in Chapter 22.

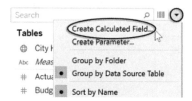

The Calculated Field dialog box appears.

» Replace "Calculation 1" in the Name field with "FTE Difference."

> **Best Practice:**
>
> *The Calculated Field needs an intuitive name to make it easy to find in a list of Dimensions or Measures.*

In the Formula section of this dialog box, assemble a calculation that subtracts Budgeted FTE from Actual FTE.

» Click the cursor in the Formula section and begin to type the measure name "Actual FTE." Tableau displays a list of options corresponding to the typed entry.

» Click the listed corresponding field name to select it.

Auto-Complete ▶

Start typing a formula and Tableau displays a list of options (functions, operators, field names, parameters, and sets) for completing the formula.

Calculated Field Dialog Box

There are three ways to enter field names into the Calculated Field dialog box:

- *Start typing and use the auto-complete function.*

- *Drag and drop the field from the Dimension or Measure window into the dialog box.*

- *Hold the CTRL key on Windows or the Command key on a Mac and drag and drop a field already in the worksheet.*

> » Type a minus sign (-) to the right of the "Actual FTE" field.

> » Complete the formula by dragging and dropping the "Budgeted FTE" field from the Data pane to the right of the minus sign (-) in the Formula window.

> » Click "OK."

◄ Non-Aggregate (Row-Level) Calculation

This formula is considered a "non-aggregate" or "row-level" calculation because no aggregation function (SUM, AVG, etc.) has been entered before each Measure name. As a result, when a non-aggregate measure field is placed in the workspace, Tableau applies the default aggregation (SUM). This can be edited, as needed, by right-clicking the field and selecting the appropriate level of aggregation.

The = sign to the left of the newly created "FTE Difference" measure indicates that this field contains a user-defined calculation.

◄ Calculated Field Display

Calculated fields display in the Data window, with an = sign to the left of the new field.

3 Create the chart

> » Drag and drop the newly created "FTE Difference" field from the Data pane onto the Rows shelf.

> » Drag and drop "City Health Center" from the Data pane onto the Columns shelf.

The chart now looks like this:

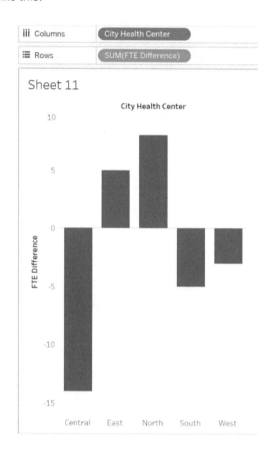

Calculated Field Aggregation ▶

Calculated Fields that are Measures need a level of aggregation, as does any other measure. Aggregation can happen at one of two points: it can be specified within a calculation formula; or, if it is not, Tableau aggregates when the Measure is dragged and dropped onto the view (as seen here, defaulting to SUM).

4 Format the chart

The default sort is alphabetical order by City Health Center. To rank the data from highest to lowest value instead:

>> Hover over the Y axis title, "FTE Difference." The Sort icon appears.

>> Click the icon once to sort descending.

Best Practice:

Sorting results, while effective in nearly all charts, becomes especially important with categorical deviation charts in order to easily compare and rank the different values.

Delete the City Health Center field label.

>> Right-click "City Health Center" header.

>> Click "Hide Field Labels for Columns."

Color-encode the bars with the FTE difference that is higher than budgeted:

» Drag and drop the "FTE Difference" field from the Data pane to Color on the Marks card.

» Click the drop-down caret of the color legend and select "Edit Colors" from the appearing menu.

» Click the checkbox for Stepped Color and change the number of Steps to "2."

» Click the checkbox for Reversed.

» Click "OK."

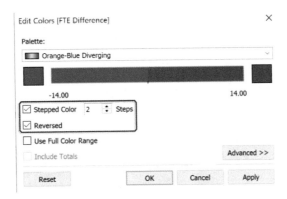

To emphasize the Zero line:

» Click "Format" on the Menu bar, then select "Lines."

» Ensure the "Sheet" tab is selected.

» Click the drop-down caret to the right of the Zero Lines option.

» The selections in this example were a slightly thicker, dashed, dark grey line.

» Click the "X" at the top right of the Format window to close it.

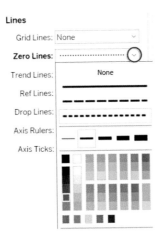

5 Add a title

» Double-click the Title Row to open the Edit Title dialog box.

» Enter the title,
"Deviation of Actual FTE to Budgeted FTE
By City Health Center."

6 Rename the worksheet tab and save the worksheet

» Double-click the worksheet tab at the bottom of the screen.

» In the highlighted text, enter the new title, "Deviation Bar: FTE Difference," then click "Enter."

» Click the "Save" icon on the Toolbar.

The final chart looks like this:

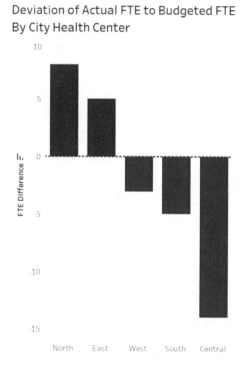

Deviation of Actual FTE to Budgeted FTE
By City Health Center

Insight: This Deviation Bar Chart enables the viewer to easily determine that North and East City Health Centers have more staff than budgeted.

10.2 Deviation Line Charts

As described in the previous section, Deviation Bar Charts, directly expressing the differences between two sets of values creates a Deviation chart. This example shows how a Deviation Line Chart is an efficient way to compare change over time.

How To: Build a Deviation Line Chart of a hospital emergency department's year-over-year percent change of patient volume by month, 2019 compared with 2018.

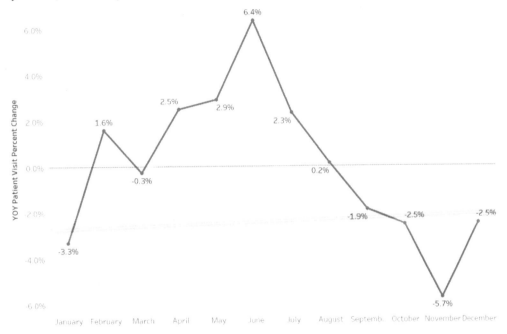

Year-over-Year Percent Change of Hospital Emergency Department Patient Volume
By Month, 2019 compared with 2018

Data source: de-identified hospital data

About the data: represents the number of patients seen in a hospital's emergency department by month for a two-year period.

1 **Create a new worksheet and connect to the data**

» At the bottom of the Tableau workspace, click the icon for a new worksheet.

» In the Data pane, select the "Ch. 10 - Patient Volume Year-Over-Year Change" dataset.

2 **Create the calculated fields**

The dataset currently contains two fields: Date and Patient Visits. The Deviation chart should depict the percent change in the number of patients seen in 2019 compared to those seen in the previous year for each month. Four Calculated Fields need to be created: one for patients seen in each of the two years; one for the numeric difference; and one for the percent difference.

» Right-click "Date" in the Dimensions window.

» Select "Create," then select "Calculated Field..." from the menu.

» Enter a field title "Patient Visits for 2019."

For this formula, the number of patient visits for the year 2019 is calculated with an IF/THEN conditional logic statement:

IF "condition X" is true, THEN return "Y"

IF the Date field shows the year 2019, then return Patient Visits for that year; otherwise, the field will return a null value (ELSE NULL).

» Enter the formula:

IF YEAR([Date]) = 2019 THEN [Patient Visits] ELSE NULL END

» Click "OK."

List of Functions ▶

Click the small gray caret on the right border of the calculation window to view a list of available functions. Click a Function to view its definition. Double-click the Function to populate it in the formula.

View the data to see how this calculation works. The new field "Patient Visits for 2019" lists only the Patient Visits for each month of the year 2019. The values for 2018 in the new field are Null.

Date	Patient Visits	Patient Visits for 2019
1/31/18	2,541	Null
2/28/18	2,312	Null
3/31/18	2,358	Null
4/30/18	2,401	Null
5/31/18	2,231	Null
6/30/18	2,357	Null
7/31/18	2,352	Null
8/31/18	2,614	Null
9/30/18	2,462	Null
10/31/18	2,616	Null
11/30/18	2,590	Null
12/31/18	2,514	Null
1/31/19	2,457	2,457
2/28/19	2,349	2,349
3/31/19	2,352	2,352
4/30/19	2,461	2,461
5/31/19	2,296	2,296
6/30/19	2,507	2,507
7/31/19	2,407	2,407
8/31/19	2,618	2,618
9/30/19	2,416	2,416
10/31/19	2,550	2,550
11/30/19	2,442	2,442
12/31/19	2,452	2,452

Follow the same steps above to create a separate calculated field for "Patient Visits for 2018," using "2018" instead of "2019" in the formula.

These two calculated fields restrict the Patient Visits data to 2019 and 2018 only.

A field is needed to calculate the difference between "Patient Visits for 2019" and "Patient Visits for 2018."

» Right-click "Patient Visits for 2019."

» Select "Create," then select "Calculated Field..." from the menus.

» Enter a title for the field: "YOY Patient Visit Difference."

» Enter the formula:

SUM([Patient Visits for 2019]) – SUM([Patient Visits for 2018])

» Click "OK."

The SUM function used in this operation is called an "Aggregate Calculation." It is used here because of the null values in many rows of the new fields (see image above).

Note

It is important to understand how Non-Aggregate and Aggregate calculations behave.

Non-Aggregate calculations evaluate each row in a data source then calculate the row-level results.

The Non-Aggregate Calculation for "YOY Patient Visit Difference" would be:

```
[Patient Visits for 2019] - [Patient Visits for 2018]
```

The calculation is performed on a single row of data at a time. It´s important to understand that performing row-level calculations with null values produces a "null" answer and can significantly affect results.

Date	Patient Visits for 2018		Patient Visits for 2019		
1/31/18	2,541	–	null	=	null
2/28/18	2,312	–	null	=	null
3/31/18	2,358	–	null	=	null
4/30/18	2,401	–	null	=	null
5/31/18	2,231	–	null	=	null
6/30/18	2,357	–	null	=	null
7/31/18	2,352	–	null	=	null
8/31/18	2,614	–	null	=	null
9/30/18	2,462	–	null	=	null
10/31/18	2,616	–	null	=	null
11/30/18	2,590	–	null	=	null
12/31/18	2,514	–	null	=	null
1/31/19	null	–	2,457	=	null
2/28/19	null	–	2,349	=	null
3/31/19	null	–	2,352	=	null
4/30/19	null	–	2,461	=	null
5/31/19	null	–	2,296	=	null
6/30/19	null	–	2,507	=	null
7/31/19	null	–	2,407	=	null
8/31/19	null	–	2,618	=	null
9/30/19	null	–	2,416	=	null
10/31/19	null	–	2,550	=	null
11/30/19	null	–	2,442	=	null
12/31/19	null	–	2,452	=	null
				SUM	**NULL**

When this field is placed in the workspace, the aggregation is automatically performed.

Aggregate calculations apply to *all rows* in a partition (grouping of values based on the Dimensions in the view).

The Aggregate Calculation for "YOY Patient Visit Difference" is:

    SUM([Patient Visits for 2019]) - SUM([Patient Visits for 2018])

The aggregation of each field is performed first (summing all rows for each field), then the calculation is performed.

Date	Patient Visits for 2018	Patient Visits for 2019		
1/31/18	2,541	null		
2/28/18	2,312	null		
3/31/18	2,358	null		
4/30/18	2,401	null		
5/31/18	2,231	null		
6/30/18	2,357	null		
7/31/18	2,352	null		
8/31/18	2,614	null		
9/30/18	2,462	null		
10/31/18	2,616	null		
11/30/18	2,590	null		
12/31/18	2,514	null		
1/31/19	null	2,457		
2/28/19	null	2,349		
3/31/19	null	2,352		
4/30/19	null	2,461		
5/31/19	null	2,296		
6/30/19	null	2,507		
7/31/19	null	2,407		
8/31/19	null	2,618		
9/30/19	null	2,416		
10/31/19	null	2,550		
11/30/19	null	2,442		
12/31/19	null	2,452		
	29,348	− 29,307	=	**41**

When this field is placed in the workspace, the appearing "AGG" on the field indicates the aggregation has been performed within the calculation.

The final calculated field displays the percent change from 2018 to 2019.

» Right-click the calculated field just created, "YOY Patient Visit Difference."

» Select "Create," then "Calculated Field" from the sub-menu.

» Enter a new title, "YOY Patient Visit Percent Change."

For this formula, the field "YOY Patient Visit Difference" should be divided by the field "Patient Visits for 2018."

However, if the formula is written as:

    SUM([YOY Patient Visit Difference])/SUM([Patient Visits for 2018])

a syntax error appears. Tableau provides information to identify the error in the formula. In this example, YOY Patient Visit Difference has already been aggregated and cannot therefore be further aggregated.

▲ Avoiding Errors in Calculated Fields

Tableau's formula editor has built-in coloring and validation to help avoid syntax errors. Such an error is highlighted with a red squiggly line, which generates directions for fixing the errors when clicked. The caret at the end of the error statement, when clicked, can also provide additional information to fix the error. A valid calculation is identified in gray text at the bottom of the formula window.

To write this formula correctly:

» Enter:

    [YOY Patient Visit Difference] / SUM([Patient Visits for 2018])

» Click "OK."

CHAPTER 10 : Deviation Charts

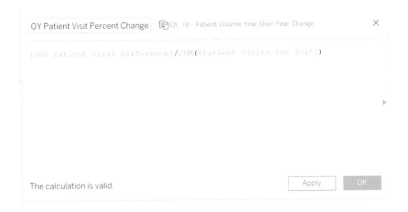

Since this field is a percentage, the number format needs to change.

>> Right-click the new calculated field "YOY Patient Visit Percent Change."

>> Select "Default Properties."

>> Select "Number Format."

>> Select "Percentage."

>> Decrease Decimal places to "1."

3 Create the chart

From the Data pane:

>> Drag and drop "YOY Patient Visit Percent Change" onto the Rows shelf.

>> Right-click and drag "Date" to the Columns shelf.

>> Select the blue "MONTH(Date)" from the Drop Field menu box, then click "OK."

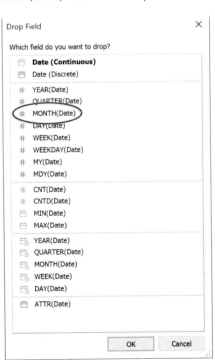

» Click the framed [T] Label icon on the Toolbar to add labels to the line.

The chart now looks like this:

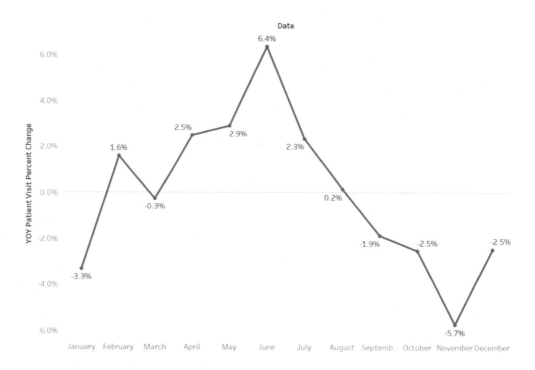

▲ The Effect of Dimensions on Aggregate Calculations

Dimensions affect how aggregate calculations perform. When the Dimension "MONTH(Date)" is added to the workspace, the calculation is partitioned to each Month. The example here examines how the calculation for the month of January is performed.

Date	Patient Visits for 2019	Patient Visits for 2018	YOY Patient Visit Difference	Patient Visits for 2018	YOY Patient Visit Percent Change
1/31/18	null	2,541			
1/31/19	2,457	null			
	2457 – 2541		= -84	/2541	-0.033

4 Format the chart

» Right-click the header "Date."

» Select "Hide Field Labels for Columns."

Add shading below the zero line to emphasize the deviation above and below zero.

» Right-click the Y axis and select "Add Reference Line" from the menu.

In the Add Reference Line, Band, or Box dialog box:

» Change the Scope to "Entire Table."

» In the Line section,

- Change Average to "Constant."

- Change Value to "0."

- Change Label to "None."

» In the Formatting section, change the Line to thin, dashed, and change Fill Below to a light gray.

» Click "OK."

5 Add a title

» Double-click the Title Row to open the Edit Title dialog box.

» Enter the title,
"Year-over-Year Percent Change of Hospital Emergency Department Patient Volume By Month, 2019 compared with 2018."

6 Rename the worksheet tab and save the worksheet

» Double-click the worksheet tab at the bottom of the screen.

» In the highlighted text, enter the new title, "Deviation Line: ED Pt Volume," then click "Enter."

» Click the "Save" icon on the Toolbar.

The final chart looks like this:

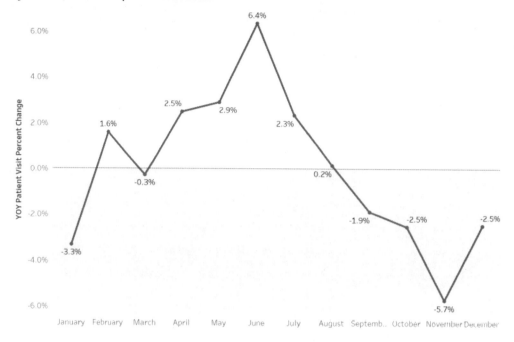

Year-over-Year Percent Change of Hospital Emergency Department Patient Volume
By Month, 2019 compared with 2018

Insight: In 2019, the Emergency Department's actual patient volume was highly variable compared with 2018. In six of the months displayed, the number of patients visiting the ED was lower than in 2018, from -0.3% in March to -5.7% in November. In the other six months of the year, patient numbers were higher than in 2018, from 0.2% in August to 6.4% in June. The general pattern shows a higher volume than the previous year in the spring and summer and a lower volume in the fall and winter.

CHAPTER 11

Area Charts

An Area Chart is an extension of a line chart. In an Area Chart, the space between each line and the next line is filled with a color to emphasize the magnitude of change in the measure over time. This chart visually displays a part-to-whole relationship where a set of layers for multiple categories flows along the corresponding time series. Since both line and Area Charts can be used to facilitate trend analysis, it is better to use the Area Chart when there is a summation relationship between the data displayed. An Area Chart is not the best way to show specific values along the trend, but it can clearly show total values to effectively display the way a dimension contributes to an overall trend.

How To: Build an Area Chart to display the change in amounts of U.S. healthcare expenditures from 1980 to 2018

U.S. Healthcare Expenditures
By Type of Service/Source of Funds
1980 - 2018

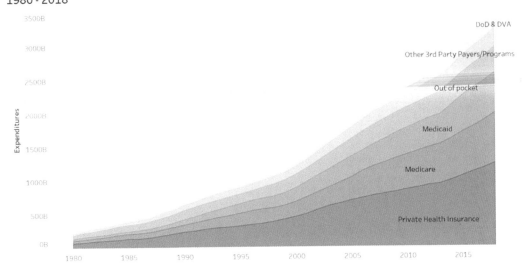

Data Source: Centers for Medicare and Medicaid Services

About the Data: The data for this exercise is from the dataset "National Health Expenditures by Type of Service and Source o Funds: Calendar Years 1980 to 2018."

1 Create a new worksheet and connect to the data

» At the bottom of the Tableau workspace, click the icon for a new worksheet.

» In the Data pane, click the "Ch. 11 - U.S. Healthcare Expenditures Trend (1980-2018)" dataset.

2 Create the chart

» While holding down the Control key, select "Date" and "Expenditures" in the Data pane.

» Go to the "Show Me" palette and select "area charts (continuous)."

» Click the "Show Me" tab again to close.

For **area charts** (continuous) try

1 date 📅

0 or more Dimensions

1 or more Measures

Tableau offers two types of Area Charts: Continuous and Discrete. Both appear on the Show Me menu. Discrete fields display data organized by row or column headers; Continuous fields display data along axes. Because the dataset in use contains data for every year from 1980 to 2018, a continuous Area Chart is the better choice here.

3 Color the chart

The resulting chart displays the sum of the Expenditures by Date. It must be disaggregated by Type of Service/Source of Funds.

» Drag and drop "Type of Service/Source of Funds" from the Data pane onto Color on the Marks card.

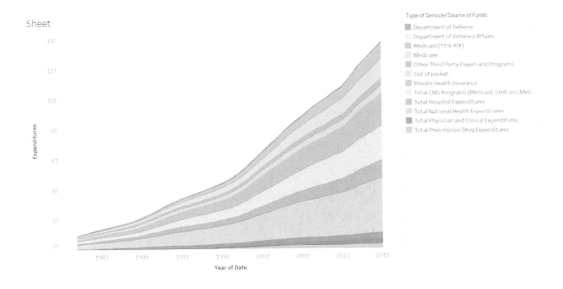

Sheet

4 Analyze the data

Notice that the Y axis´ top range is 14 trillion, and that the color legend lists different types of services as well as totals of different categories. Examine the data more closely to determine the next steps.

» Click the "View Data" icon to the right of the Search feature in the Data pane to view the underlying data. (Note: This data view was sorted first by clicking the Type of Service/Source of Funds header then the Date.)

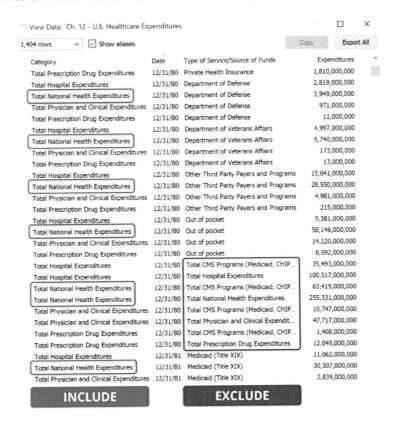

The misleadingly high expenditures are caused by overlapping categories and row-level totals in the dataset. Total National Health Expenditures is the only Category of interest for this exercise. Filtering resolves this problem.

» Click the "X" at the top right of the View Data window to close the window.

5 Filter the data

Data can be filtered from the Filter shelf by inclusion or exclusion. Decide which filter method to use after evaluating what will happen if the data set is updated with new values. The two filtering activities shown here describe filtering by inclusion and then by exclusion, and illustrate the choices made in each case.

» Drag and drop "Category" from the Data pane onto the Filters shelf.

» Click the "Total National Health Expenditures" checkbox, then click "OK."

Filter by Inclusion ▷

It is important to include only the desired data values in the report. To do so, include only "Total National Health Expenditures," thus ensuring that new values will not populate when the data is refreshed. For example, if "Hospice Expenditures" is later added as a new value in the Category field and the dataset is then refreshed, the inclusion method will prevent the new data from interfering with the current report.

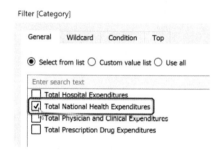

» Drag and drop "Type of Service/Source of Funds" from the Data pane onto the Filters shelf.

The Dimension "Type of Service/Source of Funds" is already in the view (on Color on the Marks card); as a result, the boxes are already checked. The new filter ("Type of Service…") is necessary to filter out "Totals" for row level Types of Service/Source of Funds.

» Click the "None" button to remove all checkmarks.

» Click the "Exclude" checkbox.

» Click all checkboxes for "Total…" fields, then click "OK."

Filter [Type of Service/Source of Funds]   ✕

General   Wildcard   Condition   Top

◉ Select from list ○ Custom value list ○ Use all   ☰

| Enter search text |
| ☐ Department of Defense |
| ☐ Department of Veterans Affairs |
| ☐ Medicaid (Title XIX) |
| ☐ Medicare |
| ☐ Other Third Party Payers and Programs |
| ☐ Out of pocket |
| ☐ Private Health Insurance |
| ☑ Total CMS Programs (Medicaid, CHIP and Medicare) |
| ☑ Total National Health Expenditures |

All   None   ☑ Exclude

◄ Filter by Exclusion

If a filtered value will never be needed, exclude it to ensure that other values will nonetheless populate when the data is refreshed. For example, if the category "Other Third Party Payers and Programs" is replaced in the dataset by more specific categories, the exclusion method will ensure that the two new fields are present in the report .

The chart now looks like this:

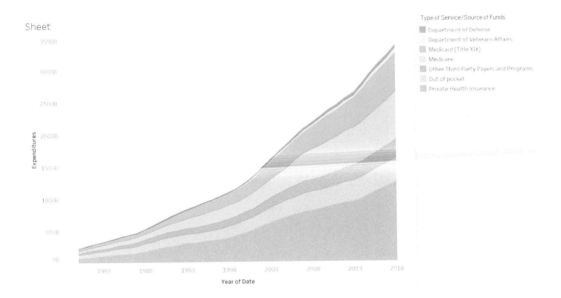

6 **Format the chart**

Add labels to each colored area:

> » Drag and drop the "Type of Service/Source of Funds" from the Data pane onto Label on the Marks card.

Because of area segment size constraints, not all labels are displayed. To see them all:

> » Click Label on the Marks card.

> » Click Options "Allow labels to overlap other marks."

137

Allow Labels to Overlap Other Marks ▶

In compressed visualizations, Tableau makes its best guess about what data labels will fit into a readable format. Choosing Allow labels to overlap other marks forces Tableau to display every labeled value. On charts where fields overlap, one solution is to manually reposition the labels where possible by dragging and dropping them to the desired location.

Some of the Type of Service labels are lengthy and can be abbreviated to ensure easier legibility. To edit the Type of Service/Source of Funds aliases:

» Right-click "Type of Service/Source of Funds" in the Data pane.

» Select "Aliases..." from the menu.

» Edit the following members:
  • Department of Defense to "DoD"
  • Department of Veterans Affairs to: "DVA"
  • Medicaid (Title XIX) to: "Medicaid"
  • Other Third Party Payers and Programs to: "Other 3rd Party Payers/Programs"

» Click "OK."

▲ **Edit Aliases**

Dimension members may be changed by assigning Aliases. This change does not affect the underlying data, but does propagate the Alias through all worksheets in the workbook using that Dimension. This feature permits clarifying display data without the need to alter underlying information. Note that every Alias value must have a unique name.

Notice the label for DVA is still not visible. DVA and DoD both have significantly slimmer areas (lesser expenditures over time) than the other Types of Services/Source of Funds. Tableau defaults the label placement to the widest spacing per area section—here, the DoD label is sitting on top of the DVA label.

» Click the "DoD" label. When the cursor changes to a +, click the label again to drag to and drop on the desired chart position.

Because these two Types of Services/Sources of Funds represent a small proportion of the total expenditures, it may be beneficial to instead group them together.

To group two field members:

» Holding down the Control key, click "DoD" and "DVA" in the Type of Service/Source of Funds color legend.

» In the appearing Command Bar, click the paperclip icon.

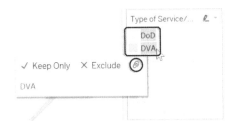

◀ Groups

Grouping data combines two or more selected Dimension members into a single member. It is a useful technique for merging similar or minimal data (such as minor categories into an "other" or "miscellaneous" member). Note that if the data is refreshed, new Dimension members will populate in the field ungrouped and may need to be manually categorized.

DoD and DVA are now grouped into a single Type of Service/Source of Funds value.

Alphabetical order is Tableau´s default sort for **Type of Service/Source of Funds**. However, sorting by lowest expenditure to highest is more useful here.

» Right-click "Type of Service/Source of Funds" field on Color on the Marks card.

» Select "Sort..." from the menu.

A Sort dialog box appears.

» For "Sort By," select "Field."

» For "Sort order," select "Ascending."

» For "Field Name," select "Expenditures."

» Click the "X" in the top right to close the dialog box.

Visual Cue for Sort

A sorted field displays the Sort icon, so it's easy to tell if sorts have been applied in the current view. To clear the sort, right-click the sorted field and select "Clear Sort." Alternatively, on the Toolbar, click the caret to the right of the Clear Sheet icon and select "Clear Sorts."

The default color scheme is discrete colors by field members of Type of Service/Source of Funds. To avoid highlighting categories with more prominent colors and to indicate that the field members are contributing parts to the whole of the area chart, edit the colors to be varying shades of a selected hue:

» Hover the cursor over the Color Legend header and click the caret that appears on the right.

» Select "Edit Colors..."

» Click the caret for the Select Color Palette menu, then change the color to Blue.

» Click the "Assign Palette" button to assign colors to all data items.

» Click "OK."

The chart now looks like this:

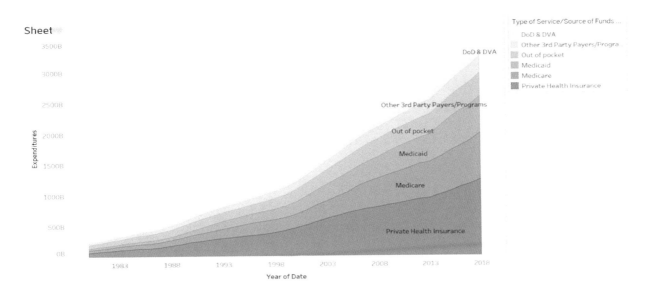

The years on the X axis can be edited for easier reading; this header is redundant, and can be removed.

» Right-click the X axis.

» Select "Edit axis...".

» Highlight and delete the Title "Year of Date."

» Click the "Tick Marks" tab at the top of the dialog box.

» In the "Major tick marks" section, click "Fixed"

» Change the Interval to: "5" years.

» Change "Tick Origin;" to "1/1/1980" by typing over the values for M/D/YYYY

» Click the "X" to close the dialog box.

7 Add a title

» Double-click the Title Row to open the Edit Title dialog box.

» Enter the title,

"U.S. Healthcare Expenditures
By Type of Service/Source of Funds
1980 - 2018."

8 Rename the worksheet tab and save the worksheet

» Double-click the worksheet tab at the bottom of the screen.

» In the highlighted text, enter the new title, "Area: US Healthcare Expenditures," then click "Enter."

» Click the "Save" icon on the Toolbar.

The final Area Chart looks like this:

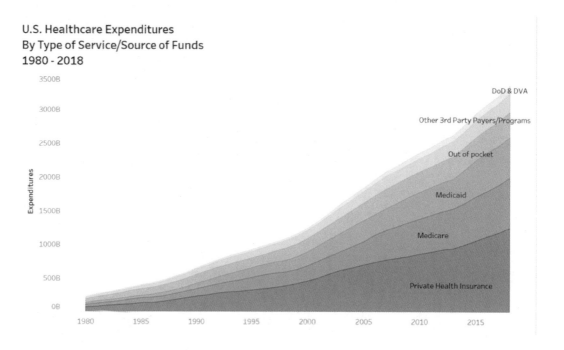

Insight: This Area Chart makes it clear that healthcare costs have risen dramatically in the last 30 years, with Private Health Insurance, Medicare, and Medicaid showing the biggest increases.

CHAPTER 12

Scatter Plots & Strip Plots

12.1 Scatter Plots

A Scatter Plot is a chart of plotted points that shows the relationship between two sets of data. Scatter Plots are useful for displaying a comparison/correlation of two measures and/or highlighting outliers in the data. Each point represents the value of one variable determining the position on the X axis and the value of the other variable determining the position on the Y axis. A Scatter Plot may show that a relationship exists, but does not and cannot prove that one variable is affecting the other. A common refrain is that "correlation does not equal causation." A "Trend Line" or "line of best fit" can be drawn to highlight the correlation between the variables. Another useful aspect of a Scatter Plot is its ability to show nonlinear relationships between variables.

Where a Scatter Plot shows the relationship between two measures, a Strip Plot shows the distribution along a scale of a single metric, highlighting where the data may cluster, show gaps, or indicate outliers. Strip Plots can be used anytime a disaggregated display of the data is warranted, and does not require use of zero at baseline, allowing for a more detailed view of the data while preventing analytical distortion.

How To: Build a Scatter Plot to analyze BMI in comparison with Systolic Blood Pressure and a Strip Plot to analyze BMI distribution by Age Groups.

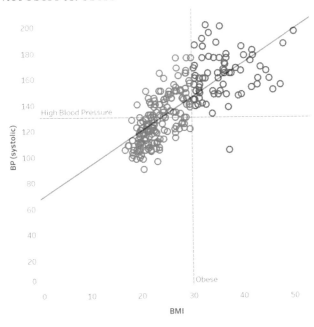

Correlation of Clinic Patient' Body Mass Index (BMI) and Systolic Blood Pressure
Not Obese vs. Obese

Distribution of Clinic Patients' Body Mass Index (BMI)
By Age Groups
Not Obese **vs.** Obese

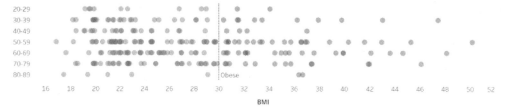

Data Source: Mock patient weight and systolic blood pressure data

About the Data: 250 mock adult patients from a hospital clinic visit were selected to record their height, weight, and blood pressure measurements for comparison.

1 Create a new worksheet and connect to the data

» Open a new worksheet.

» In the Data pane, select the "Ch. 12 - Clinic Patients' Metrics" dataset.

2 Create the chart

The measures of interest for the Scatter Plot are Systolic Blood Pressure and BMI. This dataset contains height and weight figures for each patient. A BMI can be calculated from these two measures. The formula to calculate a BMI is (body weight in kg) / (body height in meters)^2.

» Right-click "Weight(kg)" in the Data pane.

» Click "Create" to open a sub-menu.

» Select "Calculated field…"

Building a Calculated Field ▶

Building a Calculated Field based on a specific field (Dimension or Measure) automatically populates the Calculation window with that field. Starting with a specific field makes this process shorter and easier.

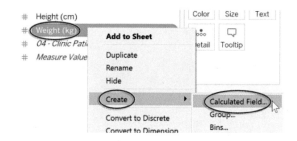

» Edit the field name to "BMI."

» In the formula window, enter:

`[Weight(kg)]/([Height(cm)]/100)^2`

» Click "OK."

From the Data pane,

» Drag and drop "BMI" to the Columns shelf.

» Drag and drop "BP (systolic)" to the Rows shelf.

» Drag and drop "Patient ID" to Detail on the Marks card.

The chart now looks like this:

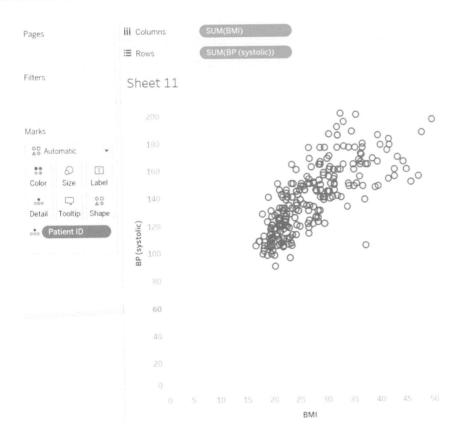

▲ Level of Detail

The Level of Detail of the view is comprised of all of the discrete dimensions present on the rows, columns, or pages shelf or the marks card. This Level of Detail indicates at what granularity the data will be aggregated. Notice that adding a dimension onto Detail on the Marks card separates out the individual marks of that dimension in the view.

Best Practice

What variable goes on what axis?

The Independent variable, sometimes referred to as the "Possible Cause Variable" goes on the X axis. The Dependent variable, sometimes referred to as the 'Response Variable," goes on the Y axis. If the terms "Independent" and 'Dependent" get confusing, try to associate the X axis with the "possible cause" and the Y axis with the "possible effect." In this example, the "possible cause" is Body Mass Index (BMI) and the "possible effect" is elevated Blood Pressure.

3 Add a Trend Line

» Adding a trend line to the scatter plot will visually identify if any relationship exists between these two variables.

» Click the Analytics Tab in the Side Bar.

» Locate "Trend Line" under Model. Click and drag onto worksheet. An option menu appears.

» Drag and drop Trend Line onto the highlighted "Linear" icon.

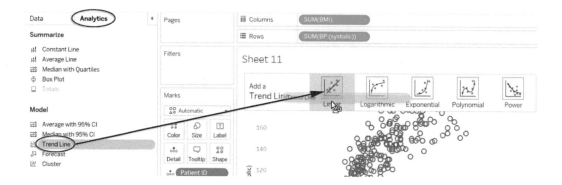

Trend Line ▶

Hover the cursor over the trend line for statistical information such as equation, R-squared, and p-value to evaluate the reliability and predictive value of the trend line.

Trend Line Information and Customization ▶

Right-click the trend line for menu options to view statistical descriptions and edit its appearance.

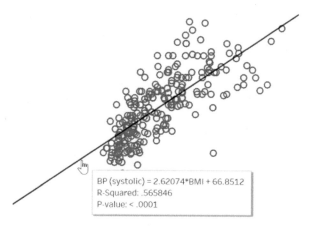

BP (systolic) = 2.62074*BMI + 66.8512
R-Squared: .565846
P-value: < .0001

Tableau also offers on-the-fly analysis to custom-select marks of interest. To activate the Toolbar for this feature:

》 Click "Worksheet" on the Menu Bar.

》 Click "Show View Toolbar."

》 Select "Show on Hover."

》 Hover the cursor over the top left section of the Scatter Plot chart to display the View Toolbar.

》 Click the caret and select the lasso option.

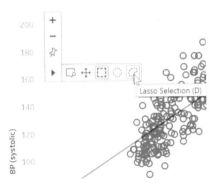

》 Select a small number of scatter plot marks. The Trend Line will adjust for the selected marks.

》 Click anywhere in the worksheet to discontinue the custom lasso.

4 Add Reference Lines

Obesity is defined as a BMI >= 30 kg/m². High Blood Pressure is defined as a Systolic BP > 130 (and a Diastolic BP > 80). Reference Lines set to these values can help determine which patients fall in both categories. To add Reference Lines:

》 With the Analytics tab in the Data pane selected, drag "Reference Line" into the workspace.

》 In the dialog box that appears, drop the Reference Line onto the junction of "SUM(BMI)" and "Table."

》 In the "Edit Reference Line, Band, or Box" dialog box, edit as follows:

In the Line section,
  • Value: click the caret and select "Constant," then enter "30" for the value.
  • Label: click the caret and select "Custom." In the blank field that appears, enter "Obese."

In the Formatting section,
  • Line: select dashed; the thinnest line option; and a lighter shade of gray.

》 Follow these steps again to add a second Reference Line, this one for SUM(BP(systolic)).

- Set the value to "130" and label the line "High Blood Pressure."

The chart now looks like this:

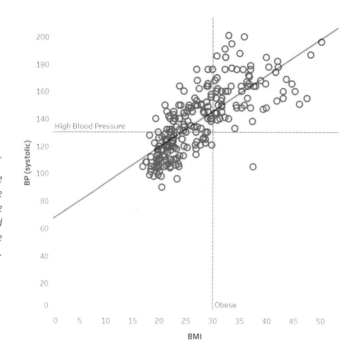

Reference Line Tooltips ▷

As with hovering over marks in the chart, hovering over a Reference Line displays a Tooltip. Its text may be edited or the tooltip may be disabled altogether via the Edit Reference Line dialog box.

5 Color-encode select data

Color-encode the marks for BMI >= 30 to more easily identify the obesity cohort. To make the distinction between patients with a BMI >= 30 and those with a BMI < 30, use a calculated field.

» Right-click "BMI" in the Data pane.

» Click "Create…" then select "Calculated Field."

» Enter the field name "Obese?"

» Enter the following calculation:

```
[BMI] >= 30
```

» Then click "OK."

Boolean Calculations

Use Boolean calculations instead of logical ones whenever possible for better performance. While a logical calculation of "IF [BMI] >=30 THEN "Obese" ELSE "Not Obese" END" would work, the resulting performance would be slower.

The "Obese?" calculated field is now a new dimension in the Data pane. Notice that the data type icon is "=T/F", indicating a Boolean data type.

» Drag and drop "Obese?" from the Data pane onto Color on the Marks card. One color is assigned to the "True" cohort (patients with BMI >= 30); another color to the "False" cohort (patients with BMI < 30).

Each group of patients now has a corresponding trend line. To have just one trend line representing the whole sample population:

» Right-click either trend line.

» Select "Edit All Trend Lines…"

» Uncheck the box "Allow a trend line per color."

» Click "OK."

To edit the colors:

» Hover over the Color Legend header until a caret appears at the right side of the header.

» Click the caret.

» Select "Edit Colors."

» Click the caret for "Select Color Palette" and choose "Color Blind."

» Click the Data Item "False" to highlight and select the medium-dark gray color.

» Click the Data Item "True" to highlight and select the dark orange color.

» Click "OK."

The color legend labels currently read "False" and "True." Changing the labels to "Obese" and "Not Obese" is clearer. To edit the labels:

» Right-click the "Obese?" calculated field in the Data pane.

» Select the "Aliases…" option.

» Click "False" under the "Value (Alias)" column, then change to "Not Obese." Note that an asterisk appears in the Has Alias column once the name has been changed.

» Click "True" under the "Value (Alias)" column and change to "Obese."

» Click "OK."

6 **Add a title**

» Enter the title:

"Correlation of Clinic Patients´ Body Mass Index (BMI) and Systolic Blood Pressure Not Obese vs. Obese"

» Highlight "Obese" and click the caret for the Color icon.

» Select "More Colors."

» Click the "Pick Screen Color" button.

» Hover cursor over the "Obese" color in the color legend, then click to save the color.

» Follow the same steps to edit the font color for "Not Obese."

7 **Rename the worksheet tab and save the worksheet**

» Double-click the worksheet tab at the bottom of the screen.

» In the highlighted text, enter the new title, "Scatter Plot: BMI & SBP," then click "Enter."

» Click the "Save" icon on the Toolbar.

The final chart looks like this:

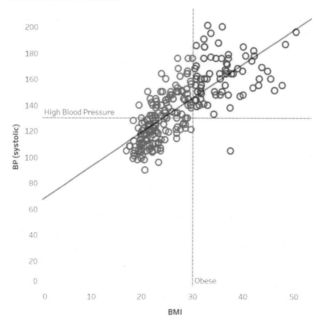

Correlation of Clinic Patient' Body Mass Index (BMI) and Systolic Blood Pressure
Not Obese **vs. Obese**

Insight: This Scatter Plot chart displays what seems to be a positive correlation between BMI and systolic blood pressure. With the exception of one patient, all the obese patients (BMI >=30) in this clinic sample have a high systolic blood pressure.

12.2 Strip Plots

ere a Strip Plot will be utilized to evaluate the distribution of BMI among the different age groups of the clinic patients to identify any patterns and/or outliers.

1 Create a new worksheet and connect to the data

» Open a new worksheet.

» Continue to utilize the "Ch. 12 - Clinic Patients' Metrics" dataset.

2 Create the chart

From the Data pane:

» Drag and drop "BMI" on to the Columns shelf.

» Drag and drop "Patient ID" on to Details on the Marks card.

» Click the drop-down menu on the Marks card and change the marks from Automatic to Circle.

The chart looks like this:

Each dot represents an individual clinic patient. There is a heavy density of patients in the 19 to 28 BMI range. To better visualize the distribution, adjust the opacity of the circles' color.

» Click Color on the Marks card.

» Adjust the Opacity slider to about 40% or as desired.

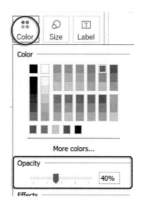

The chart now looks like this:

To stratify the Strip Plot by age groups, the age groups first need to be created from the Measure "Age."

» Right-click "Age" in the Data pane.

» From the appearing menus, select "Create," then select "Bins…"

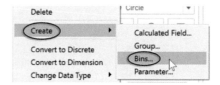

In the Edit Bins dialog box, the "New field name" is automatically created; this name may be customized if desired. Below the new field name is "Size of bins" with a calculated value that creates 15 bins. This value may be customized as well.

» Change the New field name to "Age Groups."

» Change "Size of bins" to "10."

» Click "OK."

Binning ▶

Tableau simplifies the process of grouping the values in a Measure into uniform bins by automatically creating a new field that breaks the Measure into equally spaced ranges. This new field appears as a Dimension because Bins are treated as discrete categories. (If desired, a Parameter can be used to dynamically change bin size for added interactivity.)

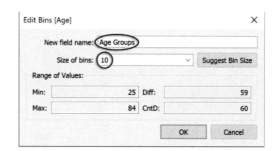

The bins will now group the number of patients by 10-year age ranges.

Best Practice

When creating bins, make sure to choose a size small enough to show detailed distribution, but not so small as to provide too much specificity. The Min, Max, and Diff values can aid in the selection of an appropriate bin range.

"Age Groups" appears as a new field in the Data pane. Notice the data type icon to its left, indicating it is a binned field.

»   Drag and drop the "Age Groups" field to the Rows shelf. The Strip Plot is now disaggregated by the Age Groups bins.

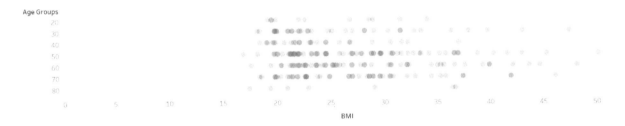

Edit the "Age Groups" aliases for better clarity of the age ranges.

»   Right-click "Age Groups" in the Data pane.

»   Select "Aliases…" from the menu.

»   Click the value in the Value (Alias) column and edit to display the age ranges, then click 'OK."

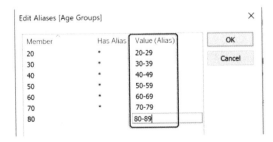

3 Format the chart

Unlike a bar chart, the axis for a Strip Plot does not have to start at zero. The BMI values for this cohort of patients begins at 17. To edit the axis:

» Right-click the X axis and select "Edit Axis..." from the appearing menu.

» In the Range section, uncheck the box for "Include zero." The axis range automatically adjusts for the range of BMI values in the dataset.

» Click the "X" in the top right corner to close the dialog box.

Add a Reference Line to delineate Obesity (BMI >= 30).

» Right-click the X-axis and select "Add Reference Line" from the appearing menu.

» In the "Edit Reference Line, Band, or Box" dialog box, edit as follows:

In the Line section,

• Value: click the caret and select "Constant," then enter "30" for the value.

• Label: click the caret and select "Custom." In the blank field that appears, enter "Obese."

In the Formatting section,

• Line: select dashed; the thinnest dashed line option; and a lighter shade of gray.

To highlight the obese patient population,

» Drag and drop the field "Obese?" (previously created in the Scatter Plot section of this chapter) to Color on the Marks card.

The chart now looks like this:

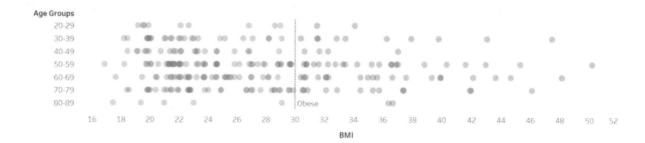

4 Add a title

» Double-click the Title Row to open the Edit Title dialog box.

» Enter the title:

"Distribution of Clinic Patients' Body Mass Index (BMI)
By Age Groups
Not Obese vs. Obese"

» Highlight "Obese" and click the caret for the Color icon.

» Select the orange square (below the default color palette) that was created in the Scatter Plot exercise.

» Highlight "Not Obese" and click the caret for the Color icon.

» Select the gray square created in the Scatter plot exercise.

Because Age Group is used in the title, the field label can be hidden.

» Right-click the field label "Age Group."

» In the menu, select "Hide Field Labels for Rows."

5 **Rename the worksheet tab and save the worksheet**

» Double-click the worksheet tab at the bottom of the screen.

» In the highlighted text, enter the new title, "Dot Plot: BMI Distribution by Age," then click "Enter."

» Click the "Save" icon on the Toolbar.

The final chart looks like this:

Distribution of Clinic Patients' Body Mass Index (BMI)
By Age Groups
Not Obese vs. Obese

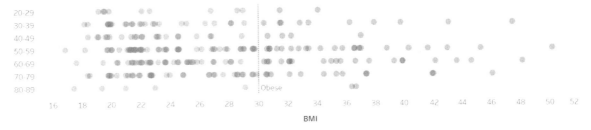

Insight: In this Strip Plot chart, it is easy to see that the predominance of total clinic patients and obese patients fall in the 50 to 79 age range.

CHAPTER 13

Tooltips

Tooltips reveal useful details or additional context when a data point is hovered over within a worksheet or dashboard. Tooltips are helpful for presenting data that would be too granular, potentially distracting, or space-consuming if displayed in the primary visualization.

A Tooltip is made up of the "Body," which contains the details of the selected mark(s) and can include additional fields or even entirely different visualizations to support and supplement the marks. Two optional components are the Command Buttons and Action Filter Links. The Command Buttons can be displayed to allow the user to filter, create groups or sets, and/or view underlying data. Action Filter Links display only when an action is configured to run on "Menu" (Actions are discussed in the Dashboards Basic Interactivity chapter).

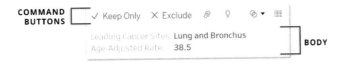

Tooltip Formatting

Tableau creates default Tooltips for every chart. Each Tooltip is organized to display many of the Dimensions and Measures present on a worksheet when the cursor is hovered over a particular mark on a chart. Below is an example of a Tooltip on a cancer mortality rate bar chart. The two fields defaulted in the Tooltip, "Leading Cancer Sites" and "Age-Adjusted Rate," are the two fields used to create this chart.

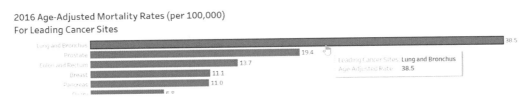

For better readability, Tooltips can be formatted with both static and dynamic text using tools in the Edit Tooltip dialog box. Supporting information and visualizations can be added; unnecessary fields can be removed. Below is a reformatted example.

2016 Age-Adjusted Mortality Rates (per 100,000)
For Leading Cancer Sites

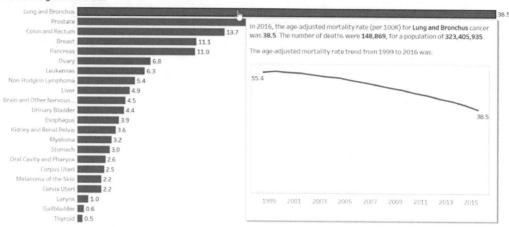

To create this chart and Tooltip:

1 Create the charts

» At the bottom of the Tableau workspace, click the icon for a new worksheet.

» In the Data pane, select the "Ch. 13 - U.S. Cancer Mortality Rates (1999-2016)" dataset.

The bar and line charts used in this exercise are built the same way as the Bar chart in Chapter 5 and the Line chart in Chapter 7. Screenshots will be omitted for the steps that parallel those chapters.

Create the Bar chart:

From the Data pane,

» Drag and drop "Leading Cancer Sites" to the Rows shelf.

» Drag and drop "Age-Adjusted Rate" to the Columns shelf.

» Click the "Sort Descending" icon in the Toolbar to sort the bars from highest to lowest.

» Click the "[T]" on the Toolbar to add labels.

The bars currently display the sum aggregation of rates for several years of data. To filter to the most recent year in the dataset (2016):

» Drag and drop "Year" to the Filters shelf.
  • In the appearing dialog box, select the "Years" option, then click "Next."
  • Click the checkbox for "2016" and click "OK."

Format the chart:

» Right-click "Age-Adjusted Rate" in the Data pane, select "Default Properties," then "Number Format."

» Select "Number (Custom)" and format the numbers to one decimal place.

» Right-click "Leading Cancer Sites" field label and select "Hide Field Labels for Rows."

» Right-click the X-axis and click "Show Header" to remove its checkmark.

Add a title and rename the worksheet tab:

» Double-click the title row and add the title:

"2016 Age-Adjusted Mortality Rates (per 100,000)
For Leading Cancer Sites"

» Rename the Sheet tab to "Bar: Cancer Mortality Rates."

The bar chart looks like this:

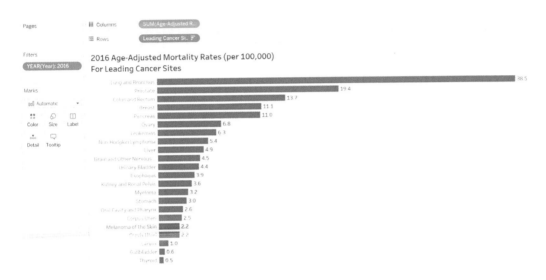

Create the line chart that will be placed into the Tooltip

» At the bottom of the Tableau workspace, click the icon for a new worksheet.

From the Data pane,

» Drag and drop "Leading Cancer Sites" and then "Age-Adjusted Rate" to the Rows shelf.

» Drag and drop "Year" to the Columns shelf.

- Right-click the "Year" field and select "Year" from the date value section.

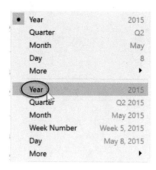

Format the chart:

» Click "Label" on the Marks card.

- Click the check box to "Show mark labels."
- In the Marks to Label section, select "Line Ends."

» Right-click the X axis and select "Edit Axis..."

» Delete the title "Year of Year."

» Right-click "Leading Cancer Sites" field label and select "Hide Field Labels for Rows."

Add a title and rename the worksheet tab:

» Double-click the title row and add the title:

"Age-Adjusted Mortality Rates (per 100,000)
For Leading Cancer Sites
1999 - 2016"

» Rename the Sheet tab to "Tooltip Line: Cancer Mortality Rates."

The line chart looks like this:

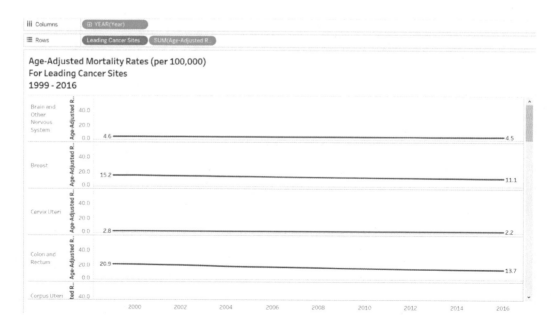

Format the Tooltip

Navigate back to the Bar chart. For a field to appear in the Tooltip, it must be present on the worksheet. For fields that are desired to display solely in the Tooltip, drag them to Tooltip on the Marks card.

» Drag and drop "Deaths" and "Population" from the Data pane to Tooltip on the Marks card.

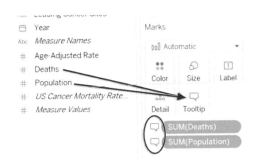

◄ Tooltip icon

Fields residing on the Tooltip card display its icon to the left of the field on the Marks card.

» Click "Tooltip" on the Marks card to open the Edit Tooltip dialog box.

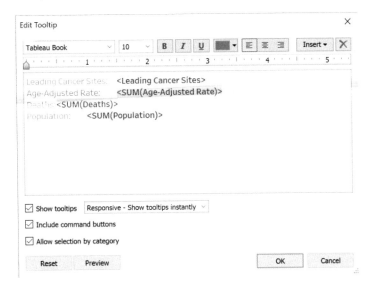

◄ Tooltip details

The Tooltip defaults the list of fields to alphabetical order, first by Dimensions, then by Measures. The text contained within < > is dynamic: it changes according to user selection in the chart. The Insert option displays fields available to add to the Tooltip.

» Edit the Tooltip to read as follows:

In 2016, the age-adjusted mortality rate (per 100K) for <Leading Cancer Sites> cancer was <SUM(Age-Adjusted Rate)>. The number of deaths were <SUM(Deaths)>, for a population of <SUM(Population)>.

The age-adjusted mortality rate trend from 1999 to 2016 was:

Insert the line chart into the Tooltip:

» Click the cursor below the text where the chart is to be inserted.

◄ Tooltip text editing

Dynamic text (text within the < >) can be added via:

1. The Insert dropdown menu option

2. Copy/past or cut/paste text present in the default Tooltip view

3. Manual entry

» Click the "Insert" caret, then select "Sheets." The Sheets option lists all worksheets that have been created in the workbook.

» Select the worksheet "Tooltip Line: Cancer Mortality Rates."

» Click "OK."

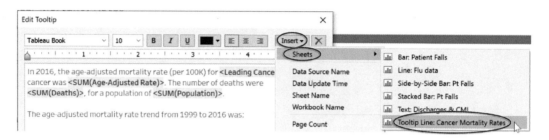

A reference to the target worksheet has been placed in the Tooltip body.

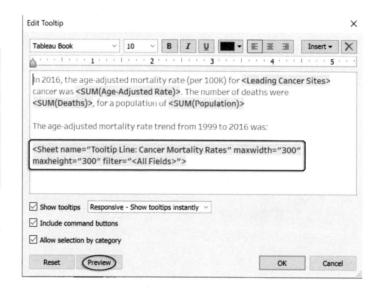

Best Practice

Use color, spacing, font, and plain language to encode information quickly and effectively. Supporting information can be added for clarity.

Tooltip Preview ▶

Use the "Preview" button to preview the Tooltip during editing.

At the bottom of the Edit Tooltip dialog box, there are several "Show tooltips" display options:

Tooltip Display Options and Command Buttons ▶

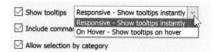

When a Tooltip is set to "Responsive," moving the cursor over a mark displays the Tooltip instantly, without Command Buttons. Click a mark or marks to display Command Buttons (unless that option has been manually turned off).

When a Tooltip is set to show "On Hover," the Tooltip will not appear until the cursor lingers over a mark. Doing so makes the entire Tooltip appear, including the Command Buttons (unless that option has been manually turned off).

Tooltips can be hidden by unchecking the "Show tooltips" checkbox.

◄ Include Command Buttons

Tooltips can embed interactive functions such as those allowing the user to filter, create groups or sets, or view underlying data. These functions can be seen at the top of the Tooltip. If these interactive functions are not desired, uncheck the "Include command buttons" box to disable them.

Format the Tooltip

» Hover over a bar to view the Tooltip. Notice that the chart is automatically filtered by the "Leading Cancer Sites" dimension to only show one line at a time within the tooltip.

The line chart needs some adjustment to improve its appearance, specifically: increasing the chart width, hiding the Y axis (the lines are labeled), hiding the Leading Cancer Sites dimension (the label is displayed in the Tooltip text), and editing the "Year" axis to display more years.

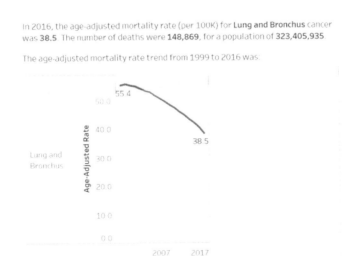

Navigate to the Tooltip Line chart worksheet.

» Right-click the Y axis and click "Show Header" to remove its checkmark.

» Right-click any Leading Cancer Sites field name and click "Show Header" to remove its checkmark.

» Right-click the X axis and select "Edit Axis…"
  • Select the Tick Marks tab.
  • Under the Major Tick Marks section, select the "Fixed" radio button.

- Click the "Show Times" checkbox to remove the checkmark.
- Change the Tick origin to "1/1/1999" and change the Interval to "2" years.

Navigate back to the Bar chart worksheet.

» Click Tooltip on the Marks card.

» Edit "maxwidth" to "500."

Tooltip Sizing ▶

The ideal height and width to render the chart in the tooltip will depend on the size and legibility of the particular visualization being embedded. Make sure to preview your tooltips and set a maxheight and maxwidth that will display nicely for all marks.

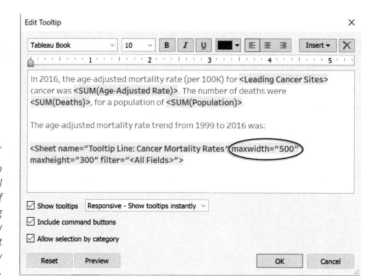

The Tooltip now looks like this:

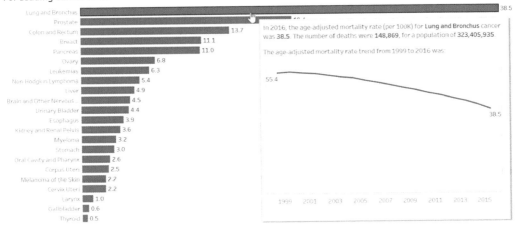

Intermediate Charts

CHAPTER 14

Box-and-Whisker Plots

A Box-and-Whisker Plot illustrates the distribution of a data set, highlighting the spread of percentiles; minimum value; 25th, 50th, and 75th percentiles; and maximum value. "Boxes" enclose the middle 50% of the data, known as the middle two quartiles of the distribution. "Whiskers" are the lines that encode the top and bottom range of data values. The whiskers can be placed at a location to display the most widely separated data points in the distribution of the data or at a location that is 1.5 times further out than the width of the adjoining box, known as the interquartile range (IQR).

Although Box-and-Whisker Plots look similar to Bar Charts, they are very different. Whereas a Bar Chart encodes and displays a single value, a Box-and-Whisker Plot features a range of values from lowest to highest, and allows comparison of the distribution of those values to other value ranges and distributions.

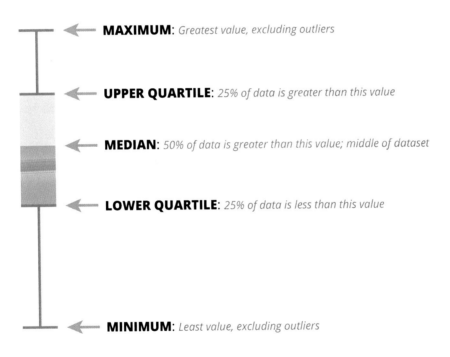

MAXIMUM: *Greatest value, excluding outliers*

UPPER QUARTILE: *25% of data is greater than this value*

MEDIAN: *50% of data is greater than this value; middle of dataset*

LOWER QUARTILE: *25% of data is less than this value*

MINIMUM: *Least value, excluding outliers*

How To: Build a Box-and-Whisker Plot chart showing the distribution of cardiovascular patients' ages by race.

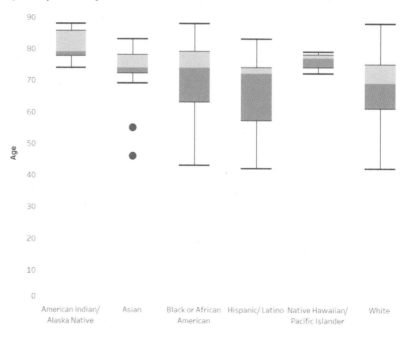

Age Distribution of Cardiovascular Clinic Patients
By Race/Ethnicity

Data Source: *De-identified outpatient clinic data*

About the Data: *Age and race of selected outpatient clinic patients being examined for cardiovascular disease.*

1 **Create a new worksheet and connect to the data**

» At the bottom of the Tableau workspace, click the icon for a new worksheet.

» In the Data pane, select the "Ch. 14 - Clinic Patients' Demographics" dataset.

2 **Create the chart**

» Holding down the Control key, click the following fields in the Data pane:
- "Pt ID"
- "Race/Ethnicity"
- "Age"

» Click the "Show Me" tab.

» Select the "Box-and-Whisker Plot" icon.

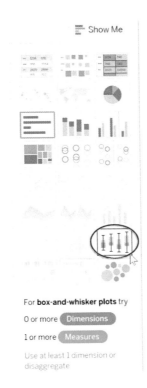

For **box-and-whisker plots** try

0 or more (Dimensions)

1 or more (Measures)

Use at least 1 dimension or disaggregate

» Click "Show Me" again to close the tab.

The chart initially looks like this:

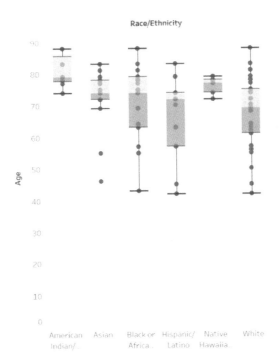

◄ **Box-and-Whisker Creation**

The Show Me button creates a basic Box-and-Whisker Plot based on the data selected. Individual marks (blue dots) plot each patient's age on the vertical axis. All elements of the visualization, including the blue dots, are controlled through the Edit Reference Line, Band, or Box menu.

3 Format the whiskers

Currently the chart displays the underlying individual values; these are not necessary and can be hidden.

» Right-click the Y axis.

» Select "Edit Reference Line."

» In the Edit Reference Line dialog box, Under Plot Options, check the box "Hide underlying marks (except outliers)."

» In the "Formatting" section of the Edit Reference Line dialog box, format the chart with desired colors (Gray blue was used in this example).

The chart now looks like this:

Interquartile Range (IQR) ▷

Tableau automatically formats the whiskers to be 1.5 times the Interquartile Range (IQR). The IQR is the length of the box section (Q3-Q1), and can be used to indicate how spread out the values are. There is a statistical assumption if some values are too far away from the middle grouping—more than one and a half times the length of the box—they are assumed to be "outliers."

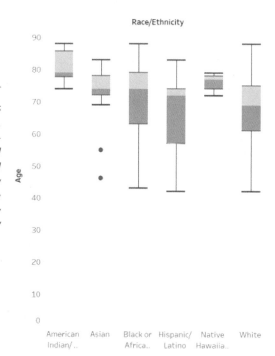

To remove the Header:

» Right-click the "Race/Ethnicity" header at the top of the chart.

» Select "Hide Field Labels for Columns."

To widen the chart:

» Hover over the right border of the chart until the cursor changes to a bi-directional arrow.

» Click and drag the chart until the Race/Ethnicity labels are fully visible.

4 **Add a title**

» Double-click the Title Row to open the Edit Title dialog box.

» Enter the title,
"Age Distribution of Cardiovascular Clinic Patients
By Race/Ethnicity."

5 **Rename the worksheet tab and save the worksheet**

» Double-click the worksheet tab at the bottom of the screen.

» In the highlighted text, enter the new title, "Box & Whisker: Clinic Pt Age," then click
"Enter."

» Click the "Save" icon on the Toolbar.

The final chart looks like this:

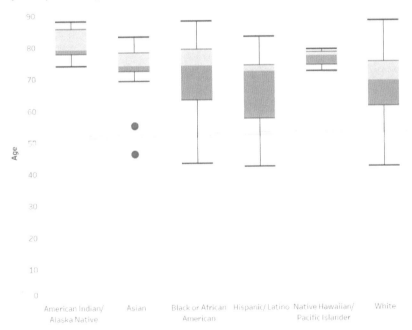

Age Distribution of Cardiovascular Clinic Patients
By Race/Ethnicity

Insight: The Box-and-Whisker Plot makes clear the distribution of age by race/ethnicity of cardiovascular patients. Here in particular, the overall age range is similar for American Indian/Alaska Native, Asian, and Native Hawaiian/Pacific Islander. Black or African Americans, Hispanic/Latinos, and Whites have a much wider age range, with Whites having a lower median age. The Asian cohort also contains two outlier patients with much younger ages (55 and 45).

CHAPTER 15

Maps

Maps are an intuitive and increasingly widely used way to visualize data, especially if location is crucial to the problems being analyzed. Geographic Maps are simply scatter plots that use longitude and latitude as X and Y coordinates and maps as background images.

There are two types of Maps: Filled and Symbol. A Filled Map, sometimes called a choropleth map, is a modification of a traditional marks map. Its study areas are filled with the measure of interest, and colors are used with different hues or diverging progression to assist in identifying areas of the measure performance. Filled Maps are the most common way to map regional data. Symbol Maps use size- and/or color-encoded shapes to represent data.

Tableau geocodes at the following levels; Country/Region; State/Province; City; Congressional District (U.S.); County; CBSA (Core-Based Statistical Area)/MSA (Metropolitan Statistical Area); Area Code (U.S.); ZIP Code/Postcode; and Airport (International Air Transport Association [IATA] and International Civil Aviation Organization [ICAO]), and NUTS Europe (Nomenclature of Territorial Units for Statistics).

How To: Build a Dual Axis Map for 2018 Massachusetts motor vehicle accidents with injury counts by county with an overlay of the location of trauma centers

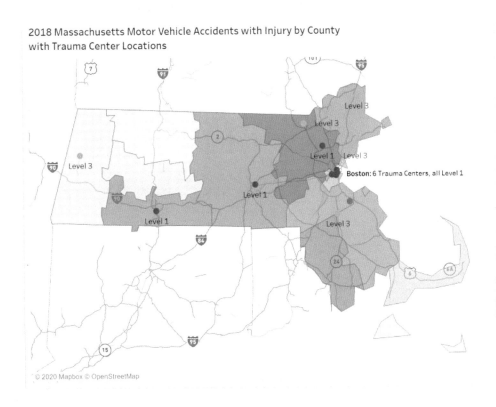

2018 Massachusetts Motor Vehicle Accidents with Injury by County with Trauma Center Locations

Data Source: www.mass.gov/crash-data, and a created data source of Massachusetts trauma centers by county.

About the Data: Counts of motor vehicle accidents with documented injury or transportation to medical facilities for 2018 by Massachusetts county. The Massachusetts trauma centers' data source was created via address search and latitude and longitude sourcing.

1 Create a new worksheet and connect to the data

At the bottom of the Tableau workspace, click the icon for a new worksheet.

> » In the Data pane, select the "Ch. 15 - MA Motor Vehicle Accidents with Injury (2018) & Trauma Hospitals" dataset.

The data in use here is from two different tables: 2018 MA MVA by County and MA Trauma Hospitals. When creating the data source (see Chapter 3 Connecting to Data for details), a relationship was automatically established on the "County" field – the dimension present in both tables. The Data pane displays fields from both tables located below their corresponding titles .

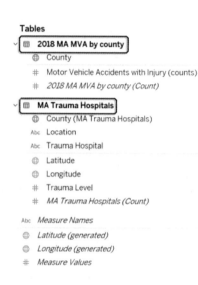

Geographic Fields ▷

Tableau must identify a Dimension as geographic to use it for maps; once it has done so, it automatically geocodes the data. When the data has been loaded, Tableau determines geographic fields using field names such as country, state, county, city, zip code, or airport codes. It places a global icon next to the field name in the Data pane. Tableau will then generate corresponding latitude and longitude fields, placing them below the data source fields in italics. These generated fields will automatically be added to the worksheet when creating a map from the Show Me menu.

2 Create the chart

In the Data pane, under "2018 MA MVA by County:"

> » Holding down the Control key, click "County" and "Motor Vehicle Accidents with Injury (counts)."

> » Click the "Show Me" tab and select "Filled Map."

176

» Click "Show Me" again to close.

The initial map displays several counties with no data. A small indicator in the bottom right of the view conveys "9 unknown," indicating that Tableau does not have sufficient information to plot these values on the map.

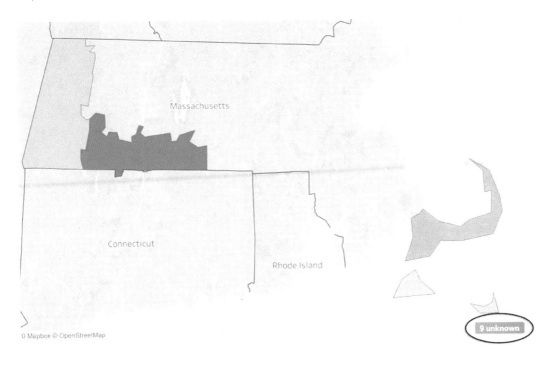

To resolve this:

» Click the "9 unknown" indicator.

In the appearing dialog box, click "Edit Locations..."

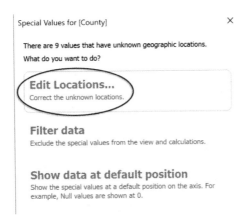

Tableau indicates that these county names are "ambiguous," meaning they are common names that occur in multiple states. Manually setting the state will allow Tableau to plot these missing locations.

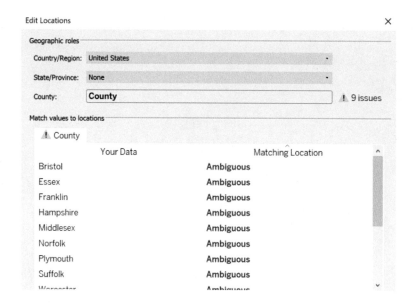

In the Edit Locations dialog box,

» Click the caret to the right of State/Province.

» Click the radio button next to "Fixed" then select "Massachusetts" from the drop-down menu.

» Click "OK."

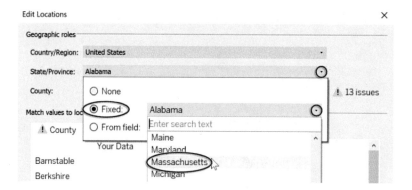

The map now looks like this, with the range in motor vehicle accidents with injury counts represented by color variation.

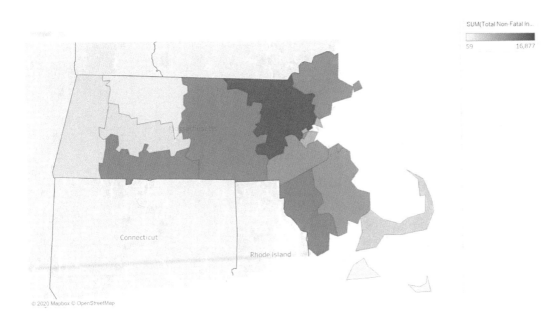

3 Create a map with the trauma hospital locations

The precise locations of the Massachusetts trauma hospitals can be displayed using the data source's geographic fields of "Trauma Hospital Latitude" and "Trauma Hospital Longitude." In order to utilize these, a second map needs to be created (it will then be overlaid on the primary map).

» Holding down the Control key, click and drag the "Latitude(generated)" field on the Rows shelf and drop it to its right to create a duplicate field. A duplicate map will be displayed below the original one.

Instead of displaying a second choropleth map, the trauma center locations will be presented as a symbol map with small circle indicators showing their precise location within each county. To edit the trauma center map,

» On the Marks card, click the "Latitude (generated)(2)" header to select its Marks card.

» Click the drop-down caret to the right of "Automatic" and select "Circle."

The circles currently represent each county (with the shading representing the MVA with Injury counts for each county). These fields need to be removed and replaced with the Trauma Hospital and Trauma Level fields.

» Click and drag off "County" and "SUM(Motor Vehicle Accidents with Injury (counts))" from the "Latitude (generated)(2)" Marks card.

The second map currently looks blank. The next steps will add the trauma hospital locations.

» Holding down the Control key, click "Trauma Hospital Latitude" and "Trauma Hospital Longitude" to select both.

» Drag and drop them onto "Detail" on the Marks card. The aggregation will be set to "AVG"; this is okay.

The second map is currently showing a single circle—the intersection of the average latitude and longitude of the trauma centers.

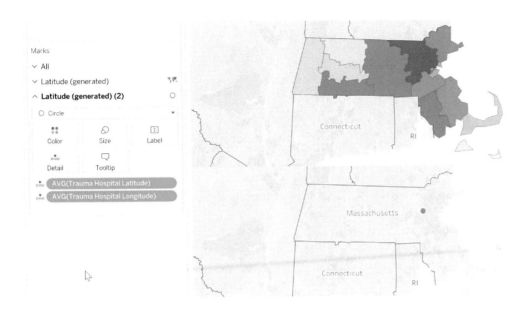

» Drag and drop "Trauma Level" to Color on the Latitude (generated)(2) marks card.

» Drag and drop "Trauma Level" to Label on the same Marks card.

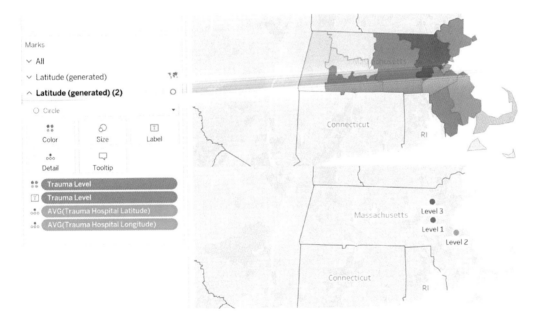

The map currently displays the aggregation of all Level 1, all Level 2, and all Level 3 trauma centers. To display the locations of each individual facility:

» Drag and drop "Trauma Hospital" to Details on the Marks card.

The default colors for the hospitals' locations will compete with the choropleth map colors. To edit the circle colors:

» Double-click in the white space of the color legend to open the color palette.

» Click the caret to the right of "Automatic" color palette and change to "Seattle Grays."

» Click "Level 1" in the Select Data Item section to highlight. Then click a dark gray square.

» Perform the same steps for the Level 2 and Level 3 data items, changing their colors to progressively lighter shades of gray.

» Click "OK."

4 Create the dual axis map

The MA Trauma Hospitals map can now be overlaid on the choropleth map.

» Right-click the "Latitude (generated)" field farthest to the right on the Rows shelf.

» From the menu, select "Dual Axis."

Dual Axis Charts ▶

The presence of two measures on the Rows or Columns shelf offers the possibility of creating a Dual Axis chart. Selecting "Dual Axis" causes Tableau to place the two charts one on top of the other, with a second axis appearing on the right or top of the chart depending on its orientation. These two charts do not have to be of the same type. The Dual Axis technique can overlay lines on a scatter plot, bars on an area chart, or a geographic symbol map on a filled map. This technique can also be used to plot two separate fields on the same axis with the same chart type.

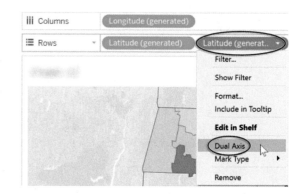

5 Format the map

Adding major highways to the map view will provide useful context to this MVA map, indicating if there is any correlation between highway density and higher counts of motor vehicle accidents per county.

» On the Menu bar, click "Map."

» Select "Map Layers..."

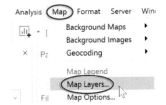

◀ Map Customization

Tableau offers several ways to customize maps. Multiple options are available for background maps (light, dark, street, satellite, etc.), custom geocoding, adding/importing Map Services, and adding/hiding many Map Layers' features.

Under "Background," "Style," click the caret and select "Outdoors."

» Under "Map Layers," uncheck:

- Base
- Terrain
- State/Province Names
- Cities
- Points of Interest

To emphasize the highways, reduce the opacity of the choropleth map.

>> On the Marks card, click the first "Latitude (generated)" header, corresponding to the filled map.

>> Click "Color" and reduce opacity to "60%."

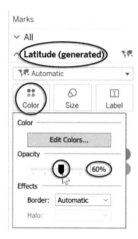

There are several trauma centers in the Boston area that are clustered together and are difficult to interpret.

Add an annotation to the map to indicate the number and levels of the clustered trauma centers.

>> Hover the cursor over white space on the map and right-click.

>> In the appearing menu, click "Annotate."

>> Select "Area" from the submenu.

>> In the Edit Annotation dialog box, enter: "Boston: 6 Trauma Centers, all Level 1."

>> Set the font to Tableau Regular, size 8, left-aligned, bold "Boston" then click "OK."

>> Adjust the width and the height of the annotation box to a single row and set it to the right of the clustered circles.

>> Click anywhere outside of the annotation box to hide the borders.

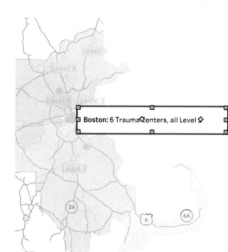

Annotation ▶

Tableau's annotation feature allows the report creator to add context or additional details directly on a chart or highlighting data points of interest. Right-click anywhere in the chart to annotate a mark, point, or area.

To hide the very faint gray background on the Annotation box,

> » Right-click the annotation box and select "Format…"

> » In the Box section, click the caret to the right of "Shading" and select "None."

> » Click the "X" in the top right of the Format Annotation pane to close it.

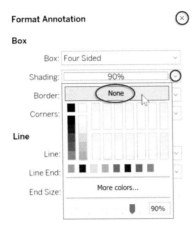

The map looks like this:

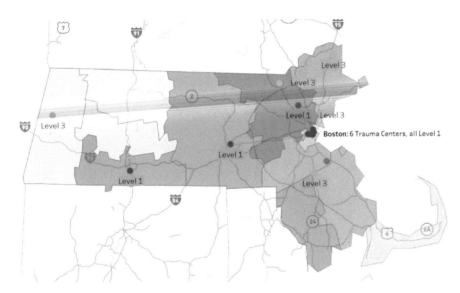

To hide the very faint gray background on the labels,

> » On the Marks card, select the header "All."

> » Click "Color."

> » In the Effects section, click the caret to the right of "Halo" and select "None."

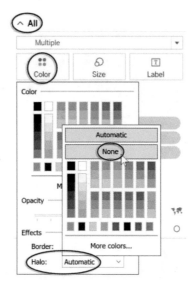

To give the trauma hospital location circles slightly more prominence, a border can be added to each circle.

> » Select the "Latitude (generated)(2)" Marks card header.

> » Click "Color."

> » In the Effects section, click the caret to the right of the "Border" option and select a medium-dark gray.

6 Add a title

> » Double-click the Title Row to open the Edit Title dialog box.

> » Enter the title, "2018 Massachusetts Motor Vehicle Accidents with Injury by County with Trauma Center Locations."

7 Rename the worksheet tab and save the worksheet

> » Double-click the worksheet tab at the bottom of the screen.

> » In the highlighted text, enter the new title, "Map: MA MVAs with Trauma Centers," then click "Enter."

> » Click the "Save" icon on the Toolbar.

The final map looks like this:

2018 Massachusetts Motor Vehicle Accidents with Injury by County
with Trauma Center Locations

© 2020 Mapbox © OpenStreetMap

Insight: On this Dual Axis Map, trauma centers are clustered where the highest volume of
motor vehicle incidents with injury occur in Massachusetts.

CHAPTER 16

Bullet Graphs

esigned by Stephen Few, a Bullet Graph is a variation of the bar chart that provides a multi-faceted display of data in a linear design, eliminating the need for meters or gauges. The Bullet Graph features three elements: a primary performance measure, a target, and a range for context. The graph compares the performance measure, represented by a horizontal bar, to another value, represented by a vertical line, and relates performance to quantitative ranges. These ranges are displayed as varying intensities of a single hue such as gray, to make them clearly visible to colorblind users.

The following diagram displays the different parts of a Bullet Graph:

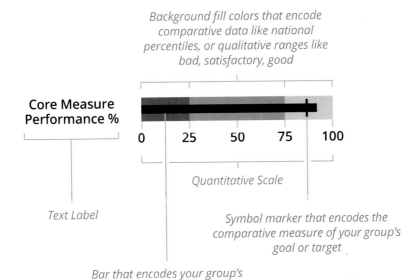

Background fill colors that encode comparative data like national percentiles, or qualitative ranges like bad, satisfactory, good

Core Measure Performance %

0   25   50   75   100

Quantitative Scale

Text Label

Symbol marker that encodes the comparative measure of your group's goal or target .

Bar that encodes your group's performance on measure

How To: Build a Bullet Graph displaying a Physician Group's performance on HEDIS Measures for Comprehensive Diabetes Care compared to a target goal and quantitative performance (poor, fair, good).

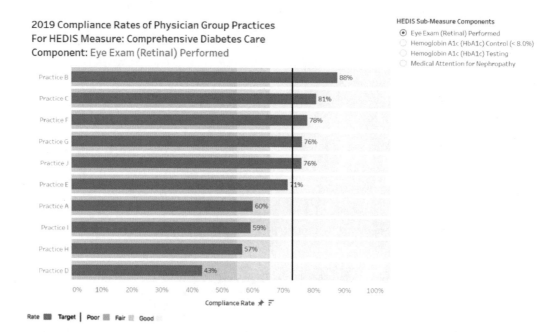

Data Source: *Mock physician group data for HEDIS measure "Comprehensive Diabetes Care" and mock target and quantitative performance ranges.*

About the Data: *The Healthcare Effectiveness Data and Information Set (HEDIS) is a set of performance measures designed to provide consumers and regulators with information to reliably compare competing managed-care health plans. HEDIS measures form a report card that evaluates a health plan's success in providing preventive care via the physicians in a plan's provider network.*

1 Create a new worksheet and connect to the data

At the bottom of the Tableau workspace, click the icon for a new worksheet.

» In the Data pane, select the "Ch. 16 - HEDIS Diabetes Measures" dataset.

2 Create the chart

» While holding down the Control key, in the Data pane, click:
- • "Physician Group"
- • "Compliance Rate"
- • "Target"

» Click the "Show Me" tab and select "Bullet Graph."

» Click the Show Me tab again to close.

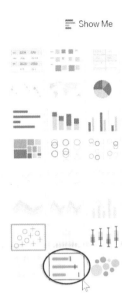

The chart initially looks like this:

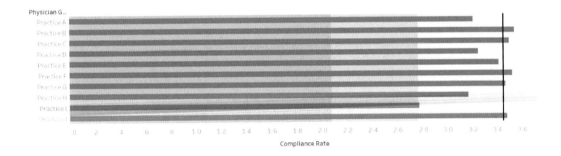

Bullet Graph Creation

The Show Me feature automatically (1) adds any Dimension to the Rows shelf to divide data according to categories; (2) adds one Measure to the Columns shelf to serve as the primary metric (blue bar); (3) adds one Measure to Details on the Marks card to create the target and distribution reference lines.

If after these steps Tableau has created a Bullet Graph that is the inverse of what was intended, the two Measure fields can be switched by right-clicking the X axis and selecting Swap Reference Line Fields.

3 Filter the data

The bars currently represent the aggregation of the four component measures of HEDIS Comprehensive Diabetes Care for each Physician Group. A filter menu can be added for the end-user to select the desired measure for viewing.

> » Right-click "HEDIS Sub-Measure Components" in the Data pane.

> » Select "Show Filter" from the menu. The filter will appear to the right of the Bullet Graph.

» Hover the cursor over the filter menu header and click the caret that appears in the top right corner.

» Select the "Single Value (list)" option.

Click the filter menu header caret again.

» Click "Customize."

» Click the "Show 'All' Value" option to remove the checkmark.

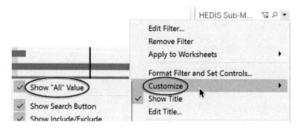

The chart now looks like this:

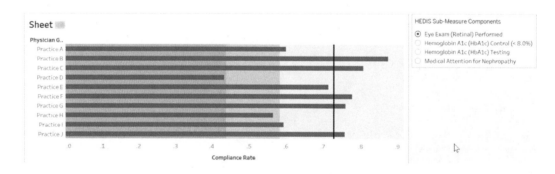

4 Edit the chart components

To add labels to the bars:

» Click the framed "[T]" icon on the Toolbar to add labels to the bars.

The Rate and Target Measures should be expressed as percentages.

» Right-click "Compliance Rate" in the Data pane.

» Select "Default Properties," then "Number Format."

» Select "Percentage."

» Change the Decimal places to "0."

» Repeat these steps for the "Target" field in the Data pane.

The shading of the Reference Bands in this chart encodes comparative data, such as percentages, quartiles, etc. In this case, Reference Bands need to be set at 75% and 90%.

» Right-click the "X axis."

» Select "Edit Reference Line."

» Select "60%,80% of Average Target."

By displaying 75% and 90% (instead of 60% and 80%) of the target value for each Core Measure, the Reference Bands will make clearer both quantitative and qualitative performance as compared to target.

» Ensure that the "Distribution" box is selected. ("Distribution" refers to a grouping of Reference Bands.)

» For Scope, select "Per Cell."

» For Computation, click the caret to the right of Value.
  - On the drop-down menu, select "Percentages."
  - Change Percentages to "75,90"

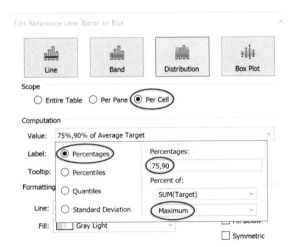

◄ Reference Distribution

Use the Distribution button at the top of the Edit Reference... dialog box to encode confidence intervals, percentiles, standard deviations, and more. The choice of Distribution over Band permits layering of additional calculations without the need to create new calculated fields.

  - On the second drop-down menu below "Percent of," click the caret and select "Maximum."

» Under Formatting, change Fill to "Gray Very Light."

» Click "OK."

The chart now looks like this:

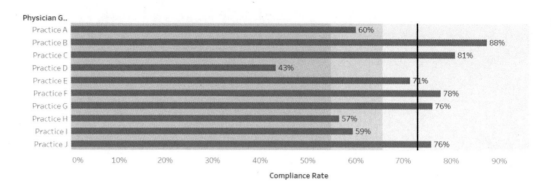

The background shades of gray indicate qualitative scale:

- Dark gray = Poor

- Medium gray = Fair

- Light gray = Good

5 Format the chart

To make the horizontal bars thicker:

» On the Menu bar, click "Format."

» Click "Cell Size."

» Select "Taller" from the submenu.

To increase white space between horizontal bars:

◀ **Cell Sizing**

Cell Size can be adjusted in small increments by using the Format menu or by manually dragging a Row or Column border.

» In the Menu bar, click the "Format" button again.

» Select "Borders."

» Select the "Rows" tab.

» In the "Row Divider" section, click "Pane."

» Select the image of the widest line and change the color to "White."

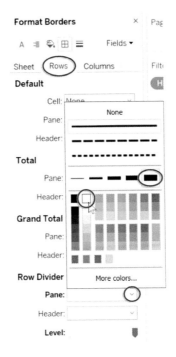

Using Row Dividers to Create Spacing

Tableau does not have a feature specifically designed to create spacing between reference lines, bands, or distributions. To enhance readability by increasing this space, insert a thick white row.

Sort the Physician Groups from highest to lowest.

» Click the Sort descending icon on the Toolbar.

The label "Physician Group" will appear in the title, so the field label can be hidden.

» Right-click "Physician Group" field label.

» Click "Hide Field Labels for Rows."

Test the filter by selecting each of the options. Notice the adjustment of the X axis as different HEDIS Measure Components are selected. The axis must have a fixed value to ensure accurate comparison. To lock the axis:

» Right-click the X axis and select "Edit Axis."

» Under the "General" tab, in the Range section, click the "Fixed" radio button.

» Change the Fixed end value to "1.05" (to allow room for labels on high-percentage bars).

6 **Add a title**

» Double-click the Title Row to open the Edit Title dialog box.

» Enter the title,

"2019 Compliance Rates of Physician Group Practices
For HEDIS Measure: Comprehensive Diabetes Care
Component: "

The title can be formatted to reflect the filter selection.

» With the cursor in the space after "Component:", click the "Insert" button.

» Select "HEDIS Sub-Measure Components" from the Insert menu.

» Highlight the inserted "<HEDIS Sub-Measure Components>" text and change the font color to dark blue.

7 **Rename the worksheet tab and save the worksheet**

» Double-click the worksheet tab at the bottom of the screen.

» In the highlighted text, enter the new title, "Bullet: HEDIS Measures," then click "Enter."

» Click the "Save" icon on the Toolbar.

The final chart looks like this:

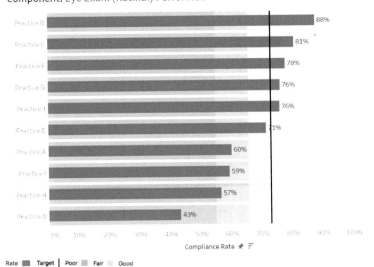

2019 Compliance Rates of Physician Group Practices
For HEDIS Measure: Comprehensive Diabetes Care
Component: Eye Exam (Retinal) Performed

HEDIS Sub-Measure Components
- ⊙ Eye Exam (Retinal) Performed
- ○ Hemoglobin A1c (HbA1c) Control (< 8.0%)
- ○ Hemoglobin A1c (HbA1c) Testing
- ○ Medical Attention for Nephropathy

Rate ▓ Target | Poor ▓ Fair ░ Good

▲ Custom Color Key

It is not currently possible to create a customized color key based on background shading from within Tableau. Use any image software (Photoshop or Paint) to create a color key, then save it as an image. The above view was created in a dashboard; the image was added as an Object and floated below the chart. This topic is covered in the Dashboard chapter.

Insight: This Bullet Graph allows the viewer to see Physician Group compliance rates for a selected Comprehensive Diabetes Care sub-measure (horizontal blue bars). For the selected sub-measure component "Eye Exam (Retinal) Performed," five practices are above target (B, C, F, G, and J). Practice E is below target but still within the "Good" range. A, I, and H are below target, in the "Fair" range, while Practice D is below target, in the "Poor" range.

CHAPTER 17

Table Calculations

Table Calculations are computations applied to the values visibly present on a work-sheet. Regardless of what chart type is used to actually visualize the data on a work-sheet, dragging and dropping fields onto the workspace returns a "table" of headers and values based on the combination of dimensions and measures present to create a given chart. Unlike other types of aggregate calculations and calculated fields that query an underlying Tableau data source, Table Calculations can be thought of as secondary calculations that leverage only this "table" of aggregate data available on the active worksheet. They are dependent on the amount, type, and orientation of data present. Table Calculations can be used to generate running totals, year-over-year comparisons, percent of totals, index calculations, and much more. Table Calculations can be added to the view using either predefined quick calculations or by specifying a custom definition. Quick Table Calculations are one-click shortcuts that eliminate the need to create common formulas manually. More complex Table Calculations can be made via the "Add Table Calculation" option .

Two examples of predefined Quick Table Calculations are shown below.

17.1 Percent of Total

This Table Calculation computes a percent of total—in this case, of full-time equivalent (FTE) employees among city health centers. The sum value of all the bars must equal 100%, conveying a part-to-whole relationship for each health center.

Percent of Total of City Health Centers' FTEs

Data Source: *Mock city health center data*

About the Data: *Mock city health center data based on actual numbers of full-time employees (FTE) for five city health centers.*

1 **Create a new worksheet and connect to the data**

» At the bottom of the Tableau workspace, click the icon for a new worksheet.

» In the Data pane, select the "Ch. 10 - City Health Center Full-Time Equivalent (FTE) Counts" dataset.

2 **Create the chart**

From the Data pane,

» Drag and drop "City Health Center" to the Rows shelf.

» Drag and drop "Actual FTE" to the Columns shelf.

» Click the Sort Descending icon on the Toolbar.

» Click the [T] icon on Toolbar to add labels.

The bar chart now looks like this:

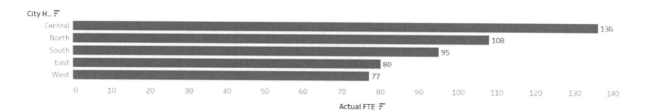

The labels for each bar identify the raw number of employees. Even though the data is rendered as a bar chart, these values make up the "table" of data that will be leveraged to create a Table Calculation to compare the Percent of Total Actual FTE for each city health center.

3 Perform a Quick Table Calculation

» Right-click the "SUM(Actual FTE)" field on the Columns shelf.

» Click "Quick Table Calculation."

» Select "Percent of Total."

Quick Table Calculation ▶

In generating a Quick Table Calculation, Tableau makes its best guess as to how it should compute the results. For Percent of Total calculation, it can perform the calculation on each row of data down the table, across the table, or by specifying a particular field.

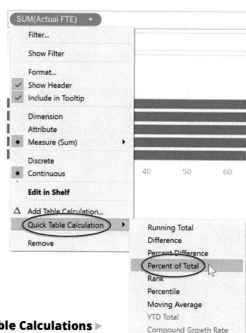

Grayed-Out Table Calculations ▶

Since table calculations are dependent on the source worksheet view, some of the predefined quick calculations may be unavailable if the worksheet view does not support the calculation. If this is the case, the unavailable calculations will be visible in the menu, but will be grayed out.

»   Right-click the "SUM(Actual FTE)" field again.

»   Click "Compute using" from the drop-down menu.

Tableau computes this Percent of Total calculation using Table (Down). In this example, "Compute using Table (Down)" works because each city health center is oriented down the worksheet; however, a more precise method is to compute using "City Health Center."

»   Select "City Health Center."

◄ Dimensions in a Table Calculation

Because Table Calculations are applied to the values computed in a worksheet, they depend on the structure and layout of the worksheet itself. Dimensions that control the operation of a Table Calculation are not part of calculation syntax; instead, they are specified in the "Compute Using" menu, which tells Tableau on what Dimension(s) it needs to perform the calculation and in what direction the calculation should be performed.

201

Best Practice

While using Table (Down) and Table (Across) to compute table calculations may work, it is a better practice to explicitly tell Tableau what field or fields to use to perform the calculation. This ensures that if column orientation is later changed or dimensions are added, the Tableau calculation will still use only the fields chosen for its computation.

»   Right-click "SUM(Actual FTE) Δ" field on the Columns shelf.

»   Select "Format."

»   Select the "Pane" tab.

»   In the Default section, click the caret to the right of "Numbers."

»   Select "Percentage" and decrease Decimal places to "1."

◄ Δ symbol

The delta "Δ" symbol is a visual cue indicating that the field contains a table calculation. Double-click the field to see the underlying calculation formula.

4 Format the chart

»   Right-click the "City Health Center" header.

»   Select "Hide Field Labels for Rows."

»   Right-click the X axis.

»   Uncheck "Show Header."

5 Confirm the calculation

To double-check the calculation, display a Grand Total showing that the percentages add up to 100%.

» Click the "Analytics" tab at the top of the Data/Analytics pane.

» Click and drag "Totals" onto the workspace. An option display will appear.

» Drop "Totals" onto the "Column Grand Totals" image.

» Confirm that the Grand Total equals 100%.

To remove the Grand Total:

» Left-click on the "Grand Total" label.

» Click "Remove."

6 Add a title

» Double-click the Title Row to open the Edit Title dialog box.

» Enter the title, "Percent of Total of City Health Centers' FTEs."

7 Rename the worksheet tab and save the worksheet

» Right-click the worksheet tab at the bottom of the workspace, then select "Rename."

» Enter an intuitive title, then click the "Save" icon on the Toolbar.

The final chart looks like this:

Percent of Total of City Health Centers' FTEs

Insight: Using the percent of total table calculation makes it easy to see that Central City Health Center has the highest percent (27.4%) of the city health centers' FTEs whereas West has the lowest (15.5%).

17.2 Running Total

A Running Total Table Calculation computes a cumulative total along a specified dimension. This report presents the progression of groups of motor vehicle incident deaths from 2010 to 2018 across U.S. census regions. This exercise also highlights how, unlike with other types of calculations in Tableau, Table Calculations require the report developer to define a scope and direction for the Table Calculation that will influence the final data output. A running total summing data across the worksheet will return a different result than the same Table Calculation summing data down the page.

Running Total of Motor Vehicle Incident Deaths For Years 2010 - 2018, by U.S. Census Region

	Midwest	Northeast	South	West
2010	7,443	4,534	16,657	6,698
2011	14,634	9,078	33,298	13,625
2012	22,182	13,585	50,629	20,654
2013	29,389	17,931	67,202	27,897
2014	36,382	21,975	84,070	35,390
2015	43,798	26,096	102,155	43,525
2016	51,609	30,354	121,616	52,322
2017	59,645	34,602	140,690	61,195
2018	67,324	38,714	159,519	69,979

Data Source: CDC Wonder

About the Data: CDC Wonder, developed by the Centers for Disease Control and Prevention (CDC), is an integrated information and communication system for public health. It provides the public with access to data from the CDC, to help promote information-driven decisions. The data for this exercise is from the dataset Multiple Cause of Death, by Census Region, where the underlying cause of death is from the UDC - ICD-10 113 Cause list: Motor vehicle accidents, for the years 2010 - 2018.

1 Create a new worksheet and connect to the data

» At the bottom of the Tableau workspace, click the icon for a new worksheet.

» In the Data pane, select the "Ch. 17 – U.S. Motor Vehicle Incident Deaths by Region (2010-2018)" dataset.

2 Create the chart

In this dataset, "Year" is not in the standard date format, but rather as a numeric value for the year only. As such, Tableau has set the field as continuous (green) integer; this will create an axis when used in the view. To use the "Year" field values as headers, the field must be changed to discrete.

» Right-click "Year" in the Data pane and select "Convert to Discrete."

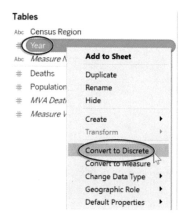

» Drag and drop "Year" onto the Rows shelf.

» Drag and drop "Census Region" onto the Columns shelf.

» Drag and drop "Deaths" onto Text on the Marks card.

» Hover the cursor over the right border of the chart until it changes to a bi-directional arrow. Click and drag to adjust width until column headers are fully visible.

3 Show Grand Totals

» Click the "Analytics" tab in the Data/Analytics pane.

» Drag "Totals" onto the workspace to open an image display.

» Drop "Totals" onto the "Column Grand Totals" image.

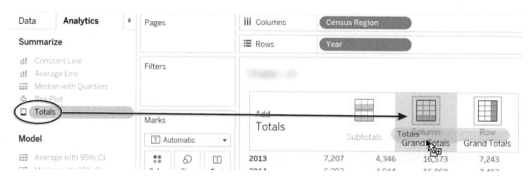

Best Practice

Although adding a Grand Total is not necessary in creating a Running Total Table Calculation, it is a good idea to include one while building the chart so that the accuracy of the calculation can easily be checked. This Grand Total will be removed for the finished visualization.

The table now looks like this:

| Year | Census Region | | | |
	Midwest	Northeast	South	West
2010	7,443	4,534	16,657	6,698
2011	7,191	4,544	16,641	6,927
2012	7,548	4,507	17,331	7,029
2013	7,207	4,346	16,573	7,243
2014	6,993	4,044	16,868	7,493
2015	7,416	4,121	18,085	8,135
2016	7,811	4,258	19,461	8,797
2017	8,036	4,248	19,074	8,873
2018	7,679	4,112	18,829	8,784
Grand Total	67,324	38,714	159,519	69,979

◀ **Totals**

Totals can also be created from the Analysis tab on the Menu bar. Additional options are available here, including formatting and location / placement choices.

4 Perform the Quick Table Calculation

To generate the Running Total:

» Right-click the "SUM(Deaths)" field on the Marks card.

» Click "Quick Table Calculation."

» Select "Running Total."

◀ **Running Total Aggregation**

Tableau's Running Total Calculation defaults to a Running Sum. Manually editing the Table Calculation permits changing the aggregation to a running average, minimum, or maximum, as needed.

Evaluate how the table calculation is being computed. The running total here is defaulting to table across. The desired result should be running down the table, computing along the Year dimension.

Year	Census Region			
	Midwest	Northeast	South	West
2010	7,443	11,977	28,634	35,332
2011	7,191	11,735	28,376	35,303
2012	7,548	12,055	29,386	36,415
2013	7,207	11,553	28,126	35,369
2014	6,993	11,037	27,905	35,398
2015	7,416	11,537	29,622	37,757
2016	7,811	12,069	31,530	40,327
2017	8,036	12,284	31,358	40,231
2018	7,679	11,791	30,620	39,404
Grand Total	67,324	106,038	265,557	335,536

» Right-click the "SUM(Deaths)" field again.

» Click "Compute Using."

» Select "Year."

Refresher ▶

As discussed in the previous section, Tableau makes its best guess as to how to compute the Table Calculation. In this case, Tableau chose to calculate a running total along Table (Across); this choice, however, does not yield the desired result which is by Year. This total can be adjusted accordingly with the Compute Using menu option, which is used to control the scope and direction of the Table Calculation.

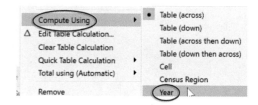

Validating the results with the column grand total, the 2018 values should (and do) match the grand total results for each census region.

To further double-check the Running Total:

» Drag and drop " Deaths" from the Data Pane onto the Workspace to make it easy to compare the new Table Calculation to the original measure.

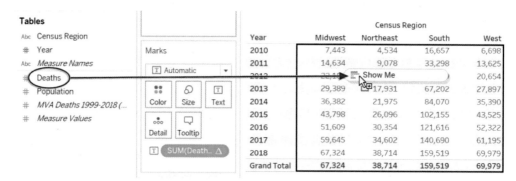

» Drag and drop the "Measure Names" field from the Rows shelf to the Columns shelf.

The chart now looks like this:

	Census Region							
	Midwest		Northeast		South		West	
Year	Deaths	Running Sum of ...	Deaths	Running Sum of ...	Deaths	Running Sum of ...	Deaths	Running Sum of ...
2010	7,443	7,443	4,534	4,534	16,657	16,657	6,698	6,698
2011	7,191	14,634	4,544	9,078	16,641	33,298	6,927	13,625
2012	7,548	22,182	4,507	13,585	17,331	50,629	7,029	20,654
2013	7,207	29,389	4,346	17,931	16,573	67,202	7,243	27,897
2014	6,993	36,382	4,044	21,975	16,868	84,070	7,493	35,390
2015	7,416	43,798	4,121	26,096	18,085	102,155	8,135	43,525
2016	7,811	51,609	4,258	30,354	19,461	121,616	8,797	52,322
2017	8,036	59,645	4,248	34,602	19,074	140,690	8,873	61,195
2018	7,679	67,324	4,112	38,714	18,829	159,519	8,784	69,979
Grand Total	67,324	67,324	38,714	38,714	159,519	159,519	69,979	69,979

Best Practice

Temporarily adding the original field (here, Deaths) next to the Table Calculations (Running Sum of Deaths) confirms that the running total is calculating as intended. Under Midwest, for example, adding the 2011 Deaths (7191) to the 2010 Running Sum (7443) confirms that the 2011 Running Sum (14,634) is correct. Notice that the last Running Sum row for Midwest for 2018 is 67,324, the same as the Grand Total. Once the correct calculation has been confirmed, the Deaths field (without the table calculation) and the Grand Total row can be removed.

After validating the accuracy of the table calculation,

» Drag the "SUM(Deaths)" field (without the calculation symbolized by the triangle) off the Measure Values shelf.

» Left-click the "Grand Total" label and select "Remove."

5 Format the chart

Hide Headers and Column Field Label:

» Right-click the "Year" header.

» Select "Hide Field Labels for Rows."

» Right-click "Census Region" header.

» Select "Hide Field Labels for Columns."

6 Add a title

» Double-click the Title Row to open the Edit Title dialog box.

» Enter the title,
"Running Total of Motor Vehicle Incident Deaths
For Years 2010 - 2018 by U.S. Census Region."

7 Rename the worksheet tab and save the worksheet

» Right-click the worksheet tab at the bottom of the workspace, then select "Rename."

» Enter an intuitive title, then click the "Save" icon on the Toolbar.

The final chart looks like this:

Running Total of Motor Vehicle Incident Deaths
For Years 2010 - 2018, by U.S. Census Region

	Midwest	Northeast	South	West
2010	7,443	4,534	16,657	6,698
2011	14,634	9,078	33,298	13,625
2012	22,182	13,585	50,629	20,654
2013	29,389	17,931	67,202	27,897
2014	36,382	21,975	84,070	35,390
2015	43,798	26,096	102,155	43,525
2016	51,609	30,354	121,616	52,322
2017	59,645	34,602	140,690	61,195
2018	67,324	38,714	159,519	69,979

Insight: In this Running Total table calculation, it is clear that from 2010 to 2018, the South had significantly more deaths than the other three regions.

CHAPTER 18

Pareto Charts

Pareto Analysis is a decision-making technique used to identify a limited number of variables that produce the most significant overall effect. It uses the Pareto Principle, also known as the 80/20 rule—the idea that 80% of a project´s benefit can be achieved by doing 20% of the work or, conversely, that 80% of problems can be traced to 20% of causes. In healthcare, Pareto Charts can be applied to the design of medical processes to identify errors and incidents, or to analyze performance data in health organizations. The objective of a Pareto Chart is to separate a few major problems from the many possible ones, so that improvement efforts can be focused based on data rather than on perception.

In Tableau, a Pareto Chart is created from raw data using table calculations. Essentially, a bar chart and a line chart are built and turned into a dual axis chart, where the line is the running total combined with a percentage of the total.

How To: Build a Pareto Chart to identify where to focus improvement efforts for laboratory testing.

Root Causes of Repeat Laboratory Samples

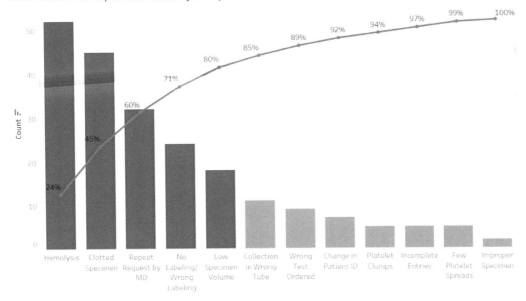

Data Source: *De-identified hospital laboratory data*

About the Data: *Problems with samples of blood, urine, and other specimens from patients sent for analysis in a hospital laboratory required a re-sampling of the specimens. This data contains a list and count of the reasons that the specimens had to be re-sampled.*

1 **Create a new worksheet and connect to the data**

» At the bottom of the workspace, click the icon for a new worksheet.

» In the Data pane, select "Ch. 18 - Repeat Lab Samples" dataset.

2 Create the chart

From the Data pane:

» Drag and drop "Root Cause of Repeat of Lab Samples" onto the Columns shelf.

» Drag and drop "Count" onto the Rows shelf.

» Click the "Sort descending" icon on the Tool bar.

3 Perform table calculations

» Right-click "SUM(Count)" field on the Rows shelf.

» In the context menu, select "Add Table Calculation."

Add Table Calculation ▶

Specifications for a Table Calculation can be added by using either Add Table Calculation or Quick Table Calculation. Choosing Add Table Calculation brings up a menu from which the type of calculation, the method of computation, or other custom details can be chosen. Quick Table Calculation automatically provides the computation and other details.

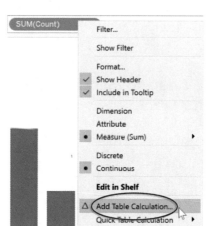

The Table Calculation dialog box appears, and the chart automatically adjusts to the default Calculation Type, "Difference From."

In the Table Calculation dialog box:

» In the Calculation Type section, click the caret to the right of the default selection "Difference From" and change the selection to "Running Total."

» In the Compute Using section, select "Specific Dimensions."

Since the only Dimension is "Root Cause of Repeat Laboratory Samples," it is automatically checked.

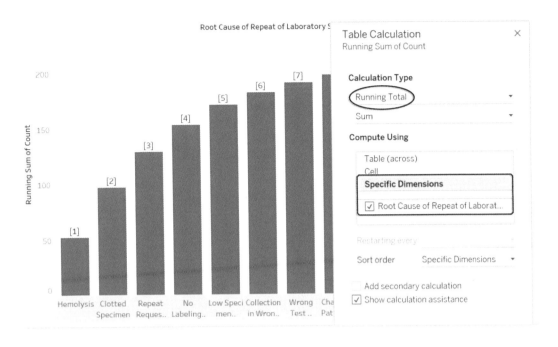

▲ Real-Time Table Calculations

Table Calculation changes made from the dialog box are displayed instantly. Yellow highlighting and corresponding bracketed numbers indicate what direction the calculation is computing along. The Show calculation assistance check box controls this display, also in real-time.

» Click the box near the bottom of the dialog box for "Add Secondary Calculation." This will expand the Table Calculation dialog box to add that calculation.

» In the Secondary Calculation Type section, click the caret to the right of the default selection "Difference From" and change to "Percent of Total."

» In the Compute Using section, select "Specific Dimensions." The only Dimension in the menu (Root Cause of Repeat Laboratory Samples) will be checked.

Perform a Secondary Table Calculation ▶

Adding a secondary Table Calculation works just like adding a primary one. The results computed take into account the computations already performed in the Primary Calculation Type settings. In this example, a Percent of Total calculation is being added as a secondary calculation to a Running Total calculation. This means that instead of displaying a running sum of the raw numbers from the Count field, the calculation will compute a running percent of the Count going from left to right across the worksheet.

Running Total and Moving Calculation are the only table calculations that can have a secondary calculation; the others are considered to be terminal calculations.

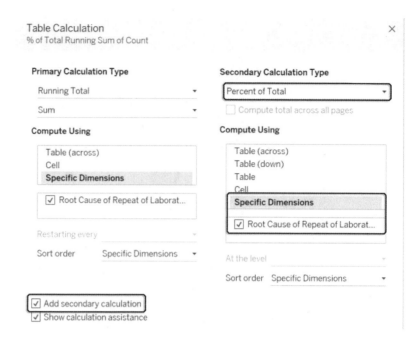

To close the dialog box, click the "X" in the top right corner.

To change the bars to a line:

» In the Marks card, click the caret to the right of "Automatic" mark type.

» Select "Line."

This is the "Pareto" part of the chart.

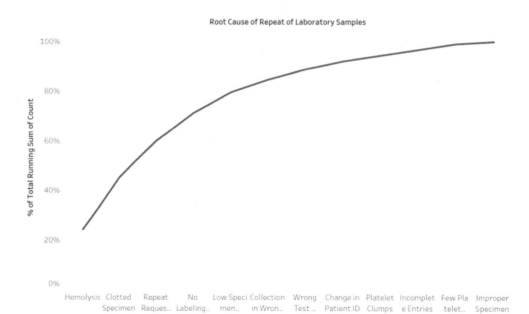

Refresher

In order to create this Pareto Line, the results in the original bar chart were sorted so that root causes appear from largest on the left to smallest on the right. Combining this display with the Percent of Total Running Sum table calculation creates the Pareto Line. Proof of its accuracy is provided by the gradual progress towards 100% along the horizontal axis.

4 Create the Dual Axis chart

» Drag and drop "Count" from the Data pane onto the Rows shelf to the right of the "SUM(Count)Δ" field already on the shelf. (The Δ symbol on the SUM(Count) field denotes a Table Calculation resides on that field.) Two line charts are created: "Percent of Total Running Sum of Count" and "Count."

» Click the "SUM(Count)" field just added to the Row shelf, highlighting it to display its own Marks card.

» Click the caret to the right of Line to display the drop-down menu.

» Change Line to "Bar."

The chart now looks like this:

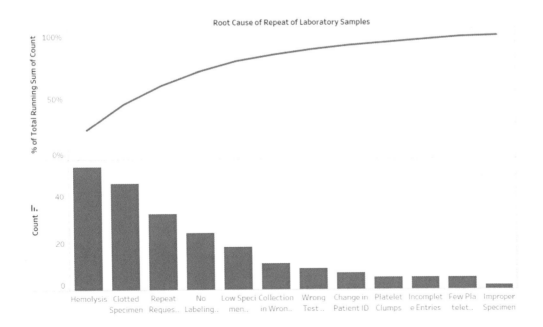

To overlay the line chart on the bar chart, a dual axis must be created:

» Right-click the "SUM(Count)" field on the Rows shelf.

» Select "Dual Axis" from the drop-down menu.

This will overlay the bar chart on the Pareto line and add the corresponding axis for the bar to the right side of the chart.

Dual Axis Charts ▶

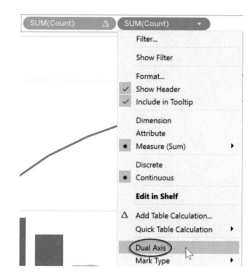

The presence of two measures on the Rows or Columns shelf offers the possibility of creating a Dual Axis chart. Selecting "Dual Axis" causes Tableau to place the two charts one on top of the other, with a second axis appearing on the right or top of the chart depending on its orientation. These two charts do not have to be of the same type. The Dual Axis technique can overlay lines on a scatter plot, bars on an area chart, or a geographic symbol map on a filled map. This technique can also be used to plot two separate fields on the same axis with the same chart type.

When units of the two axes are similar (and the data types are the same), the latter should be synchronized on the same scale (by right-clicking the secondary axis and selecting Synchronize Axis). It may sometimes be impossible to do this if the formats of the two axes (for example, Count and Percent) are incompatible.

Tableau automatically orients the two charts so that one chart is in front of the other. This order can be changed by right-clicking one of the dual axes and selecting Move Marks to Front/Back.

The primary (left) Y-axis should display the counts for the bar chart; the secondary (right) Y-axis, the percentages for the Pareto line. To swap the axes:

» Drag the "SUM(Count) Δ" field to the right of the "SUM(Count)" field on the Rows shelf.

Display the Percent of Total Running Sum values to help identify the root causes that collectively contribute to 80% of the repeat laboratory samples. To add the percentages to the line:

» Click the "SUM(Count) Δ" field on the Rows shelf to highlight the Line view on the Marks card.

» Click the Label selector on the Marks card then click the box for "Show mark labels."

» Right-click the "SUM(Count) Δ" field on the Rows shelf.

» Select "Format" from the drop-down menu.

» Select the Pane tab then click the caret to the right of "Numbers" in the Default section.

» Select "Percentage" and change Decimal places to "0."

To arrange the values above the line:

» In the Format pane, click the caret to the right of "Alignment" in the Default section.

» In the Vertical alignment section, click the icon farthest to the right to position the percentages above the line.

» Click the "x" in the top right of the Format pane to close it.

Increase the chart size to better display Root Cause labels.

» On the Toolbar, click the Fit caret to the right of "Standard" and change to "Entire View."

» If the Root Cause labels are displaying vertically, right-click any Root Cause label and select "Rotate Label" to change the labels from vertical to horizontal.

The chart now looks like this:

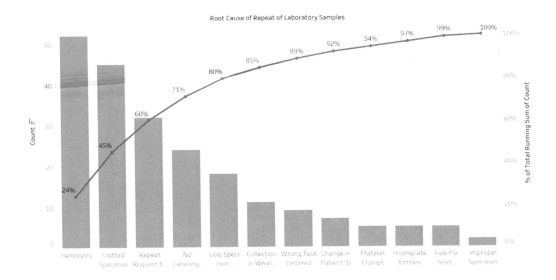

5 Highlight 80% contribution with color

Visual highlighting can be added to this classic Pareto chart by using a calculated field to color-encode the laboratory errors that contributed to 80% of repeat draws.

» Click the "SUM(Count)" field on the Rows shelf to highlight the label header on the Marks card.

» While holding down the Control key, drag and drop "SUM(Count) Δ" from the Rows shelf to Color on the Marks card.

Dual Axis Visual Cue ▶

Tableau changes the oval field shape of the two measures to flat edges, denoting the Dual Axis chart.

Refresher ▶

Holding the Control key while dragging and dropping a field will copy it to a new location.

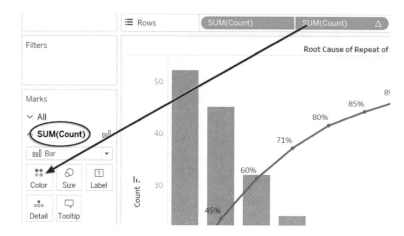

The chart color changes intentionally to a color gradient because "SUM(Count) Δ" is a continuous measure.

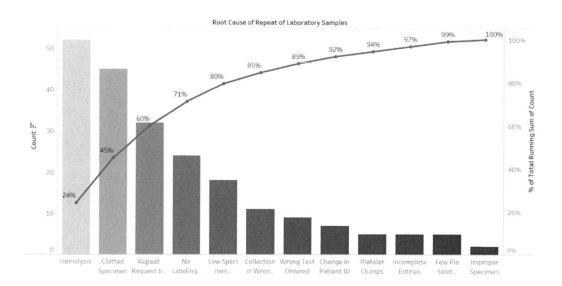

» Right-click "SUM(Count) Δ" on Color on the Marks card.

» Select "Edit in Shelf" from the menu that appears.

» Add the following to the end of the formula displayed in the field; "<=.8." This will distinguish the counts below or equal to 80% from those greater than 80%.

◄ **Interactive Editing**

Pressing Ctrl and Enter while in the Edit in Shelf function applies the formula within the field while leaving the Edit window open for further editing if necessary.

▲ **Customize Table Calculations**

When Table Calculations are selected, Tableau writes a calculated field formula in the background. Clicking the Edit in Shelf button permits the user to edit this formula as needed (scroll left to view the entire calculation). Pressing the Enter saves the change to the formula in the field.

To save the formula as a new calculated field in the Data pane, hold down Ctrl, then drag and drop the edited field to the Data pane. Rename with an intuitive title.

The calculation is now a Boolean value. Notice it is a discrete field on Color on the Mark card, creating a color palette, not a color gradient. Bar colors now highlight the root causes contributing to 80% of the repeat labs, separating them from those contributing to the remaining 20%.

6 Format the Chart

To edit the colors:

» Click the caret to the right of the "Measure Names" color legend.

» Select "Edit Colors."

» Change the color palette to "Color Blind."

» Click the Data item "% of Total Running Sum of Count" to highlight.

» Select the gray square on the Color Palette.

» Click "OK."

» Perform the same steps for the bars color legend, changing "True" to a dark blue and "False" to a light gray.

Increase the column header border height to make complete headers visible:

» Hover the cursor over the X axis until a vertical bi-directional arrow appears. Click and drag the axis to the appropriate height to view full label names.

To hide the Column header:

» Right-click the column header "Root Cause of Repeat Laboratory Samples."

» Select "Hide Field Labels for Columns."

Because the line values are labeled, the secondary Y-axis is not needed. To hide it:

» Right-click the secondary Y-axis.

» Click "Show Header" to remove its checkmark.

7 Add a title

» Double-click the Title Row to open the Edit Title dialog box.

217

》 Enter the title, "Root Causes of Repeat Laboratory Samples," then click "OK."

8 Rename the worksheet tab and save the worksheet

》 Double-click the worksheet tab at the bottom of the screen.

》 In the highlighted text, enter the new title, "Pareto: Repeat Lab Samples," then click "Enter."

》 Click the "Save" icon on the Toolbar.

The final chart looks like this:

Root Causes of Repeat Laboratory Samples

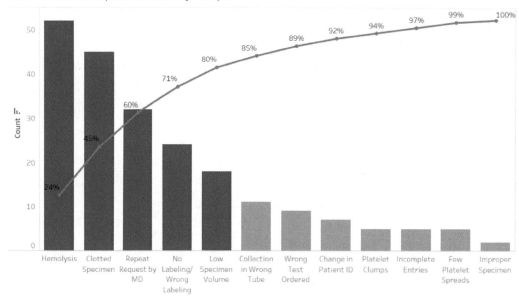

Insight: 80% of the repeat laboratory samples (shown in blue) have just five root causes: Hemolysis, Clotted Specimen, Repeat Request by MD, No Labeling/Wrong Labeling, and Low Specimen Volume. These represent the largest area for improvement to decrease the occurrence of repeat lab samples.

CHAPTER 19

Forecasting

Tableau uses built-in algorithms to forecast time-series data. This feature identifies any patterns that can be used to make predictions based on historical data. It is less common, but also possible to create a forecast without a date field using a dimension with integer values to order the measure being forecasted.

The forecasting feature relies on a statistical concept called Exponential Smoothing. The details of this statistical technique will not be covered in this book; in general, the overall effect is an adjustment technique that produces a smoothed time series, where recent observations are given relatively more weight in forecasting than are older ones. Exponential smoothing is effective when the measure to be forecast exhibits trends or seasonality over the period of time on which the forecast is based.

Any time-series chart containing a minimum of five data points can be used to create a forecast. The Analytics pane contains a Forecast option that can be dragged and dropped onto the workspace to add a Forecast to the time-series chart. Alternatively, a Forecast can be added by right-clicking a mark or the white space within the work area and selecting Forecast -> Show Forecast.

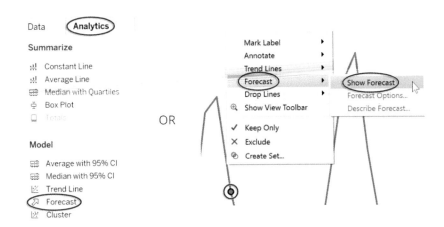

Tableau displays the forecast of estimated future values in a line of lighter color coupled with a shaded band representing the prediction interval. This interval represents the likelihood that the values will be within the shaded band.

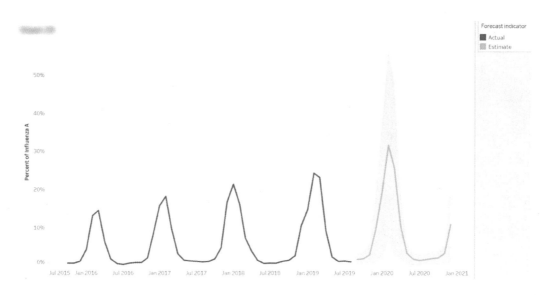

The default Forecast can be edited by right-clicking in the workspace, hovering the cursor over "Forecast" in the menu that appears, and selecting "Forecast Options…"

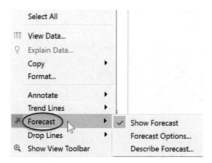

Forecast Options

The Forecast Options dialog box offers several ways to customize a forecast, including adjusting both the length of the forecast and the source data´s aggregation. The Forecast Model can be edited to exclude seasonality or create a custom model, using additive or multiplicative model types for both Trend and Season.

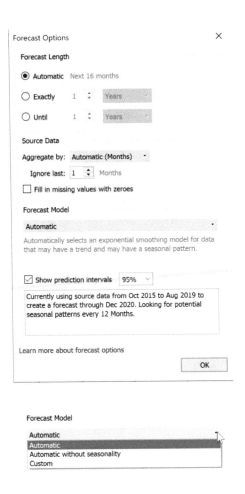

Describe Forecast

In the "Describe Forecast" dialog box, two tabs contain information for this description: Summary and Model.

- The Summary tab lists options used for creating the forecast and summary data.

- The Model tab describes the Model used to create the forecast and displays statistical data for Quality Metrics and Smoothing Coefficients.

Other Forecast Options

Additional forecasting options and settings can be selected by right-clicking the forecasted measure and choosing from the list of features under "Forecast results."

Requirements and Considerations for Forecasting

1) **Data Types:** Forecasts can be created with a minimum one date dimension and one measure present in the view. If no date dimension is available, a dimension field with integers can be used.

2) **Sufficient Data:** A trend forecast requires at least 5 data points; a seasonal forecast, at least 2 seasons or one season plus 5 periods.

3) **Granularity:** Selection of a level of granularity in the form of a date unit (Year, Month, Quarter, etc.) is required.

4) **Trimming:** If the data cuts off in the middle of the specified date unit (for example, the most recent month is incomplete for a monthly forecast), Tableau can trim the data. Select the option Ignore Last to ensure that the partial period does not decrease the accuracy of the forecast.

5) **Granularity Adjustments:** If there is not enough data to forecast at a particular granularity (for example, only six quarters of data are available), Tableau will instead base the forecast on a monthly algorithm, then aggregate the results by quarter. This happens by default and requires no special configuration.

6) **Improved Accuracy:** The more data points in the forecast model, the more accurate the prediction is likely to be.

SECTION 5

Dashboards & Stories

CHAPTER 20

Dashboards

A Dashboard, when properly designed, enables at-a-glance display and monitoring of crucial information. A well-designed Dashboard includes only what is necessary; condenses information without compromising its meaning; and employs display mechanisms that, even when small, can be easily read and understood. Tableau further defines a Dashboard as a combined display of worksheets in a single screen.

This section and the two that follow demonstrate how to construct a Hospital Surgical Site Infection Summary Dashboard. The process emphasizes the best design practices and uses many of Tableau´s interactive features to create an engaging user experience.

Section 1 builds and formats a simple Tableau Dashboard from four worksheets. Section 2 adds basic interactivity to the Dashboard using quick filters and action filters. Section 3 adds interactivity between two separate Dashboards with links, a back button, an information button, and a dynamic title.

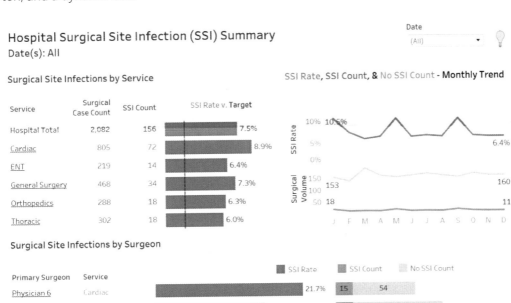

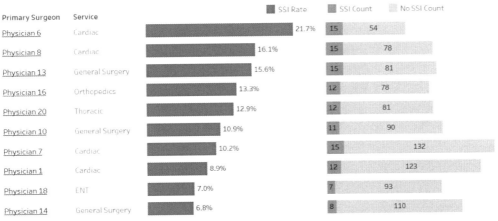

Special note for building the Dashboard example in this chapter: The data file entitled "Tableau for Healthcare – Dashboard Starter Workbook" contains five pre-built worksheets. Four of these will be assembled in the primary Dashboard; the fifth will be part of a second Dashboard to illustrate interactivity between dashboards.

20.1 Dashboards: Basic Building and Formatting

How To: Build and format a simple Dashboard showing surgical case counts, surgical site infection counts, and rates.

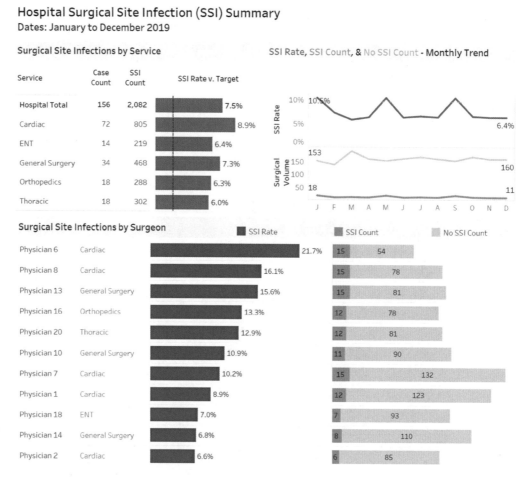

Hospital Surgical Site Infection (SSI) Summary
Dates: January to December 2019

Surgical Site Infections by Service

Service	Case Count	SSI Count	SSI Rate v. Target	
Hospital Total	156	2,082		7.5%
Cardiac	72	805		8.9%
ENT	14	219		6.4%
General Surgery	34	468		7.3%
Orthopedics	18	288		6.3%
Thoracic	18	302		6.0%

SSI Rate, SSI Count, & No SSI Count - Monthly Trend

SSI Rate: 10% 10.5% ... 6.4%

Surgical Volume: 153 ... 160

18 ... 11

J F M A M J J A S O N D

Surgical Site Infections by Surgeon

■ SSI Rate   ■ SSI Count   ■ No SSI Count

Physician 6	Cardiac	21.7%	15	54
Physician 8	Cardiac	16.1%	15	78
Physician 13	General Surgery	15.6%	15	81
Physician 16	Orthopedics	13.3%	12	78
Physician 20	Thoracic	12.9%	12	81
Physician 10	General Surgery	10.9%	11	90
Physician 7	Cardiac	10.2%	15	132
Physician 1	Cardiac	8.9%	12	123
Physician 18	ENT	7.0%	7	93
Physician 14	General Surgery	6.8%	8	110
Physician 2	Cardiac	6.6%	6	85

Data Source: *De-identified hospital surgical data*

About the Data: *The four worksheets created for this dashboard exercise display surgical site infection data that includes the number of surgical procedures performed, the count of surgical site infections, and the calculated surgical site infection rate. The date range is January to December 2019. Data is displayed by service and surgeon.*

1 Connect to the workbook and open a new dashboard

» From the Tableau for Healthcare training files, double-click the Tableau workbook "Tableau for Healthcare – Dashboard Starter Workbook.twbx" to open it.

» There are two ways to open a new Dashboard:

Option 1: Click "Dashboard" on the File row, then select "New Dashboard."

Option 2: At the far right of the bottom row of tabs, click the Dashboard icon.

Tableau Dashboard Workspace

When a new Dashboard is opened, the multipurpose pane on the left side of the screen changes to show features and controls needed to create a dashboard.

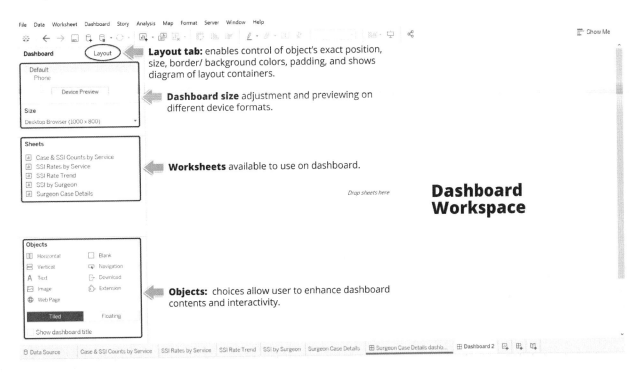

Objects Pane

- **Horizontal/Vertical:** these are layout containers that enable grouping of dashboard items for improved positioning and resizing. Horizontal layout containers place worksheets side-by-side; vertical layout containers stack worksheets.

- **Text/Image/Webpage:** insert text, images, and/or embedded webpages anywhere on the dashboard.

- **Blank:** can be used to balance sheet placement and white space on the dashboard.

- **Navigation:** create buttons for easy navigation to selected dashboards, stories, and/or worksheets.

- **Download:** create dashboard buttons enabling the viewer to export the active dashboard to a PDF, PowerPoint slide, crosstab, or image.

- **Extension:** use third party web apps to increase dashboard functionality.

- **Tiled vs. Floating:** tiled worksheets are displayed side-by-side, with no overlaps, in the Dashboard workspace. The active gray space previously described provides a grid-like area for placement of worksheets. Tiled is Tableau's default layout and is recommended for placing worksheets and filters. Floating objects, in contrast, can be placed anywhere on the Dashboard, and can overlap others; this ability is some-times useful in the display of legends or buttons.

2 Create the dashboard

Worksheets are the building blocks of the Dashboard. The Hospital Surgical Site Infection Summary dashboard will be created from four of the five worksheets pre-built for this exercise.

>> In the left column, "Sheets" section, click "Case & SSI Counts by Service," then drag and drop it onto the Dashboard workspace.

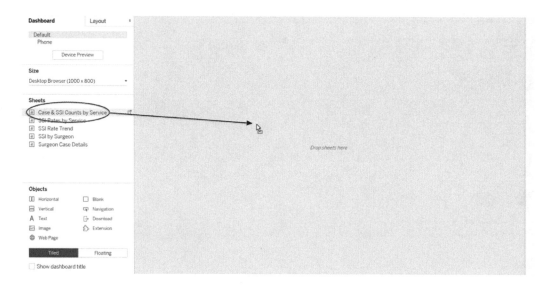

▲ **Worksheet Preview**

Hover over a selected Dashboard Worksheet to view a thumbnail image of the corresponding chart.

Notice that when a worksheet is dragged onto the Dashboard workspace, the color of the workspace changes to gray. This color change highlights the active area for worksheet placement.

When the worksheet has been placed on the Dashboard workspace, notice the gray border of the worksheet and the two tabs. The gray border indicates the highlighted worksheet and its corresponding dashboard real estate. The top center tab allows for the relocation of the worksheet; the side tab has options for removing the sheet from the dashboard, navigating directly to the worksheet, and a drop-down caret for a menu list of options.

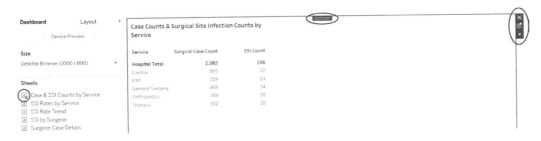

▲ Active Worksheets on Dashboard

Checkmarks in the Sheets section highlight worksheet(s) currently displayed in the dashboard workspace.

» Next, drag the worksheet "SSI Rates by Service" to the Dashboard workspace.

» Drop the worksheet to the right of the "Case & SSI Counts by Service" worksheet.

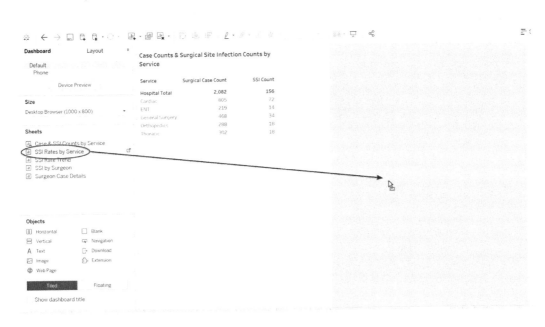

▲ Dashboard Worksheet and Object Placement

As worksheet or objects are moved onto the Dashboard workspace, it is useful to experiment with placement to make location options clear. Try dragging a worksheet or object to the workspace and moving it around from place to place before dropping it, observing the movement of the active gray areas. A worksheet or object may be dropped in any active gray space.

» Drag and drop "SSI Rate Trend" worksheet onto the Dashboard to the right of the current two worksheets.

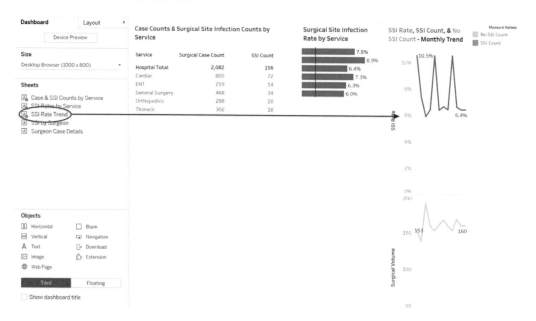

▲ Worksheets with legends and/or filters

Worksheets with color or size legends and/or filters will carry them over to the dashboard, placing them in a vertical layout container at the far-right of the workspace. Considerations will need to be made to include or remove the legends/filters as they support or detract from the view.

The fourth worksheet should now be placed below the current worksheets.

However, unless the bottom of the display is visible, it is virtually impossible to place a worksheet there.

» Using the right scroll bar, vertically scroll to the bottom of the Dashboard.

» Drag and drop the "SSI by surgeon" worksheet onto the Dashboard in the gray highlighted section below the three worksheets already present.

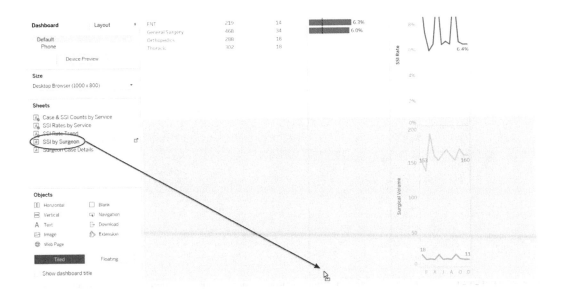

▲ Worksheet placement

Worksheet placement becomes trickier as more worksheets are added to the view. Continue to move the cursor over the dashboard workspace (here it is moved towards the bottom) until the desired gray drop-zone indicator appears.

The dashboard now looks like this:

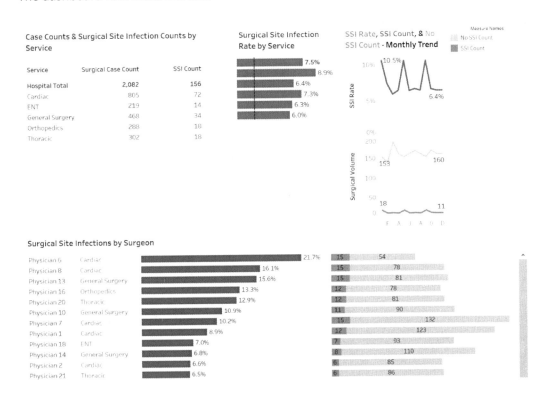

3 Adjust the dashboard display size

» Near the top of the left Dashboard pane, find the "Size" section.

» Click the caret to the right of "Desktop Browser (1000 x 800)" to view display-size options. (Tableau defaults the Dashboard size to Desktop.)

Dashboard Size Options ▷

There are three high-level overall size options:

Fixed size: *contains a menu of many common resolutions to help inform choices.*

Automatic: *dynamically adjusts the size of the dashboard based on the user's screen size.*

Range: *permits setting a minimum and/or maximum resolution to provide flexibility.*

» For this example dashboard, select "Fixed size."

The default "Desktop Browser (1000 x 800) appears below it.

» Click the caret to the right to view the many fixed size options.

» Select "Letter Portrait (850 x 1100).

Best Practice

Dashboard resolution can vary widely depending on the screen size of the device used to display reports. Consider the range of devices used by the target audience and build compatibility with the smallest resolution for that range. If reports are customarily printed, Letter Portrait and Letter Landscape are generally successful.

▲ Device Preview

Using the "Device Preview" tool, the report builder can view the dashboard layout through the lens of several common device options, such as tablet, phone, and desktop, with standard brands/sizings in each category. Custom device sizing can also be created. A gray box reveals how the dashboard will look on the selected device.

4 Format the dashboard

Dashboard real estate is high value; it is therefore crucial to format with the goal of reducing white space and highlighting content. The example Dashboard below contains some white space that needs adjustment to ensure that the visualizations have as much room as possible. Excess white space is often generated when a worksheet is moved to the workspace. Any legends and/or filters associated with worksheets are, by default, displayed at the right edge; the resulting white space needs to be eliminated. Scroll bars, if present, can be off-putting and impede at-a-glance comprehension, so eliminating them where possible is desirable as well.

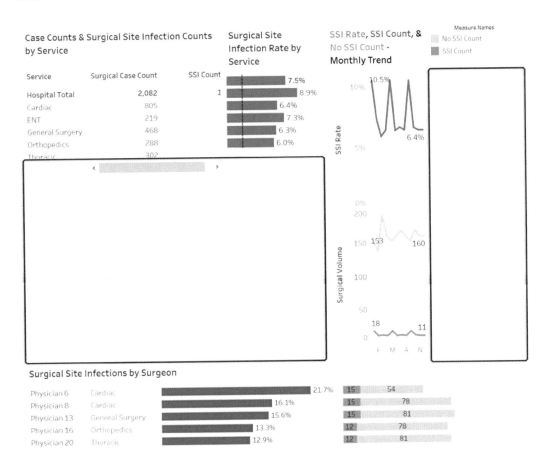

» Click the "Case & SSI Counts by Service" worksheet on the Dashboard to highlight. A gray border appears around the worksheet indicating that it is active. In the right corner, a tab will appear.

» Click the caret at the bottom of this tab to display a drop-down menu.

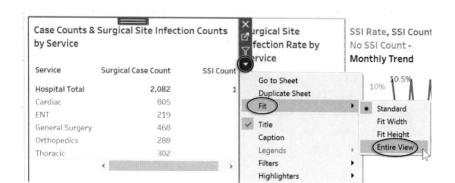

Dashboard Adjustments ▶

Nearly every object on a dashboard has this drop-down caret, providing many options to fine-tune appearance and control the object's behavior.

» Select "Fit."

» Select "Entire View."

» Follow the same steps for the remaining worksheets on the dashboard.

Refresher

When selecting a Fit option, keep in mind that a worksheet may grow if data is increased in the future. If for example many hospitals or services are added, displaying the worksheet in Entire View could make it cramped and illegible. Consider Fit Width instead: a scrollbar will enable the user to see additional data.

The color legend in the far right column corresponds to the SSI Rate Trend worksheet. The trend lines are color-coded in the title, making the color legend unnecessary.

» Click the "Measure Names" color legend to highlight.

» Click the "X" in the top right corner to delete the legend.

The width and height of the worksheets need adjustment for visual balance.

» Hover the cursor over the right border of the "Case Counts & Surgical Site Infection Counts by Service" worksheet until the cursor changes to a bi-directional horizontal arrow.

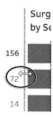

» Click and drag the border to the desired width.

» Hover the cursor over the other worksheet borders and click and drag them to the desired width and height.

The dashboard now looks like this:

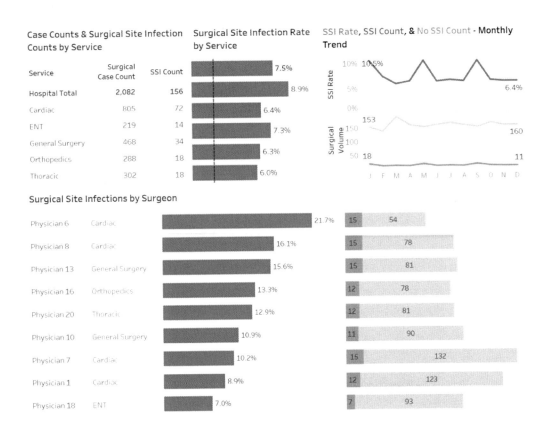

Service	Surgical Case Count	SSI Count
Hospital Total	2,082	156
Cardiac	805	72
ENT	219	14
General Surgery	468	34
Orthopedics	288	18
Thoracic	302	18

Case Counts & Surgical Site Infection Counts by Service

Surgical Site Infection Rate by Service

SSI Rate, SSI Count, & No SSI Count - Monthly Trend

Surgical Site Infections by Surgeon

Physician 6	Cardiac	21.7%	15	54
Physician 8	Cardiac	16.1%	15	78
Physician 13	General Surgery	15.6%	15	81
Physician 16	Orthopedics	13.3%	12	78
Physician 20	Thoracic	12.9%	12	81
Physician 10	General Surgery	10.9%	11	90
Physician 7	Cardiac	10.2%	15	132
Physician 1	Cardiac	8.9%	12	123
Physician 18	ENT	7.0%	7	93

5 Create column labels and worksheet titles

The top text table and bar chart both show aggregate data by Service and would be better presented with a single title above both worksheets. Additionally, a text box under this title and above the bar chart will provide a clearer label and align the bars with the text table rows. Use the Text option in Objects to add precise titles and labels. Because of the need for these labels, the worksheet titles for the top row of charts will be hidden.

》 Right-click the worksheet title for "Case Counts & Surgical Site Infection Counts by Service" and select "Hide Title" from the appearing menu.

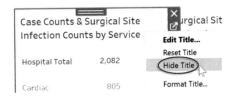

》 Perform the same steps for the bar chart worksheet title.

Add Label to bar chart:

》 Drag and drop Text from the Objects pane to above the bar chart.

236

>> In the Text dialog box, enter the label "SSI Rate v. Target" and set font to Tableau Book, size 9, bold, and center align it.

>> Set the font color for "SSI Rate" to blue to match the bar color.

   • Highlight "SSI Rate", then select the color palette.

   • Select "More Colors" then select "Pick Screen Color."

   • Click on a blue bar to capture the color.

>> Set the font color for "Target" to a dark red to match the reference line in the bar chart, following the above steps. .

>> Adjust the text box border to align with the corresponding rows of the text table.

The label should look like this:

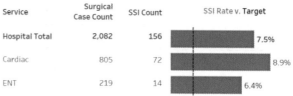

Labels ▶

Column headers have limited ability for formatting. Instead, use Text object to create precision labels, controlling font size, color, alignment, shading, and/or borders.

Add Text boxes for worksheet titles:

>> Drag and drop Text from Objects and place across the top of the dashboard.

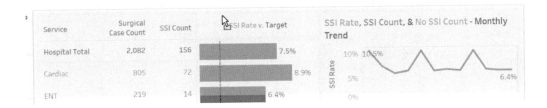

Service	Surgical Case Count	SSI Count	SSI Rate v. Target	SSI Rate, SSI Count, & No SSI Count - Monthly Trend
Hospital Total	2,082	156	7.5%	
Cardiac	805	72	8.9%	
ENT	219	14	6.4%	

» Enter the title: "Surgical Site Infections by Service" and set font to Tableau Medium, size 11, dark gray.

To correctly balance the titles for the top worksheets, a text box will be added for the line chart as well.

» Double-click the "SSI Rate, SSI Count, & No SSI Count – Monthly Trend" worksheet title.

» Copy the title (ctrl-c), then click "OK" to close the Edit Title dialog box.

» Drag Text from Objects and place to the right of the "Surgical Site Infections by Service" title text box.

» Paste the copied title and click "OK."

Hide the line chart worksheet title:

» Right-click the line chart worksheet title and select "Hide Title."

Add shading to titles to highlight them:

» Click the "Surgical Site Infections by Service" text box to highlight it.

» Click the "Layout" tab at the top of the left column.

» Under "Background," click the null icon. Select a light gray color from the palette.

Best Practice

Using titles to frame individual dashboard sections as described above is one approach to layout and design. It is sensible to take audience, data, and potential use into consideration when selecting design elements such as color, arrangement, and labeling.

» Perform the same steps for the other title text box.

» Adjust the height and width of the worksheets as needed to appropriately fit the dashboard space.

To add background color to the "Surgical Site Infections by Surgeon" worksheet,

» Right-click the worksheet title.

» From the menu, select "Format Title..."

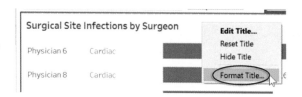

» In the Format pane to the left of the dashboard, under the Title section, click the drop-down caret for Shading.

» Select a light gray color from the color palette.

6 Adjust chart layout with padding

Notice the monthly trend line chart has column labels at the bottom of the chart displaying the first initial of each month. Unlike with the text table and bar chart, the intuitive title above the line chart means a separate column header is not needed above the trend lines. As a result, the top of the line chart is not horizontally aligned with the text table and bar chart.

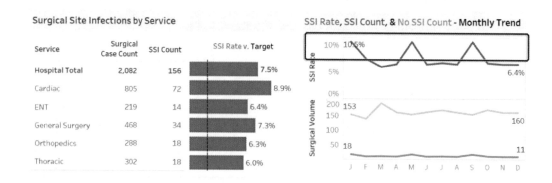

To align the top of the line chart with the top of the bar chart, use Tableau's padding function.

» Click the "SSI Rate, SSI Count, & No SSI Count – Monthly Trend" worksheet to high-light it.

» In the left side of the dashboard work area, click the "Layout" tab.

» Scroll down to the Outer Padding and Inner Padding sections.

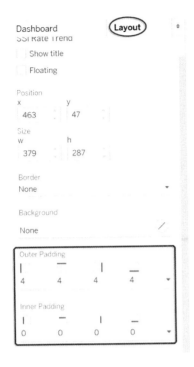

Padding

Padding enables the precise spacing of items on a dashboard. Tableau defaults the Outer Padding to 4 on all sides.

Outer Padding: adds space between the worksheet border and the outer edge of the chart.

Inner Padding: adds space between the edge of the chart features and the outer edge of the chart.

In the example below, a border and background shading was added to the example line chart to highlight the difference between Outer and Inner Padding.

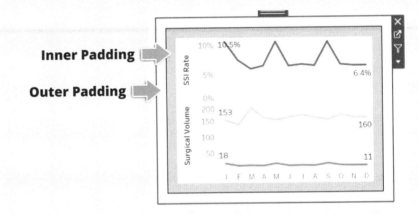

» Click the caret to the right of the Outer Padding settings.

» Uncheck "All sides equal."

» Increase the "top" value until the top of the line chart aligns with the top of the bar chart (approximately "40").

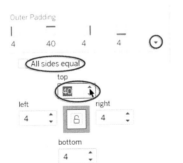

◄ **Gridlines**

To help with precision alignment, use Tableau's gridline feature. Click "Dashboard" on the Menu Bar, then select "Show Grid." Gridline sizing can be adjusted using the "Grid Options" feature, also on the Menu Bar.

Format the Surgical Site Infections by Surgeon worksheet

The Surgical Site Infections by Surgeon worksheet at the bottom of the dashboard will utilize its corresponding color legend to label the bar charts. To add and format the color legend:

» Click the "Surgical Site Infections by Surgeon" worksheet to highlight it, then click the drop-down caret in the side tab of the worksheet.

» In the menu, select "Legends," then "Color Legend (Measure Names)."

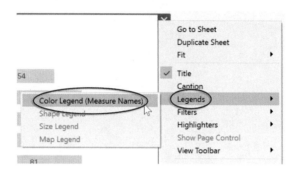

The Measure Names color legend appears in the top right column of the dashboard work-space. Relocate and format it to reduce excess white space.

» Click the "Measure Names" color legend to highlight, then click the caret in the side tab.

» From the menu, select "Floating."

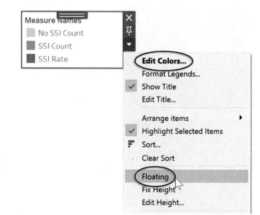

Tiled vs. Floating Layout ▷

*Tiled worksheets are displayed side-by-side, with no overlaps, in the dashboard workspace. The active gray space previously described provides a grid-like area for placement of worksheets. **Tiled** is Tableau's default layout and is recommended practice for worksheets and filters. **Floating** worksheets, in contrast, can be placed anywhere on the Dashboard, and can overlap others; this ability is useful in the display of legends.*

The Measure Names color legend is now highlighted and separated from the dashboard.

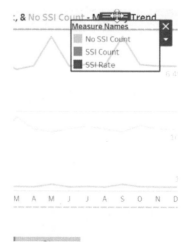

» Hover over the tab on the top middle border of the color legend and click and drag it to just above its corresponding bar charts.

» Click the caret again on the floating color legend.

» Click the "Show Title" option on the menu to remove its checkmark.

» Click the caret on the floating color legend again.

» Select "Arrange Items," then select "Single Row."

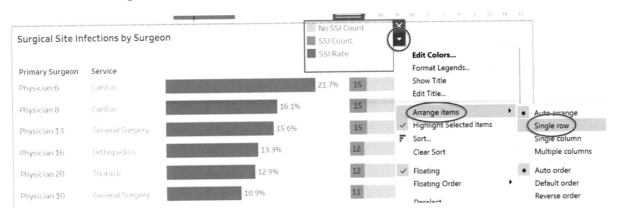

» Hover on the right border of the floating color legend until a bi-directional arrow appears.

» Click and drag to the appropriate width.

» Adjust the width, height, and location of the color legend to desired proportions.

» If the spacing between the color labels requires adjustment, hover the cursor between to display a vertical dotted border. Click and drag the border to adjust spacing as desired.

» Click anywhere outside of the dashboard workspace to de-select the floating legend.

The floating legend should look like this:

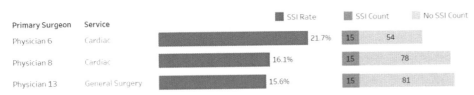

7 Add a dashboard title

» Drag and drop a Text box from the Dashboard Objects pane to the top of the Dashboard sheet. (The active gray space will appear at the very top.)

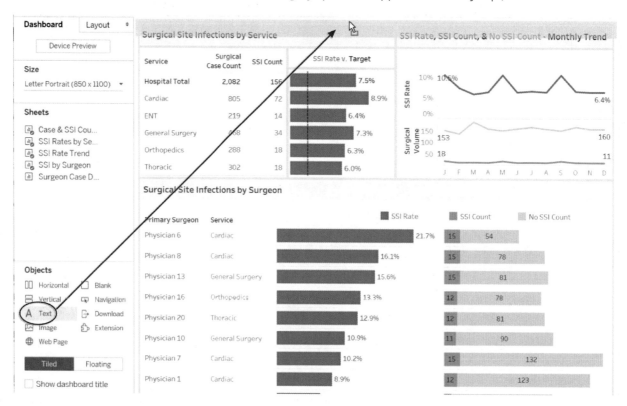

▲ Why not use "Show dashboard title"?

Checking the Show Dashboard Title button adds the title within a vertical layout container. Layout containers are a formatting feature used to organize tiled worksheets in a dashboard. They can sometimes cause confusion for new Tableau users because the alignment of objects is restricted to either horizontal or vertical. When using the default dashboard title, the vertical container prevents additional objects from being added to the right of the title. For this reason, a title using the Text Box object, which does not create a new layout container, is used for the dashboard title.

» In the Edit Text dialog box, enter the title:

"Hospital Surgical Site Infection (SSI) Summary
Date(s): January to December 2019"

» Choose font type and size. (This example uses Tableau Medium, 15-point for the title, and 12-point for the subtitle. The font color has been changed to a dark gray.)

» Click "OK."

» Hover the cursor over the bottom border of the title text box on the Dashboard until it changes to a bi-directional arrow.

» Click and drag the title text box border to desired height.

» Adjust the heights and widths of the dashboard worksheets, text box titles, and floating color legend as desired.

8 **Rename the dashboard tab and save the dashboard**

» Right-click the "Dashboard 2" tab at the bottom of the workspace.

» Select "Rename Sheet."

» Enter title, "Hospital SSI Summary."

» Press the Enter key to save.

The dashboard now looks like this. It is simply formatted and contains no interactivity. A great deal more work will be required to transform it into a powerful tool that fully informs its viewers. It is crucial to follow all remaining instructions in this chapter to create a production-ready dashboard.

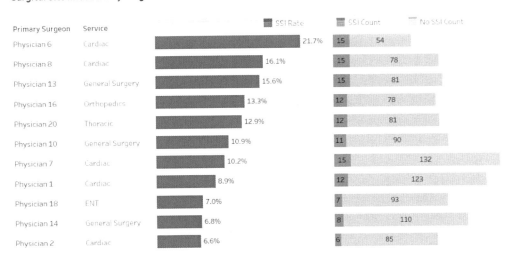

Hospital Surgical Site Infection (SSI) Summary
Date(s): January to December 2019

Insight: Organization of this Hospital Surgical Site Infection Summary dashboard allows the report viewer to see the data aggregated by Service for the entire year; trended over time; and then stratified by Surgeon.

20.2 Dashboards: Basic Interactivity

nteractivity makes Tableau dashboards more powerful. Continuing with the dashboard developed in the previous section, Dashboards: Basic Interactivity shows how to implement different types of filters—specifically multi-worksheet Filters and Actions—that give the user more flexibility in viewing both particular data and more data within the same dashboard layout.

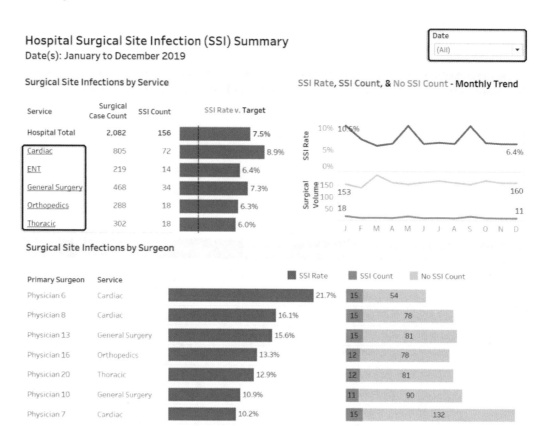

Filters for Multiple Worksheets

Filters can be either Dimensions or Measures, but typically are Dimensions, allowing for filtering of categories of data or of dates. The field used for a filter requires incorporation in a dashboard worksheet. Filters then applied to multiple worksheets enable the user to filter for a specific category of data and have that category apply to all the worksheets within the Dashboard.

The following example will incorporate a Date filter onto the dashboard. Date filters enable the user to focus on a specific day, week, month, or year of data. Here, a Date filter by month will be created.

1 Insert and format a Date Filter

To use a filter on a dashboard, the field must be utilized in one of the worksheets on the dashboard. Assessing the current worksheets on the dashboard: the "SSI Rate, SSI Count, & No SSI Count – Monthly Trend" worksheet uses a date field—set to the discrete month aggregation to create the trend line (see the Line chart chapter for a refresher on date aggregation).

» Click the line chart worksheet to highlight it on the dashboard.

» In the side tab of the highlighted worksheet, click the drop-down caret for More Options.

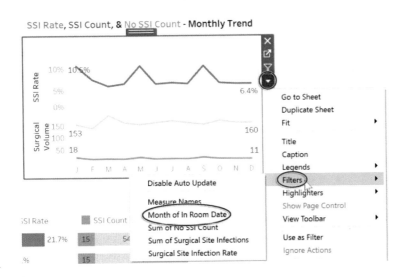

◄ Making Filters Available on a Dashboard

As demonstrated in the example to the left, a Filter will be available for use on a Dashboard only if the field is currently present on the selected worksheet.

» From the menus, select "Filters" then "Month of In Room Date."

"Month of In Room Date" appears as a filter at the right side of the dashboard. Currently this filter applies only to the line chart worksheet. To apply it to all the dashboard worksheets:

» Click the "Month of In Room Date" filter to highlight.

» Click the caret in the right corner tab.

» Select "Apply to Worksheets."

» Click "Selected Worksheets."

Refresher

Just as with worksheets, Dashboard Filters can be customized to display values as check boxes, drop-downs, custom lists, or even sliders. Filter size and placement can be adjusted just like any other Dashboard object.

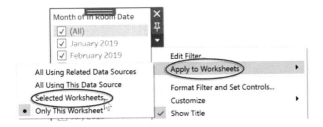

◄ Apply Filter to Multiple Worksheets

A Filter can be applied to one or more worksheet(s) that use the same data source or a related data source with at least one common linking field. Remember that a Filter can control filters on other worksheets not present on the Dashboard, so be careful to include only the worksheets that really are to be filtered.

» Click the "All on dashboard" button then click "OK."

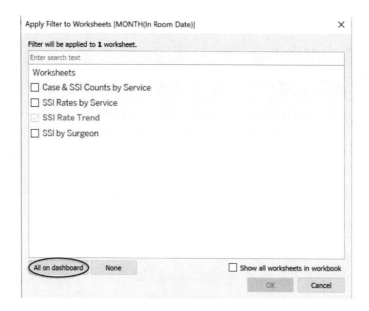

» Test the filter to ensure it performs as expected. Select several months and observe how the data displays on all worksheets.

2 Format the dashboard

The new Filter creates unnecessary, wasteful white space on the right side of the Dashboard. Eliminate this space with additional formatting.

» Click the "Month of In Room Date" Filter to highlight.

» Hover the cursor over the top center border tab until it changes to a cross shape.

» Click and drag the Filter box to the right of the Dashboard title. A gray rectangle appears to show where the Filter can be dropped.

» Release the Filter to the right of the title.

The Date filter requires a different selection option to work better within this space.

» Click the Date filter to highlight, then click the drop-down caret.

» From the menu, select "Multiple Values (dropdown)."

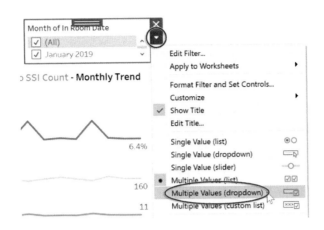

» Adjust the width of the filter as needed to fit legibly into the allotted space.

The title of the "Month of In Room Date" Filter can be shortened to "Date."

» Double-click the "Month of In Room Date" Filter title.

» Shorten the title to "Date."

The Dashboard now looks like this:

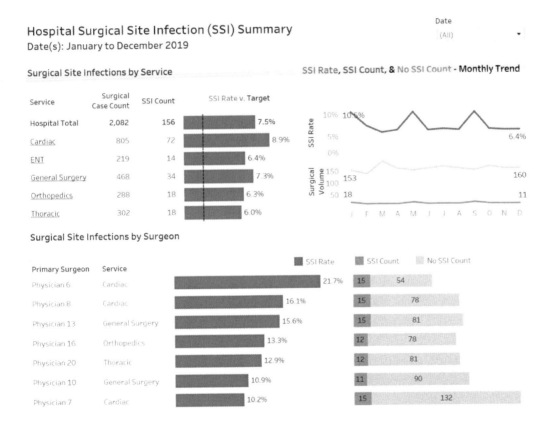

3 Add and format an Action (Intra-dashboard)

While Quick Filters reside on the periphery of the Dashboard in a menu section, Action Filters reside within the dashboard itself. These allow the user to select data in one worksheet to filter results in another one. Action Filters are useful for minimizing the clutter of multiple Quick Filters while still enabling the user to control what data is displayed. For this example, an Action Filter will be set up using the Service field.

》 Click the "Surgical Site Infections by Service" text table worksheet to highlight.

》 Click the "Use as Filter" funnel icon.

Use as Filter Feature ▷

This feature designates a particular worksheet as the source of an Action Filter that will affect every other worksheet in the Dashboard. Tableau automatically applies every single dimension as a filter to the other worksheets, assuming they share a data source. In this example, choosing Use as Filter creates an Action Filter that applies Service to the other worksheets in the Dashboard. If the user clicks Cardiac, the other worksheets filter for Cardiac.

Rather than searching for Use as Filter on the drop-down menu, save time by clicking the funnel icon in the tab of the worksheet.

Surgical Site Infections by Service

Service	Surgical Case Count	SSI Count
Hospital Total	2,082	156
Cardiac	805	72
ENT	219	14
General Surgery	468	34
Orthopedics	288	18
Thoracic	302	18

To edit the action filter behavior:

》 Click "Dashboard" on the Menu row.

》 Select "Actions…"

》 Click the "Filter 1 (generated)" title to highlight.

》 Click the "Edit…" button.

Edit Actions ▷

In the Actions context box in the screenshot, notice Filter 1 (generated). When the Use as Filter option was selected, Tableau generated an Action Filter applying all possible dimensions from the original worksheet to the target worksheets. For additional options, the Action Filter can be edited or even removed.

Highlight, URL, Set, and Parameter Actions can also be created via this menu. Highlight Actions intensify the colors of all marks of interest while fading those of others; URL Actions navigate to a website or web-hosted file via a new browser tab. Set Actions and Parameter Actions pass a user-selected value into the Set or Parameter. An example of a Set Action can be seen in Chapter 24.

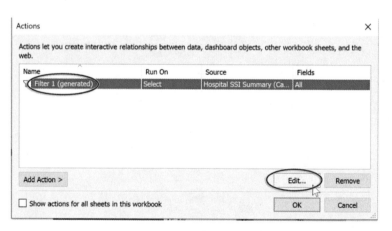

Follow these steps in the Edit Filter Action dialog box:

» Change Name to "Service Filter."

» Under Source Sheets, ensure that only the "Case & SSI Counts by Service" box is checked.

» Under Run action on, click the "Select" button.

» Under Target Sheets, uncheck the boxes for "Case & SSI Counts by Service" and "SSI Rates by Service."

» Under Clearing the selection will: make sure that "Show all values" is selected.

» Under Target Filters, choose "Selected Fields."

◀ Elements of an Action

1) *Name:* *Provide a descriptive name so that each Action on a list can be easily identified by other developers.*

2) *Source Sheets:* *Start here to select the worksheet that will initiate the Action.*

3) *Run action on:* *This option specifies what user prompt (Hover, Select, or Menu) starts the action. Select is the most frequently chosen trigger.*

4) *Target Sheets:* *Designates the worksheets to be filtered when the Source Sheet is activated. The dropdown menu permits selecting worksheets on the same dashboard as the Source Sheet's; on a different dashboard from the Source Sheet's; or on individual worksheets not present on a dashboard.*

5) *Clearing the selection will:* *When the Action on the Source Sheet is deselected, this option allows the user to leave the filter displayed on the Target Sheets; show all data on the Target Sheets; or remove all data until a new Action is initiated.*

6) *Target Filters:* *This section enables transmitting either all possible fields to the Target Sheets or only specific ones. (Actions can pass only Dimensions that are present somewhere on the Source Sheet.)*

249

▲ Selected Fields

When working with multiple data sources, and to ensure precision, use the Selected Fields option (under Target Filters in the Edit Filter Action dialog box) to focus exclusively on one or more fields. Applying only Selected Fields gives more control over exactly what will be sent from Source to Target worksheets. Using this menu, Tableau can pass an Action across different data sources. The fields for Source and Target must be defined in the Add Filter dialog box.

» Click the "Add Filter..." button at the bottom of the dialog box.

» Under each of the two "Field" options, choose "Service" from the drop-down menu.

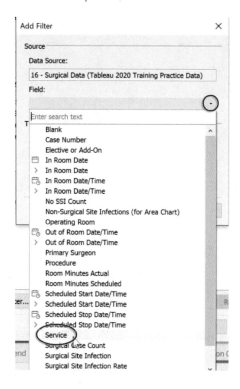

» Click "OK" to close all three open dialog boxes.

After the addition of the Service Action, click any one of the Services in the Case & SSI Counts by Service worksheet to test that selected target worksheets filter for the selected Service. Click the same Service again to undo the Action.

It will not, however, be immediately evident that this Action is present; to make it more obvious, format each Service name as a hyperlink. Clicking any Service hyperlink redisplays the Dashboard viewed through the Service Action.

» Right-click any Service name.

» Select "Format" from the menu.

» In the Format window, select the "Header" tab.

» Click the caret to the right of "Font."

» Click the underline option, "U."

» Select a bright blue square from the color palette. (Select the "More Colors" option to reveal all choices.)

Now each Service name looks like a hyperlink, inviting the user to click it and thus engage the Action.

The dashboard now looks like this:

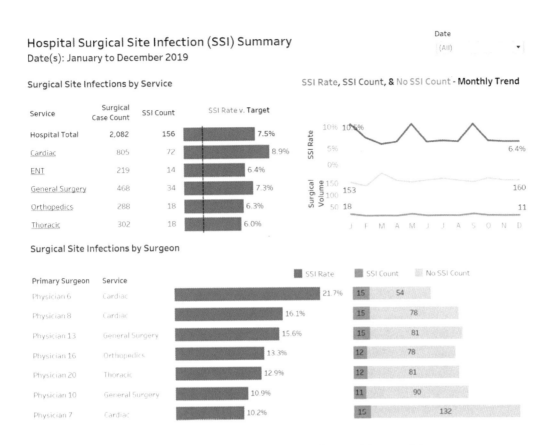

The third and final part of the Dashboards section, Advanced Interactivity, covers maneuvering to a second dashboard and creating a navigation button, an information button, and a dynamic title. This section guides the user in completing preparation of this example Dashboard for production.

20.3 Dashboards: Advanced Interactivity

In addition to their other functions, Tableau Dashboards convey the ability to interact with and navigate between dashboards or between a dashboard and a worksheet. This section details how to create the following features to transform this standalone dashboard into a production-ready application:

- Action to navigate to another dashboard

- Back Button to return to a previous dashboard

- Information Button to reveal or hide additional text

- Dynamic Title that changes based on filter selections

Hospital Surgical Site Infection (SSI) Summary
Date(s): All

Surgical Site Infections by Service

Service	Surgical Case Count	SSI Count	SSI Rate v. **Target**
Hospital Total	2,082	156	7.5%
Cardiac	805	72	8.9%
ENT	219	14	6.4%
General Surgery	468	34	7.3%
Orthopedics	288	18	6.3%
Thoracic	302	18	6.0%

SSI Rate, SSI Count, & No SSI Count - **Monthly Trend**

Surgical Site Infections by Surgeon

Primary Surgeon	Service	SSI Rate	SSI Count	No SSI Count
Physician 6	Cardiac	21.7%	15	54
Physician 8	Cardiac	16.1%	15	78
Physician 13	General Surgery	15.6%	15	81
Physician 16	Orthopedics	13.3%	12	78
Physician 20	Thoracic	12.9%	12	81
Physician 10	General Surgery	10.9%	11	90
Physician 7	Cardiac	10.2%	15	132
Physician 1	Cardiac	8.9%	12	123
Physician 18	ENT	7.0%	7	93
Physician 14	General Surgery	6.8%	8	110

Best Practice

In addition to design and layout, report interactivity is a crucial element in creating a high-impact dashboard suite. This interactivity includes filtering within a dashboard; drilling down to more detailed dashboards, then returning to the starting point; and hovering to obtain additional information. This section will help designers turn individual reports into a unified user experience.

Continuing with the construction of the Hospital Surgical Site Infection Summary Dashboard, this section creates an Action allowing the user to navigate from the existing SSI Summary Dashboard to a more granular dashboard ("Surgeon Case Details") provided in the current example workbook. The Action is engaged by clicking a primary surgeon´s name in the source Dashboard to drill down to surgical case details.

1 Add and format an Action (Inter-dashboard)

» Open the "Hospital Surgical Site Infection (SSI) Summary" dashboard.

» Click "Dashboards" on the Menu bar.

» Click "Actions..." (the "Service filter" that appears under "Name" was created in the previous section)

» Click the "Add Action" button.

» Select "Filter..."

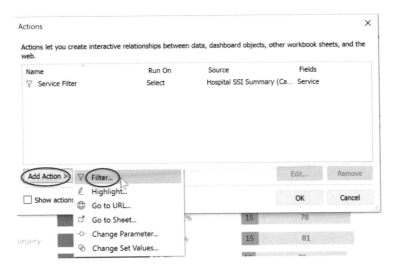

▲ Types of Actions

From the Actions menu, a Filter, Highlight, URL , Sheet, Parameter, or Set Action can be added.

Filter: Passes data from the Source to the Target worksheet(s) in order to navigate to and filter results on the latter.

Highlight: Passes data from the Source to the Target worksheet(s) in order to highlight the selected results without filtering the data.

URL: sends the user to a website defined in the URL Action dialog box. This web address can encode data from a field in the data source if configured to do so.

Sheet: navigates the user to the selected worksheet.

Set: allows the user to dynamically change what is in or out of a created set. See Chapter 24 for a Set Action exercise.

Parameter: the user can dynamically change the value of a parameter by interacting with the chart.

» Name the filter "Surgeon Drill-down."

» Under Source Sheets / Hospital SSI Summary, uncheck all boxes except for "SSI by Surgeon"

» Under Run action on, click the "Select" box.

» Under Target Sheets, click the caret and select "Surgeon Case Details dashboard." This will display the only target worksheet, "Surgeon Case Details," which will be checked. The Action will be directed to the worksheet(s) checked that reside within the target dashboard. In this case, the single worksheet within this dashboard will be checked by default.

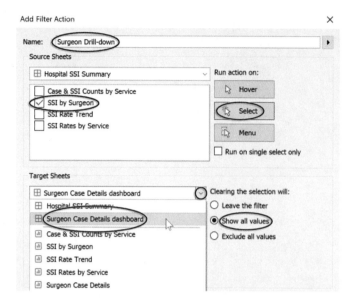

Refresher ▶

Remember that applying an Action sends a set of criteria to the Target worksheet. In this exercise, slightly more complexity is added because the Target is a worksheet in another Dashboard. The second Dashboard must be selected before the filter can be applied.

» Under Target Filters, click "Selected Fields."

» Click the "Add Filter…" button.

» Under Source, click the caret beneath "Field."

» Select "Primary Surgeon" from the drop-down menu.

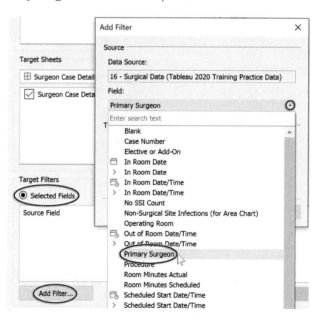

Ensure that the Target Field is also "Primary Surgeon."

» Click "OK."

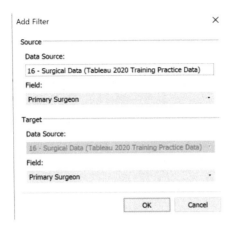

◀ Action Field Mapping

Tableau matches the field name in the Target Field if that name precisely replicates the selection in the Source Field. Here, it matches Primary Surgeon. If, however, this is not the right choice because the Target Field is different, another Field name can be substituted. Similarly, if the Source and Target Data sources are different, the Target Field can be manually mapped.

The Filter Action box should now look like this:

255

» Click "OK."

The Action for "Surgeon drill-down" is now present on the Actions list in addition to the Service filter.

» Click "OK" again.

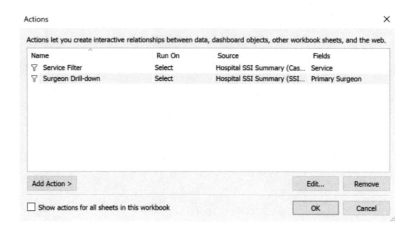

» Test the Action by clicking on a Primary Surgeon name on the Hospital SSI Summary dashboard. This should navigate to the Surgeon Case Details dashboard and filter for the selected Primary Surgeon. From the tabs at the bottom of the screen, choose the Hospital SSI Summary dashboard tab to return to the primary dashboard.

To signal the link, format the Primary Surgeon column in a blue, underlined font (signaling "hyperlink").

» Click the "Surgical Site Infections by Surgeon" worksheet on the Hospital SSI Summary dashboard to highlight.

» Select "Format" from the Menu bar.

» Select "Font…"

» Click the "Fields" caret.

» Select "Primary Surgeon."

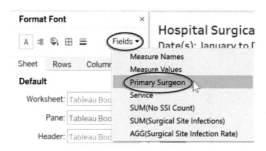

» Select the "Header" tab.

» Click the "Default Font" caret.

» Select a blue square on the color palette. (Click "More Colors…" to view the full color palette.)

» Click the "Underline" icon.

» Click the "X" to the right of the Format window title to close this window.

The Surgical Site Infections by Surgeon worksheet on the Dashboard now looks like this:

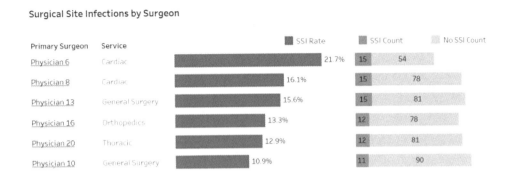

Creating Navigation Buttons to Improve Dashboard Interactivity

Navigation buttons aid the end-user to seamless maneuver through a dashboard suite or to and from specific worksheets. Tableau's navigation buttons allow for plenty of customization, using text or images, borders and background formatting, and adding supporting text in the form of tooltips. This section will describe the creation of a Back Button to navigate the user from the Surgeon Case Details dashboard to the Hospital SSI Summary dashboard.

2 **Create and format a Back Button**

Best Practice

Incorporating Back Buttons into dashboards provides a seamless experience for report users by allowing them to quickly drill into and out of their data.

The Navigation option in the Objects pane is used to create the Back Button on the Surgeon Case Details dashboard.

» Drag and drop "Navigation" from the Objects pane to the right of the Surgeon Case Details dashboard title.

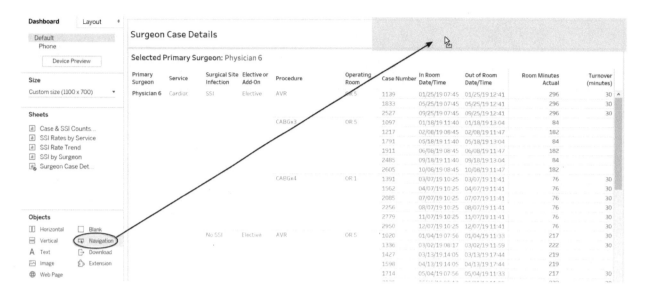

» In the appearing highlighted "Navigation" object, click the drop-down caret to open the "More Options" menu.

» Select "Edit button…"

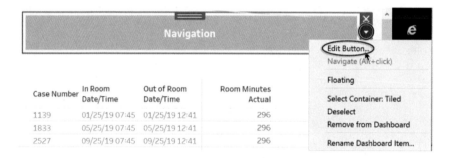

The Edit Button dialog box offers options for navigation locations, button styles, formatting, and tooltip text. Perform the following steps to edit the Back Button:

» In the section "Navigate to", click the drop-down caret and select "Hospital SSI Summary."

Navigation options ▶

Navigation buttons are not limited to dashboards, but can be used to maneuver to different worksheets in the workbook. Be mindful that the drop-down menu selections include both worksheets and dashboards present in the workbook.

» For "Button Style," click the drop-down caret and select "Image Button."

» Under "Image," click the "Choose" button.

» Select the "My Tableau Repository" folder (often found under the "Documents" folder), then the "Shapes" folder.

The Back Button will use an image of a green, left-pointing arrow.

» Within the Shapes folder, select the "Arrows" folder, then scroll down the images to the green, left-pointing arrow.

» Select a left-pointing arrow then click the "Open" button.

» Click the "Apply" button in the Edit Button dialog box to see how the image appears.

» In the Tooltip section, enter "Click to navigate back to the Hospital SSI Summary dashboard."

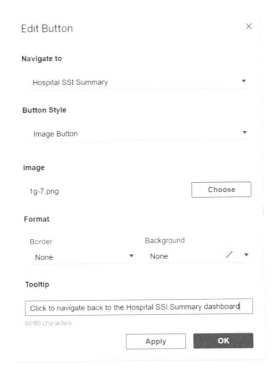

» Click "OK."

» Adjust the width of the navigation button box as desired.

Surgeon Case Details

Selected Primary Surgeon: Physician 6

Test the Back Button to ensure it performs as desired.

» Hover over the button to check the tooltip text.

» Hold down the "Alt" key ("Option" button on a Mac), then click the Back Button. Navigation should be directed to the Hospital SSI Summary dashboard.

Note: report consumers using Reader, Server, or Tableau Online will need only a single click to activate the navigation. To test this functionality, view the dashboard in Presentation Mode.

Creating Specialized Worksheets to Improve Dashboard Interactivity

Up to this point, worksheets have been created to visualize data. In the following sections, they will be built for other purposes. Instructions follow for two separate worksheets designed to add additional information and interactivity to the Dashboard: Information Button and Dynamic Title.

3 Create and format an Information Button

Information buttons are useful for including a detailed written description of dashboards. Information buttons take up minimal real estate; pop-up messages provide the necessary space to relay information. Because there is a character limit in the Navigation button option, the Information Button will be created via a worksheet, utilizing the worksheet's Tooltip function to display the detailed text.

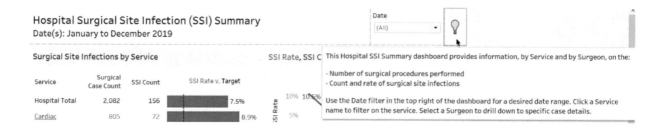

Best Practice

Most dashboards do not have the space to display full written descriptions or lengthy instructional text. Further, once it is read, this type of text often distracts from the dashboard's message. Using an information button to hide the text is a great way to save space and enhance focus.

The Information Button will be created using two processes:

1) Build a separate worksheet with an Information Button shape, but no data.

2) Add this worksheet to the Dashboard and format it to look like a stand-alone button.

» Open a new, blank worksheet.

» Click the drop-down caret to the right of the Search window in the Data pane and select "Create Calculated Field" from the appearing menu.

» Enter the following in the Calculated Field dialog box:

Name: "Blank"

Formula: "" (a set of double quotation marks)

» Click "OK."

◀ Blank Calculated Field

The "Blank" calculated field, a string field where all values are set to "", is handy for performing formatting tricks in Tableau. In this example, the field helps create a worksheet with a single shape (an Information Button) and no data. This field can also be used as a placeholder Dimension to manipulate header spacing.

» Drag the calculated field "Blank" to Details on the Marks card.

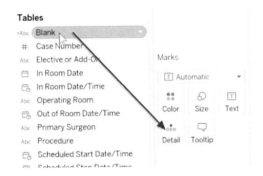

Tableau automatically formats this field as a square. Change the square to the desired shape.

» Click the Marks Type caret to the right of "Automatic."

» Select "Shape."

» Click the "Shape" box that now appears on the Marks card.

» Select "More Shapes…"

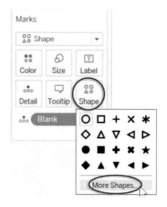

» Under "Select Shape Palette," click the caret to the right of "Default."

» Select "Bug Tracking."

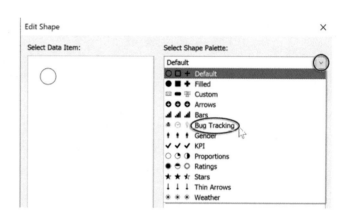

Adding Custom Shapes ▶

Tableau offers a selection of shapes that can be incorporated into the navigation button or into worksheets. If none of the included shapes suits the designer's needs, custom shapes can be added by importing image files into the My Tableau Repository \ Shapes folder. (Make sure to restart Tableau after new shapes have been added.) Tableau's default light bulb shape will be used in this exercise.

» Select the light bulb image.

» Click "OK."

» Click Size on the Marks card.

» Move the slider about halfway to the right.

» Rename the worksheet "Information Button."

4 Add and format the Information Button onto the dashboard

» Open the Hospital SSI Summary Dashboard.

» Drag and drop the "Information Button" worksheet to the right of the Dashboard title and of the Date quick filter.

262

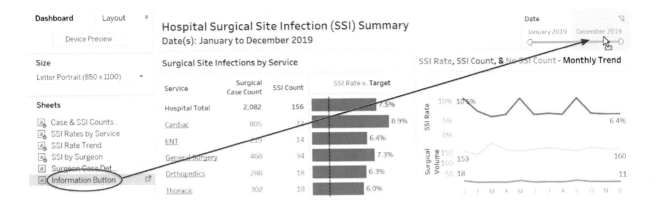

» Click the drop-down caret on the border of the highlighted Information Button worksheet.

» Click "Title" to remove its checkmark.

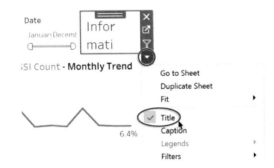

» Click the worksheet drop-down caret again and select "Fit."

» Select "Entire View."

To re-size the Information Button border on the Dashboard:

» Click the Information Button worksheet to highlight.

» Click the left edge and drag it to re-size as desired.

If the Information Button icon need further resizing:

» Navigate to the Information Button worksheet.

» Click Size on the Marks card and adjust the slider as desired.

» Adjust the borders of the Date quick filter as needed.

5 Edit the Tooltip for the Information Button

» Navigate back to the Information Button worksheet.

» Click Tooltip on the Marks card.

» Uncheck the box next to "Include command buttons."

» Change the text to read:

"This Hospital SSI Summary dashboard provides information, by Service and by Surgeon, on the:

- Number of surgical procedures performed

- Count and rate of surgical site infections

Use the Date filter in the top right of the dashboard for a desired date range. Click a Service name to filter on the service. Select a Surgeon to drill down to specific case details."

» Click the "Preview" button to view how the Tooltip will look.

» Click "OK."

» Hover the cursor over the Information Button on the dashboard to display the Tooltip.

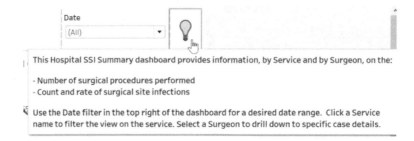

6 Create and format a Dynamic Title

A worksheet title can be filtered according to data in that worksheet. Dynamic Titles enable the user to see and confirm what is being filtered in the Dashboard.

Hospital Surgical Site Infection (SSI) Summary
Date(s): October 2019, November 2019, December 2019

Date

▲ **Dynamic Titles**

These Titles are created by using a worksheet that appears to have no data on it. All the data to be displayed is hidden in Details on the Marks card. Adjusting the transparency of Color on the Marks card to zero ensures that no data is showing. This will make sense once the worksheet is added to the dashboard, because only the Title is displayed there.

This section creates a separate worksheet designed to display a Dynamic Title for the Dashboard.

» Open a new worksheet and rename it "Dynamic Title."

» Right-click and drag "In Room Date" to Details on the Marks card.

» In the Drop Field box, select the date value (green icon) "Month" and click "OK."

» Right-click the newly added "In Room Date" field and change from continuous to discrete.

Date formatting ▷

Changing the date field from continuous to discrete enables the dynamic title to display the individual months selected in the Date filter.

» Click Color on the Marks card.

» Change Opacity to "0."

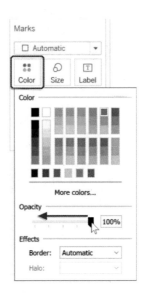

» Double-click the Title Row to open the Edit Title dialog box.

» Change the title to:

"Hospital Surgical Site Infection (SSI) Summary"
"Date(s): "

» Click the "Insert" button.

» Select "MONTH(In Room Date)" from the drop-down menu.

Refresher

In this example, the Date field is inserted into the worksheet title so that the latter changes dynamically as the dataset is filtered for different dates. The Insert menu can also enable the addition of parameters, last-updated timestamps, or the report-developer's name.

» Highlight title and change the font to "Tableau Medium."

» Change "Date(s): <MONTH(In Room Date)>" font size to "12."

» Click "OK."

7 Add and format the Dynamic Title onto the dashboard

» Open the Hospital SSI Summary Dashboard.

» Drag the new "Dynamic Title" worksheet to the right of the current Text title box.

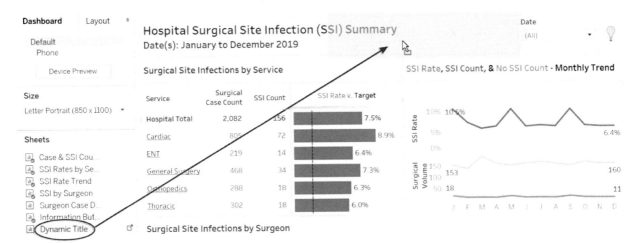

» Click the original Dashboard Title to highlight.

» Click the "X" in the top right corner to delete the text box.

» Click the new "Dynamic Title" worksheet to highlight.

» On the Toolbar, change the Fit option from "Standard" to "Entire View."

8 Link the Filters to the Dynamic Title

» Click the "Date" filter to highlight.

» Click the caret in the upper right corner.

» Click "Apply to Worksheets."

» Click "Selected Worksheets."

» Click the "Dynamic Title" box to apply the Filter to the Dynamic Title worksheet.

» Test the filter to ensure that the Dynamic Title is working correctly.

9 Final dashboard formatting tips

When the report viewer first opens a dashboard, consider the initial view. It may be helpful to pre-select filters or sort pertinent charts to draw attention to important findings.

Hide worksheet tabs so that the report viewer sees only dashboard tabs. To hide all worksheets:

» Right-click one of the dashboard tabs, and select "Hide All Sheets" from the menu.

» Repeat for the second dashboard tab.

The order of the dashboard tabs can be changed to reflect the order in which they should be reviewed.

» Click the "Hospital SSI Summary Dashboard" tab and drag it to the left of the "Surgeon Case Details Dashboard" tab.

» The final Dashboard looks like this:

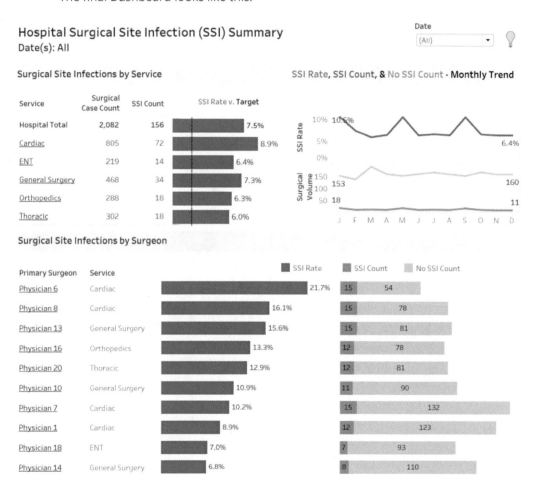

Insight: From January to December, the Surgical Site Infection rate was above target for the hospital and for each of the services. The SSI Rates peaked in January, March, and September at about 10.5%. Physician 6, a cardiac surgeon, had the highest SSI rate (21.7%) with the lower volume of procedures performed (69).

CHAPTER 21

Stories

Tableau´s Story tool enables digital storytelling formatted directly in a visualization. A Story can be incorporated into a workbook as a separate sheet type, like a worksheet or dashboard. The tool puts context in sequential progression to narrate the story of the data. Each Story Point captures a particular view or insight, guiding the audience through the analysis. As with any good story, these points create the smooth flow of a compelling visual narrative.

Stories can be put to good use in various ways. In addition to simply creating a presentation to emphasize a specific trend or element in reports, a Story can also be used to walk an audience through the functionality of a new suite of reports or dashboards or even to highlight data quality issues during development.

How To: Create a Story to describe the current opioid addiction crisis.

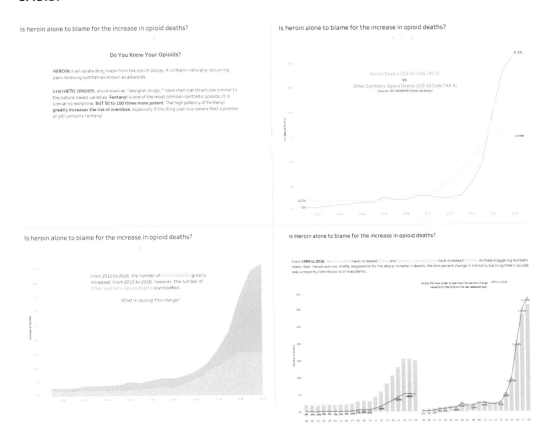

Data Source: *CDC WONDER online databases provide data and analysis to support evidence-based assessment of public health programs and population health trends.*

About the Data: *Centers for Disease Control and Prevention, National Center for Health Statistics. Multiple Cause of Death 1999-2018 on CDC WONDER Online Database, released December 2016. Data are from the Multiple Cause of Death Files, 1999-2018, as compiled from data provided by the 57 vital statistics jurisdictions through the Vital Statistics Cooperative Program.*

The Story Workspace

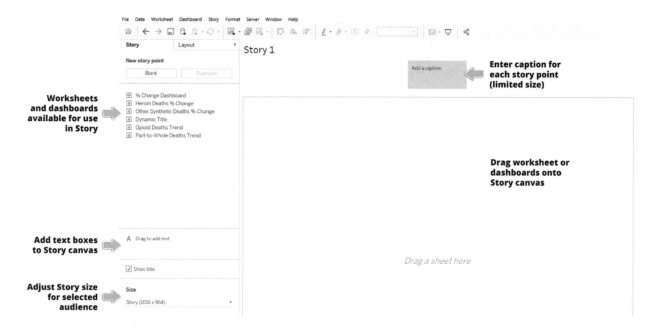

1 Create a new Story

This Story example describes the current national opioid crisis, comparing heroin deaths to synthetic opioid deaths. Two worksheets and one dashboard have been created to display heroin and synthetic opioid trends. This Story contains a considerable amount of explanation via text; therefore, Text Boxes instead of Captions are used to create it.

> » Open the "Tableau for Healthcare – Story Starter Workbook" already prepopulated with 2 worksheets and one dashboard.

To create a new Story:

Option 1:
- On the Menu bar, click "Story."
- Click "New Story."

Option 2:
- On bottom row of Worksheet/Dashboard tabs, click far-right icon to add new Story.

2 Set the Navigation Style and rename the story tab

The navigation style can be edited to find the best fit for each Story. The large amount of text in this Story makes the "Dots" style the best choice for a cleaner, less distracting appearance.

» Click the "Layout" tab at the top of the left pane.

» Click the "Dots" radio button.

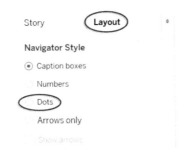

» Click the "Story" tab at the top of the left pane to return to the Story pane.

» Right-click the "Story 1" tab at the bottom of the workbook and select "Rename."

» Change name to "Opioid Deaths."

» Click the "Save" icon on the Toolbar to save the workbook.

3 Create the first Story Point

The first page of the Story is an introduction, describing the current opioid crisis using only text boxes. Three text boxes will be created.

» Drag and drop a Text box from the Story window onto the workspace.

» Enter the text, "Do You Know Your Opioids?"

» Highlight and bold the text, then change the font size to "18."

» Click "OK."

» Drag and drop the second Text box onto the workspace.

» Enter the text, "HEROIN is an opiate drug made from the opium poppy; it contains naturally-occurring pain-relieving substances known as alkaloids."

» Left-align the text, bold the word "HEROIN," and click "OK."

» Drag and drop a third Text box onto the workspace.

» Enter the text, "SYNTHETIC OPIOIDS, also known as "designer drugs," have chemical structures similar to the nature-based varieties. Fentanyl is one of the most common synthetic opioids; it is similar to morphine, BUT 50 to 100 times more potent. The high potency of Fentanyl greatly increases the risk of overdose, especially if the drug user is unaware that a powder or pill contains Fentanyl."

» Left-align the text. Bold the following text: "SYNTHETIC OPIOIDS," "Fentanyl," "BUT is 50 to 100 times more potent," and "greatly increases the risk of overdose."

271

» Click "OK."

4 Format the text boxes and add a Story title

» Right-click the first text box and select "Format description" from the menu.

» In the Format window, click the "Shading" caret, then change the color as desired (the example uses light blue).

» Click the "Borders" caret, then change the line to "None."

» Follow the same steps to edit the other two text boxes.

To adjust the width of the Text boxes:

» Click a Text box to highlight.

» Click and drag the borders to a desired width. Adjust the height in the same way.

To add a Story title:

» Double-click the Title row to open the Edit Title dialog box.

» Change the title to "Is heroin alone to blame for the increase in opioid deaths?"

» Highlight the text and change the font size to "20."

Is heroin alone to blame for the increase in opioid deaths?

‹ • • • • ›

Do You Know Your Opioids?

HEROIN is an opiate drug made from the opium poppy; it contains naturally- occurring pain-relieving substances known as alkaloids.

SYNTHETIC OPIOIDS, also known as "designer drugs," have chemical structures similar to the nature-based varieties. **Fentanyl** is one of the most common synthetic opioids; it is similar to morphine, **BUT 50 to 100 times more potent**. The high potency of Fentanyl **greatly increases the risk of overdose**, especially if the drug user is unaware that a powder or pill contains Fentanyl.

5 Add a new Story Point

» In the Story pane, under "New story point," click the "Blank" button.

» Drag and drop the "Opioid Deaths Trend" worksheet from the Story pane onto the canvas.

» Drag and drop a Text box onto the canvas.

» Enter the following description:

Heroin Deaths (ICD-10 Code T40.1) vs. Other Synthetic Opioid Deaths (ICD-10 Code T40.4)
(Source: CDC WONDER Online Database)

» Color-code the corresponding text to match the line colors.

» Format the text box to match previous text boxes.

6 Set the Story Size

The size of the Story with the Opioid Deaths Trend chart may be too large for the screen to accommodate. This is a good time to set the size of the Story. Evaluate the smallest resolution readers will use, then select a Story size. As with Dashboards, there are many size choices. The default setting is "Story (1016 x 964)."

» In the Size section at the bottom of the Story pane, click the caret to the right of the default size setting and select the desired size (in this example, Letter Landscape).

◀ Refresher

As with dashboards, a small blue checkmark indicates that the worksheet (or dashboard) is active—in this case, on the story canvas.

The Story Point now looks like this:

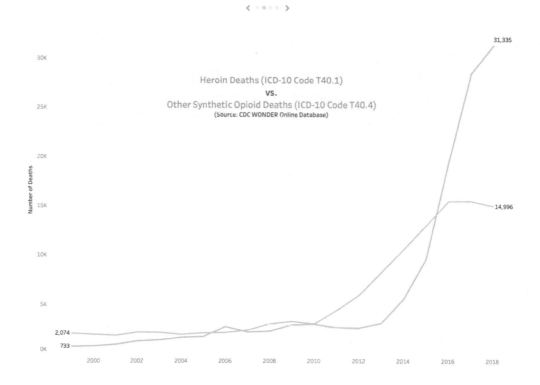

Is heroin alone to blame for the increase in opioid deaths?

Heroin Deaths (ICD-10 Code T40.1)
vs.
Other Synthetic Opioid Deaths (ICD-10 Code T40.4)
(Source: CDC WONDER Online Database)

7 Add a new Story Point

A second option for adding a new Story Point is to drag and drop a worksheet or dashboard onto the navigation bar.

» Drag "Part-to-Whole Deaths Trend" from the Story window to the navigation bar. Arrows will appear on the navigation bar indicating where the sheet can be placed. Drop the worksheet when the arrows appear at the far right.

» Drag and drop a Text box onto the canvas.

» Enter the following description:

"From 2010 to 2016, the number of Heroin deaths greatly increased. From 2015 to 2018, however, the number of Other Synthetic Opioids deaths skyrocketed. *What is causing this change?*"

» Italicize 'What is causing this change?"

» Color-code the corresponding text to match the Area chart colors.

» Format the text box to match previous text boxes.

Is heroin alone to blame for the increase in opioid deaths?

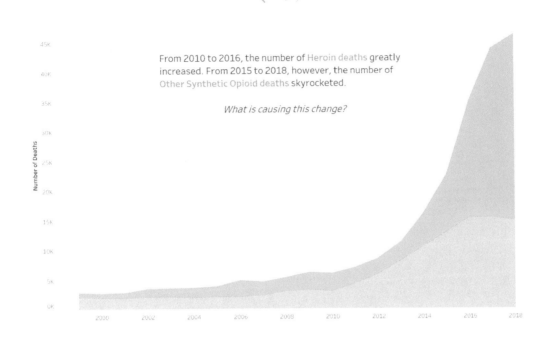

8 Add a final Story Point

» Add a new Story Point, then drag and drop "% Change Dashboard" onto the workspace.

This dashboard renders in the Story Point at its default size, which is larger than the space available in the Story workspace; a horizontal and a vertical slide bar appear. To set the dashboard to the correct size:

» Click the "% Change Dashboard" tab at the bottom of the workbook to navigate to the dashboard.

» In the Dashboard pane on the left, in the Size section, click the carets to the right of the dashboard´s set size to display the drop-down menu.

» Select the "Fit to Opioid Deaths" size option.

>> At the bottom of the workbook, click the "Opioid Deaths" tab to return to the Story.

The dashboard now fits the size of the Story.

Adjusting the Year slider changes the displays and the dynamic title. When the slider has been moved, a pop-up icon box appears above the navigation dots, offering options to:

- **Delete:** deletes the active Story Point
- **Revert:** changes the view back to the prior view
- **Update:** saves the edited view
- **Save as a New Story Point:** saves the view as a new Story Point

If the slider has been adjusted, click the "Revert" icon to return the slider to the previous setting.

>> Click the "Save" icon on the Toolbar.

The final Story Point now looks like this:

Is Heroin alone to blame for the increase in opioid deaths?

From **1999 to 2018**, Heroin Deaths have increased 623%, and Synthetic Opioid Deaths have increased 4175%. As these staggering numbers make clear, heroin was not chiefly responsible for the sharp increase in deaths; the dire percent change in mortality due to synthetic opioids was a majority contributor to this epidemic.

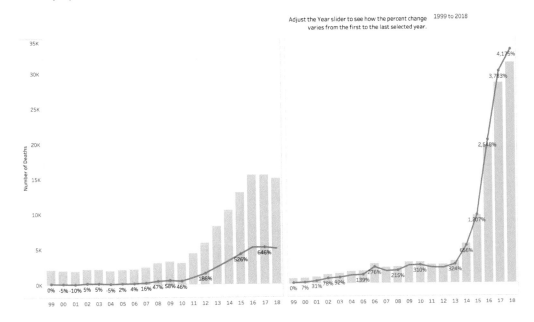

Adjust the Year slider to see how the percent change varies from the first to the last selected year. 1999 to 2018

▲ Presentation Mode

Full-screen Presentation Mode is perfect for displaying reports in front of any audience in Tableau Desktop or Reader. This mode hides the shelves, menus, and Sidebar to cleanly showcase the visualization. To activate Presentation Mode, either select the Presentation Mode icon from the Toolbar or press F7.

SECTION 6

Advanced Skills

CHAPTER 22

Calculated Fields

Tableau´s Calculated Fields are an effective way to quickly add data and information unavailable in the original data source(s) to reports and dashboards. If a dataset is missing a key piece of information, Tableau offers several ways to manipulate existing data fields to create new calculated ones. Think of this new field as an additional dataset column that supplies the missing information. As with other data fields, the new calculated field [identified by an equal sign (=) preceding its icon] will reside in the Dimensions or Measures sections of the Data pane, and can be placed on any shelf to build the visualization.

Be certain to consider dashboard and report performance when creating Calculated Fields in Tableau. If the calculations will be used in numerous views, or by a large number of report-builders, it may be prudent to create a new field in the source data. Doing so could also ease maintenance woes; adjusting a calculation once in a database is far easier than doing so in every workbook.

The following section details how to create Calculated Fields of the String, Number, Date, Type Conversion, Logical, User, and Aggregate types.

How To: Create a Calculated Field.

» Right-click any Dimension or Measure to be used in a calculation or in the blank space in the Data pane.

- If a Dimension or Measure is right-clicked, select "Create," then "Calculated Field…" from the sub-menus.
- If a blank space is right-clicked, select "Create Calculated Field" from the sub-menu.

Calculated Field dialog box overview:

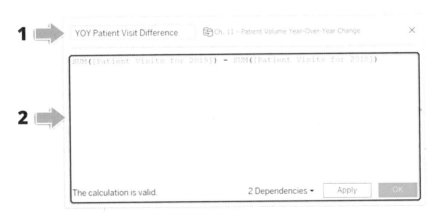

1) **Name:** Replace the default name "Calculation 1" with a descriptive one. Since the newly created Calculated Field will be listed among all the other fields in the Data pane, a descriptive name will make it easier to find.

2) **Formula:** The Formula Editor box includes validation to help avoid syntax errors and a color-coding system to help users recognize specific parts of the formula. The Formula parts consist of:

   a. **Fields:** Display in orange. All data source fields and calculated fields are available for calculations. To add a field to the Formula Editor, either:

      » Begin typing the field name in the Formula Editor box and select the name from the menu that appears. Note: the menu will list field names as well as function names corresponding to the entered letter(s).

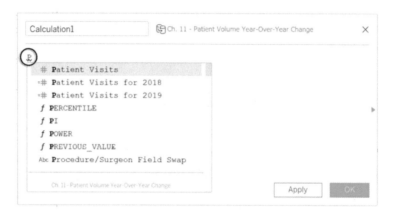

      » Drag and drop the field from the Data pane into the Formula Editor box.

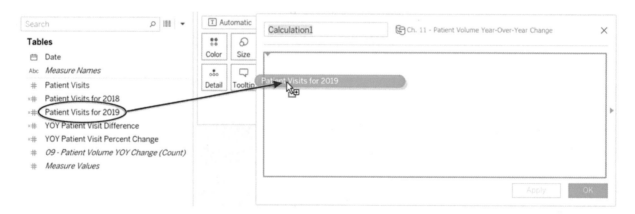

   b. **Operators:** Display in **black**. Operators are entered into the Formula Editor when the calculation calls for addition (+), subtraction (-), multiplication (*), and division (/). Operators used in logical calculations also include IF, THEN, CASE, WHEN, AND, OR, >, >=, =, <=, <, and <>. Operators are not case-sensitive.

   c. **Functions:** Display in blue. To view the list of available functions, click the caret on the right border of the Formula Editor box. If "All" is selected, an alphabetical list displays every Function available for creating a formula. Click the caret to the right of "All" and select a Function category to narrow the list of corresponding Functions. Click a Function to view its definition and formatting requirements. Double-click a Function name to add it to the Formula Editor box, or type the Function name directly.

d. **Parameters:** Display in **purple**. Parameters are placeholders for variables that can be inserted into the Formula Editor to replace constant values. Parameters are discussed in chapter 25.

e. **Comments:** Display in gray. Comments are optional. To annotate the formula with comments, start the Comment text in the Formula Editor with two forward-slash characters. As an example: "//Use this calculation for surgeon over/under scheduled time."

Help and Validation

Directly beneath the Formula, the Formula Editor displays a message confirming that the calculation syntax has been entered correctly and is valid, or that it contains errors. In the latter case, click the red caret for hints on solving the problem. As a further help, some syntax errors are underscored with a red wavy line.

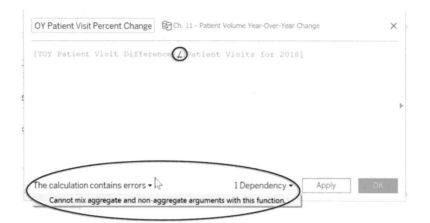

Calculation Categories

This section introduces the broad categories of calculations that Tableau offers, with specific healthcare-related examples.

» Click the caret beneath and to the right of the Functions section of the Calculated Field dialog box to see the Functions list:

- Number

- String

- Date

- Type Conversion

- Logical

- Aggregate

- User

- Table Calculation

- Spatial

A brief review of functions and examples corresponding to each category follows. Table Calculation is discussed in Chapter 17. Level of Detail Expressions under the Aggregate category are discussed in Chapter 23.

NUMBER

Mathematical calculations performed on a number field.

ABS: Returns the absolute value of the given number. Use this function to find the difference between values, whether positive or negative.

Example: A field called [ALOS Variance] represents the difference between the average lengths of stay for each month. If the calculation is **ABS([ALOS Variance])**, then on a row where ALOS Variance is –4, the calculation will return 4.

Starting Field	Calculation	Result
ALOS Variance		
-4	ABS([ALOS Variance])	4

ZN: Returns the value of a numeric field if it is not NULL; if the value is NULL, it returns 0 instead.

Example: If the calculation is **ZN([Surgery Cost])**, then on a row where Surgery Cost is NULL, the calculation will return 0.

Starting Field	Calculation	Result
Surgery Cost		
NULL	ZN([Surgery Cost])	0

STRING

Calculations performed on one or more string (text) fields.

STARTSWITH: Returns true if the string starts with the substring.

Example: If the calculation is **STARTSWITH([Staff Name],"Dr.")**, then on a row where Staff Name is "Dr. Williams," the calculation will return TRUE.

Starting Field	Calculation	Result
Staff Name		
Dr. Williams	STARTSWITH([Staff Name],"Dr.")	TRUE

REPLACE: Returns a string in which every occurrence of the substring is replaced with the replacement string. If the substring is not found, the string is unchanged.

Example: If the calculation is **REPLACE([Staff Name],"Dr.","Doctor")**, then on a row where Staff Name is "Dr. Williams," the calculation will return "Doctor Williams."

Starting Field	Calculation	Result
Staff Name		
Dr. Williams	REPLACE([Staff Name],"Dr.","Doctor")	Doctor Williams

Additional String Manipulation: Strings can also be connected using the "+" operator.

Example: If there is a field called [First Name] with a record of "James" and a field called [Last Name] with a record of "Williams" on the same row, then the calculation **[Last Name]+", "+[First Name]** will return "Williams, James."

Starting Field		Calculation	Result
First Name	Last Name		
James	Williams	[Last Name]+", "+[First Name]	Williams, James

DATE

Calculations that manipulate dates or transform dates into integers.

DATEADD: Adds an increment to the specified date and returns the new date. The increment is defined by the interval and the date_part.

Example: If the calculation is **DATEADD("month",1,[Surgery Date])**, then on a row where Surgery Date is 04-15-2020, the calculation will return 05-15-2020.

Starting Field	Calculation	Result
Surgery Date		
04-15-2020	DATEADD("month",1,[Surgery Date])	05-15-2020

DATETRUNC: Truncates the specified date to the accuracy specified by the date_part and returns the new date.

Example: If the calculation is **DATETRUNC("year",[Surgery Date])**, then on a row where Surgery Date is 04-15-2020, the calculation will return 01-01-2020.

Starting Field	Calculation	Result
Surgery Date		
04-15-2020	DATETRUNC("year",[Surgery Date])	01-01-2020

TODAY: Returns the current date. Useful for computing rolling dates and other time-related calculations relative to the current view date.

Starting Field	Calculation	Result
N/A	TODAY()	<Current Date>

TYPE CONVERSION

Calculations that change the data type of a field.

STR: Returns a String given an expression. (That is, converts an expression to a string.)

Example: **STR(60)** would convert the integer 60 to a string value of 60 that can then be linked with other strings.

Starting Field	Calculation	Result
Integer		String
60	STR(60) + " beats per minute (bpm)"	60 beats per minute (bpm)

INT: Returns an Integer given an expression. This function truncates results to the closest integer toward zero.

Example: **INT (4.7)** would convert the value 4.7 to the integer 4.

Starting Field	Calculation	Result
Value		Integer
4.7	INT(4.7)	4

LOGICAL

These calculations test for specific scenarios in order to organize data in a manner other than the way it is already displayed in the database. Common uses for logical expressions include grouping dimensions, excluding values, creating custom bins, and comparing values.

IF/THEN: Tests a series of expressions returning the <then> value for the first true <expr>.

Example: The calculation **IF [Surgery Start] > [Scheduled Surgery Start] THEN "Late Case" ELSE "On Time Case" END** will return a value of "Late Case" if the Surgery Start date/time field occurred after the Scheduled Surgery Start date/time field.

	Starting Field	Calculation	Result
Surgery Start	Scheduled Surgery Start		
4-14-2019 8:15 AM	4-14-2019 8:00 AM	`IF[Surgery Start] > [Scheduled Surgery Start] THEN "Late Case" ELSE "On Time Case" END`	Late Case
4-14-2019 10:00 AM	4-14-2019 10:05 AM		On Time Case

CASE / WHEN: Finds the first <value> that matches <expr> and returns the corresponding <return>.

Example: The calculation **CASE [Continent] WHEN "North America" THEN "Americas" WHEN "South America" THEN "Americas" WHEN "Africa" THEN "Africa" END** will return a value of "Americas" for a continent of either "North America" or "South America."

Starting Field	Calculation	Result
Continent		
North America	`CASE [Continent]`	Americas
South America	`WHEN "North America" THEN "Americas"` `WHEN "South America" THEN "Americas"`	Americas
Africa	`WHEN "Africa" THEN "Africa" END`	Africa

USER

These calculations are performed when a user is logged in to Tableau Server and viewing a report. User functions most often manage row-level security.

USERNAME: Returns the username for the current user. This is the Tableau Server or Tableau Online username when the user is signed in; otherwise, it is the local or network username for the Tableau Desktop user.

This calculation is used in conjunction with a field in the dataset that associates user names with specific rows of data. It requires that the username of the person logged on precisely matches a [Tableau Username] field contained in the data source to return TRUE. If this is the case, the user will be able to see all data associated with the "TRUE" user name. Row-level security built in to the calculation prevents this user from seeing any other [Tableau Username] data.

Example: When Doctor A is logged into the Tableau Server, if **USERNAME()=[Tableau Username]** is filtered for TRUE, then s/he will see only the "ADoctor" row of data, and not the "BDoctor" row.

Starting Field		Calculation	Result
Tableau Username	Doctor Name	When ADoctor is logged in to Tableau Server	
ADoctor	Doctor A		TRUE
ADoctor	Doctor A	USERNAME()=[Tableau Username]	TRUE
BDoctor	Doctor B		FALSE

CHAPTER 23

Aggregation and Level of Detail Expressions

omprehensive coverage of advanced aggregations in Tableau could fill an entire book. This chapter is a concise and manageable introduction to some core concepts and mechanics to perform various aggregations and Level of Detail Expressions.

Basic Calculations and Aggregation

Basics of Granularity | Level of Detail | Aggregation

Instead of building calculations into a data source, Tableau returns results by aggregating data in real time based on the Dimensions present in a worksheet. Every time a new Dimension is incorporated into a visualization, Tableau recalculates this aggregation. The most common aggregations are Sum, Average, Minimum, Maximum, Count, and Count Distinct.

The aggregation results change based on the specific combination of dimensions present on a worksheet, and this is referred to as the level of detail (LOD) of the visualization. The first image below shows a count of Patient IDs by Gender from a sample patient data source with 167 records. The second image adds another Dimension, Race/Ethnicity, increasing the granularity of the visualization.

Fewer Dimensions: more aggregated/ less granular.

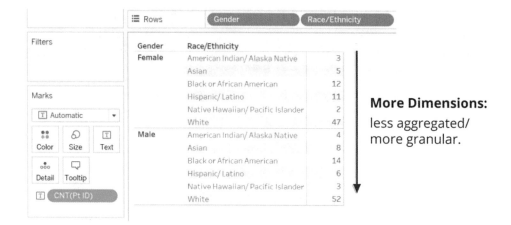

Level of Detail (LOD) Expressions

It is often necessary to calculate data at a granularity different from the level of detail resulting from the Dimensions present in the worksheet. Level of Detail Expressions can be performed at a more granular level (via INCLUDE), a less granular level (via EXCLUDE), or an entirely independent level (via FIXED) by "scoping" Dimensions directly into a calculated field. Here is the syntax for constructing an LOD expression:

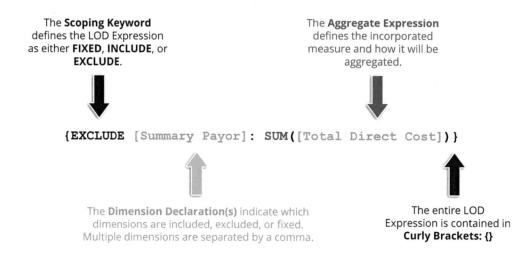

Scoping Keywords

- **FIXED** defines exactly the Dimension(s) to be incorporated in the LOD Expression. The Dimensions in the View do not affect the aggregation. FIXED LOD Expressions are calculated before Dimension filters, but after Context filters.

- **INCLUDE** defines any Dimension(s) included in the LOD Expression in addition to the Dimensions present in the View. INCLUDE LOD Expressions are calculated after Dimension filters.

- **EXCLUDE** defines any Dimension(s) excluded from the LOD Expression, regardless of whether those Dimensions are present in the View. EXCLUDE LOD Expressions are calculated after Dimension filters.

- **Table-Scoped Level of Detail** performs the expressed aggregation on the entire data source, independent of all Dimensions. This is the equivalent of performing a FIXED LOD Expression without specifying any Dimensions. A Table-Scoping LOD Expression is accomplished by framing an aggregation in curly brackets without including a scoping keyword.

Example - Manipulating Level of Detail

The table below shows Expenditures ($) created using a sample subset of the US Healthcare Expenditures data with several LOD Expressions showing the result of each calculation.

Year of Date	Type of Service/Source of Funds	Category	Expenditures	Exclude LOD: Categories	Exclude LOD: Service + Category	Fixed LOD: on Service	Fixed LOD: Table-Scoped
2016	Medicaid	Total Hospital Expenditures	$189B	$293B	$812B	$13,921B	$227,412B
		Total Physician and Clinical Expenditures	$72B	$293B	$812B	$13,921B	$227,412B
		Total Prescription Drug Expenditures	$32B	$293B	$812B	$13,921B	$227,412B
	Medicare	Total Hospital Expenditures	$272B	$518B	$812B	$20,545B	$227,412B
		Total Physician and Clinical Expenditures	$149B	$518B	$812B	$20,545B	$227,412B
		Total Prescription Drug Expenditures	$97B	$518B	$812B	$20,545B	$227,412B
2017	Medicaid	Total Hospital Expenditures	$193B	$301B	$844B	$13,921B	$227,412B
		Total Physician and Clinical Expenditures	$75B	$301B	$844B	$13,921B	$227,412B
		Total Prescription Drug Expenditures	$33B	$301B	$844B	$13,921B	$227,412B
	Medicare	Total Hospital Expenditures	$284B	$543B	$844B	$20,545B	$227,412B
		Total Physician and Clinical Expenditures	$158B	$543B	$844B	$20,545B	$227,412B
		Total Prescription Drug Expenditures	$101B	$543B	$844B	$20,545B	$227,412B
2018	Medicaid	Total Hospital Expenditures	$197B	$307B	$882B	$13,921B	$227,412B
		Total Physician and Clinical Expenditures	$77B	$307B	$882B	$13,921B	$227,412B
		Total Prescription Drug Expenditures	$33B	$307B	$882B	$13,921B	$227,412B
	Medicare	Total Hospital Expenditures	$297B	$574B	$882B	$20,545B	$227,412B
		Total Physician and Clinical Expenditures	$170B	$574B	$882B	$20,545B	$227,412B
		Total Prescription Drug Expenditures	$107B	$574B	$882B	$20,545B	$227,412B

The first column is a basic SUM aggregation of Expenditures ($) broken out by Year, Type of Service, and Categories. These three Dimensions define the default level of detail for the worksheet. Compare each calculation to the results in the table to see how the various LOD Expressions work.

The second column;

This LOD calculates the sum of Expenditures for each year and each Type of Service. Note that the same value displays for all categories within each Type of Service and Year.

The third column;

This LOD calculates the sum of Expenditures for each Year. The same value displays for Type of Service and Categories, changing only for each Year.

The fourth column;

This LOD calculates the sum of Expenditures only for Type of Service. The values change for Type of Service but remain the same for Categories and Year.

The fifth column;

This LOD calculates the total sum of Expenditures for the entire table, ignoring Year, Type of Service, and Categories.

Level-of-Detail Expression Activity

How To: Display the Number of Emergency Department Super-Utilizers (6+ visits per year), within a Health System, by Hospital, for a selected year.

Example Health System's Emergency Department (ED) Super-Utilizers for 2019
Medicaid Patients, Ages 1-64, with 6+ ED Visits per Year

Data Source: *Mock data of emergency department use for seven hospitals in a health system.*

About the Data: *Research has shown that 50% of healthcare expenditures can be attributed to 5% of the population. These "Super-Utilizers" have 3+ chronic conditions and visit the emergency department multiple times a year. These visits are frequently not for medical emergencies and are often the result of patient's lacking health insurance and access to primary care.*

1 Create a new worksheet and connect to the data

» At the bottom of the Tableau workspace, click the icon for a New Worksheet.

» In the Data pane, select the "Ch. 23 – Emergency Department Visits."

2 Create the chart

» Drag and drop "Hospital" on to the Rows shelf.

» Right-click and drag "Patient ID (Medical Record Number)" to the Columns shelf.

» In the appearing Drop Field box, select "CNTD (Patient ID (Medical Record Number))."

» Click the "[T]" on the Toolbar to add labels to the bars.

» Click the Descending Sort icon on the Toolbar to sort the bars in descending order.

Add a Grand Total row to the chart to view the total number of patients seen in the ED for all hospitals.

» Click the "Analytics" tab to the right of the Data pane tab.

» Click and drag "Totals" over the canvas and drop onto "Column Grand Totals."

The chart looks like this:

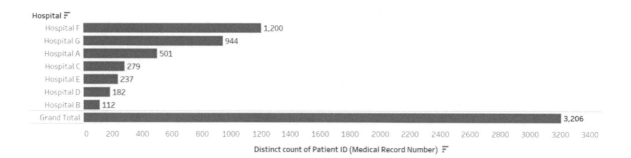

The Level-of-Detail Expression

The chart currently displays the count of all patients who have visited any of Hospitals A through G's Emergency Departments, regardless of the number of visits.

The goal is to view only those patients who have visited an emergency department six (6) or more times—the ED Super-Utilizers—across any of the seven hospitals in the health system for a selected year and to display the number of ED Super-Utilizers that visited each hospital. To do this, a calculation is required to identify those Patient ID (Medical Record Number)'s with six or more Visit IDs, independent of the Hospital dimension. A Level-of-Detail Expression calculation is needed to aggregate the count of visits by Patient ID (Medical Record Number) regardless of what other dimensions are present in the worksheet. The scoping key word that will perform this is FIXED.

The calculation is as follows:

```
{FIXED[Patient ID (Medical Record Number)]: COUNT([Visit ID])}>=6
```

The FIXED scoping key word aggregates the calculation at the level of the declared dimension "Patient ID (Medical Record Number)"—no other dimension used in the visualization will disaggregate this calculation's result. The chart utilizes the dimension "Hospital" to display the number of patients who visited each hospital's emergency department. By fixing the calculation on "Patient ID (Medical Record Number)" the formula will count the total number of visits a patient had to any of the hospitals. The aggregate expression is the count of the visit ID (each visit ID represents a unique ED visit). Once the LOD calculation has set the count of visits to the Patient ID (wrapped in curly brackets), then a simple logical statement can be added to the end of the calculation: >=6.

>> Right-click in the white space of the Data pane.

>> From the menu, select "Create Calculated Field..."

>> Edit the field name to 'ED Super-Utilizers."

>> Enter the calculation:

```
{FIXED[Patient ID (Medical Record Number)]:COUNT([Visit ID])}>=6
```

The Level-of-Detail Expression is now a Boolean data type, meaning it has two values: "T/F."

» Drag and drop the new calculated field "ED Super-Utilizers" to the Filters shelf.

» Select "True." in the Filter dialog box.

The chart is now filtered to display only those patients with six or more visits in the dataset.

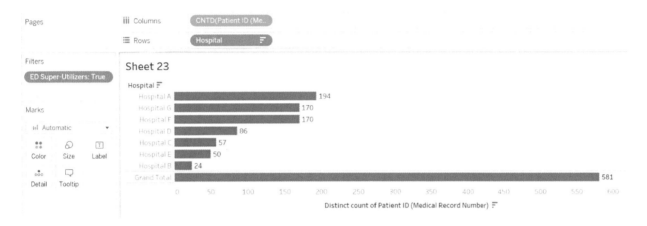

The dataset, however, contains two years of data. To see the most recent year's data,

» Drag and drop "Visit Date" to the Filters shelf.

» From the Filter Field dialog box, select "Years" then click "Next."

» Select "2019" then click "OK."

The chart looks like this:

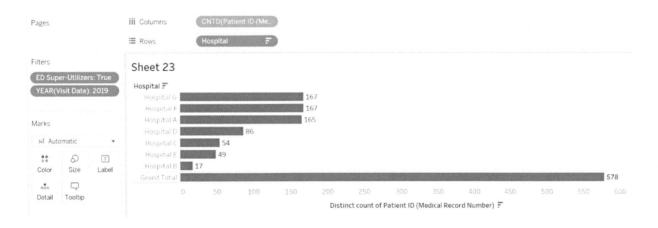

Despite the addition of the YEAR(Visit Date) Filter, the total only decreased by three patients. Is the data being displayed accurately?

Order of Operations

Tableau performs operations in a specific order—an understanding of this ensures the analytics perform as intended.

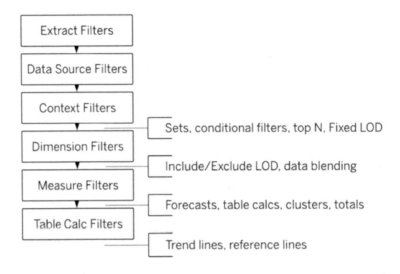

A dimension filter "Visit Date" has been added to the visualization. Based on the Order of Operations, this dimension filter applies after the Fixed LOD is performed. The result is that the ED Super-Utilizers calculation is still returning true for all patients with 6+ visits across the entire dataset. After this filter has been applied, then the "Visit Date" filter removes the three patients who only had visits in 2018. This is not the intended result.

To ensure the Visit Date filter works correctly, it needs to be changed to a Context Filter in order to perform prior to the Fixed LOD. The Fixed LOD calculation will then be performed on the results of this Context Filter—performed on "2019."

To change "Visit Date" to a Context Filter:

》 Right-click "YEAR (Visit Date): 2019" on the Filters shelf.

》 Select "Add to Context."

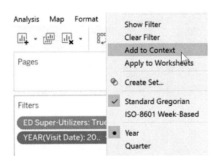

The "YEAR(Visit Date): 2019" field changes to a light-gray fill (indicating it is a Context Filter) and is placed above the "ED Super-Utilizers: True" field.

◄ Context Filter

A context filter is applied to a worksheet before dimension filters, measure filters, table calculation filters, and level of detail expressions. This can improve performance by limiting the amount of data queried for large datasets and can allow for dependent calculations as seen in this exercise. It is possible to set any dimension filter as a context filter. If using context filters for performance improvements, it is recommended to use a single context filter to significantly reduce the size of the data instead of applying many context filters.

The chart now looks like this:

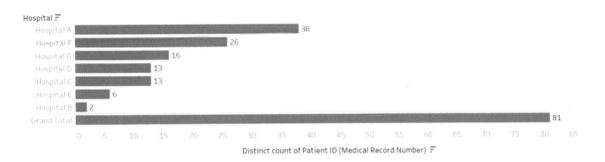

3 Format the chart

The Hospital field label is unnecessary. To hide it:

>> Right-click the "Hospital" field label.

>> Select "Hide Field Labels for Rows."

The bars are labeled, therefore the X-axis is unneeded. To hide it:

>> Right-click the X-axis.

>> Click "Show Header" to remove its check mark.

Edit the "Grand Total" header:

>> Right-click the "Grand Total" header and select "Format."

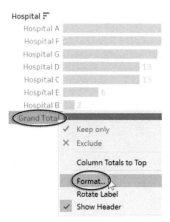

» In the "Grand Totals" section of the Format pane, change the Label to "Total Number of Super-Utilizers."

To adjust the row height,

» Hover the cursor over the row border above "Total Number of Super-Utilizers."

» When the cursor changes to a bi-directional arrow, click and drag to the desired height.

4 Add a Title

» Double-click the Title Row to open the Edit Title dialog box.

» Enter the title, "Example Health System's Emergency Department (ED) Super-Utilizers for 2019

Medicaid Patients, Ages 1-64, with 6+ ED Visits per Year"

» Change the font to Tableau Medium, size 14 for the first row of the title; size 12 for the second row.

5 Rename the worksheet tab and save the worksheet

» Double-click the worksheet tab at the bottom of the screen.

» In the highlighted text, enter the new title, "LOD Expression: ED Super-Utilizers"

》 Select "Save" to save the file.

The final chart looks like this:

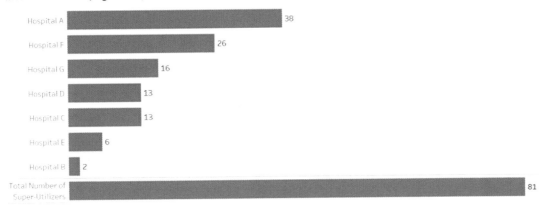

Example Health System's Emergency Department (ED) Super-Utilizers for 2019
Medicaid Patients, Ages 1-64, with 6+ ED Visits per Year

Hospital A	38
Hospital F	26
Hospital G	16
Hospital D	13
Hospital C	13
Hospital E	6
Hospital B	2
Total Number of Super-Utilizers	81

Insight: For this example Health System, there are 81 ED Super-Utilizer Medicaid Patients between ages 1-64. Almost half (38) of those ED Super-Utilizers have visited Hospital A's emergency department this year.

Set Actions

Sets are custom fields, created on dimensions, used to capture and analyze a subset of data. Deployed in a visualization, they can be used to compare members, highlight data points of interest, or define criteria to focus the user's attention. Sets are unique in that they display dimensions in two categories: IN the set and OUT of the set. Creating actions for sets allows the end-user to interact with the visualization, selecting dimension members into the IN category, while simultaneously moving the other members OUT, with results immediately reflected in the view.

How To: How to: Build a Set Action, creating a hierarchical drill path to view completed research studies' disease condition lists and patient enrollment counts for selected pharmaceutical companies.

Set actions will be used to expand only the selected sponsor value to reveal the related conditions.

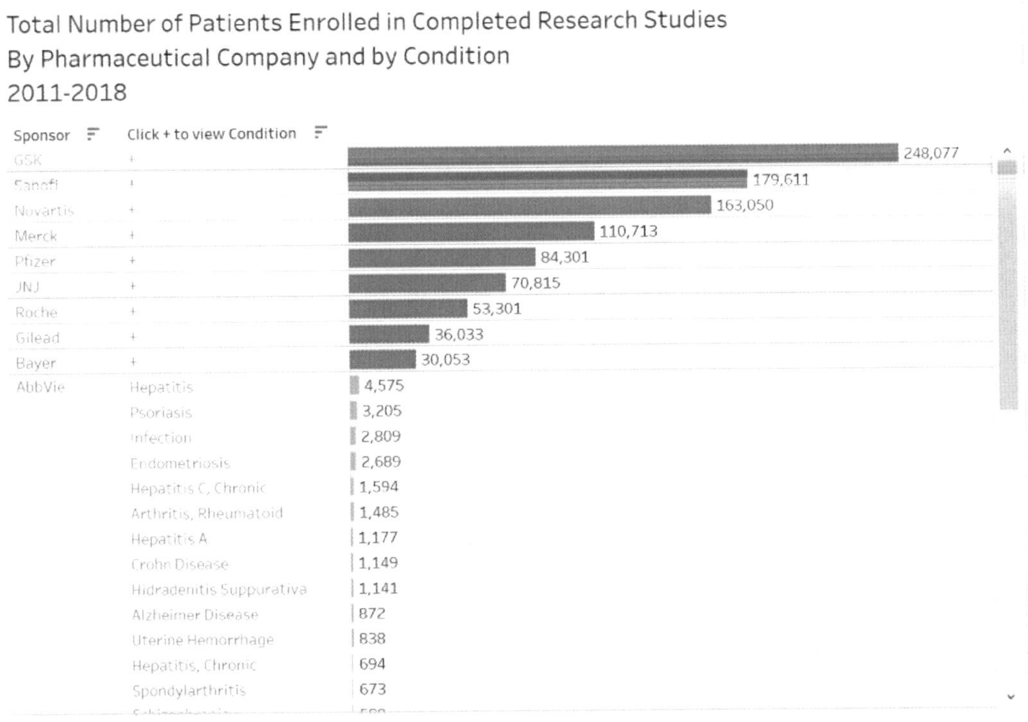
Total Number of Patients Enrolled in Completed Research Studies
By Pharmaceutical Company and by Condition
2011-2018
Sponsor
Click + to view Condition
GSK
Sanofi
Novartis
Merck
Pfizer
JNJ
Roche
Gilead
Bayer
AbbVie
Hepatitis
Psoriasis
Infection
Endometriosis
Hepatitis C, Chronic
Arthritis, Rheumatoid
Hepatitis A
Crohn Disease
Hidradenitis Suppurativa
Alzheimer Disease
Uterine Hemorrhage
Hepatitis, Chronic
Spondylarthritis
248,077
179,611
163,050
110,713
84,301
70,815
53,301
36,033
30,053
4,575
3,205
2,809
2,689
1,594
1,485
1,177
1,149
1,141
872
838
694
673

Data Source: *Harvard Dataverse. Hey, Spencer, 2019, Data for "A Bird's Eye View of Pharmaceutical Research and Development." https://dataverse.harvard.edu/dataset.xhtml?persistentId=doi:10.7910/DVN/S8C77Q*

About the Data: *Registered clinical trials for 10 large pharmaceutical companies. The data has been filtered to years 2011-2018 for Completed clinical trials only.*

1 Create a new worksheet and connect to the data

» At the bottom of the Tableau workspace, click the icon for a new worksheet.

» In the Data pane, select the dataset "Ch. 24 – Completed Pharmaceutical Studies' Enrollment by Condition."

2 Create the chart

» Drag and drop "Sponsor" onto the Rows shelf.

» Drag and drop "Enrollment" onto the Columns shelf.

» Click the Sort Descending icon on the Toolbar to sort the bars from highest to lowest.

» Double-click the worksheet tab and rename it "Pharm Enrollment by Condition."

The chart looks like this:

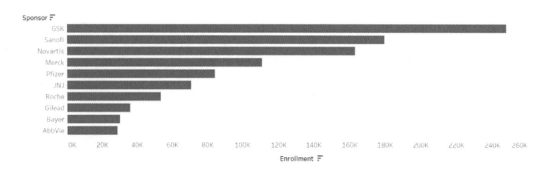

3 Create the Set

The first step is to create the Set. Sets are created on the desired Dimension to indicate which Dimension members will be in or out of the set. Here, Sponsor will be used.

» Right-click "Sponsor" in the Data pane.

» Choose "Create" then "Set..."

Creating Set Actions ▶

Create Set Actions by following the four steps below:

1) Create the Set

2) Use the Set in a calculation

3) Use the calculated field in the visualization

4) Add the Set Action to the worksheet

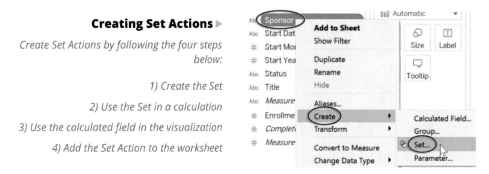

In the Create Set dialog box,

» Name the set "Sponsor Set."

» Click the checkbox next to "AbbVie" (here, the sponsor with the smallest enroll-ment volume is selected to view how the calculation in the next step performs when added to the view)

» Click "OK."

4 Use the Set in a calculation

» Right-click in the white space of the Data pane and select "Create Calculated Field..."

» Name the calculated field "Click + to view Condition."

» Enter the calculation:

```
IF [Sponsor Set] THEN [Condition] ELSE "+" END
```

» Drag and drop "Click + to view Condition" to the right of Sponsor on the Rows shelf.

The calculation with the set is performing as expected. AbbVie is the only value currently IN the set. Therefore, AbbVie is the only Sponsor displaying Conditions; the other Sponsors display the "+" symbol.

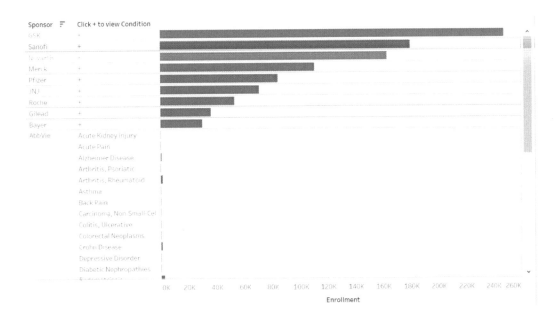

5 Add the Set Action to the worksheet

Currently the Sponsor Set is static—fixed on AbbVie. Adding a Set Action will enable the end-user to select the desired Sponsor and view the corresponding conditions.

》 Click "Worksheet" on the Menu Bar then "Actions..."

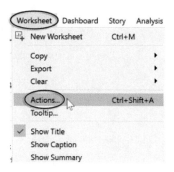

》 Click the "Add Action" near the bottom left of the Actions dialog box.

》 Select "Change Set Values..."

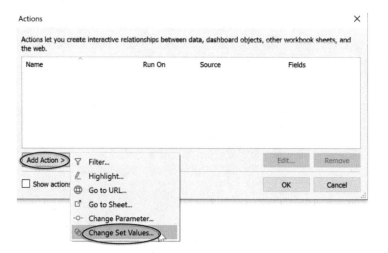

》 Name Action "Sponsor Set Action."

- **Source Sheets:** Pharm Enrollment by Condition
- **Run action on:** Select
- **Target Set:**
  - *Data Source:* Ch. 24 – Pharmaceutical Studies by Condition
  - *Set:* Sponsor Set
- **Running action will:** Assign values to set
- **Clearing selection will:** Remove all values from set

》 Click "OK."

◄ Clearing the Set Action

The bottom right section of the Add Set Action menu is not only important for defining what happens when the set is cleared; it also determines what is in the set by default when the chart is first viewed.

*- **Keep set values**: allows for existing set values to remain in the set. In this case, the set action will only add additional values to the set. Use this setting to add multiple (but not all) values to a set instead of replacing a single set value when the set action is triggered.*

*- **Add all values to the set**: allows for every value in a dimension to be included in the set by default and when the set action is not engaged.*

*- **Remove all values from the set**: allows for the set selection to be empty by default and clears the values when the set action is not engaged.*

»   Click "OK" again to close the Actions dialog box.

Test the Set Action by clicking one of the "+" next to another Sponsor.

To turn off the Set Action, click in the active Condition column to close it.

Important Note: When closing the set selection, the first click highlights the Condition name. Click again to toggle off the highlight, which in turn, deactivates the Set Action. Do not double-click as this will initiate a filter on the field.

6 Format the chart

Color-encode the bars for selected Sponsor.

» Drag and drop "Sponsor Set" onto Color on the Marks card.

To edit the bar colors:

» Double-click in the white space of the IN/OUT (Sponsor Set) color legend.

» Click the "In" data item to highlight it and change it to a teal color.

» Click the "Out" data item to highlight it and change it to a blue color.

To sort the bars for the selected Conditions:

» Right-click the "Click + to view Condition" field on the Rows shelf and select "Sort..."

» In the Sort dialog box:
  • Sort by: Field
  • Sort Order: Descending
  • Field Name: Enrollment

» Click the "X" in the top right corner to close the dialog box.

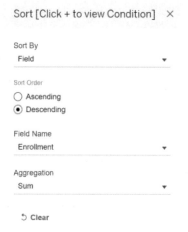

Add Labels to the bars.

» Click "Label" on the Marks Card, then click the checkbox for "Show mark labels."

The bars are labeled, therefore, hide the X axis.

» Right-click the X axis.

» Click "Show Header" to remove the checkmark.

7 Add a title

» Double-click the Title Row to open the Edit Title dialog box.

» Enter the title,

"Total Number of Patients Enrolled in Completed Research Studies
By Pharmaceutical Company and by Condition
2011-2018"

» Click the "Save" icon on the Toolbar.

The final chart looks like this:

Total Number of Patients Enrolled in Completed Research Studies
By Pharmaceutical Company and by Condition
2011-2018

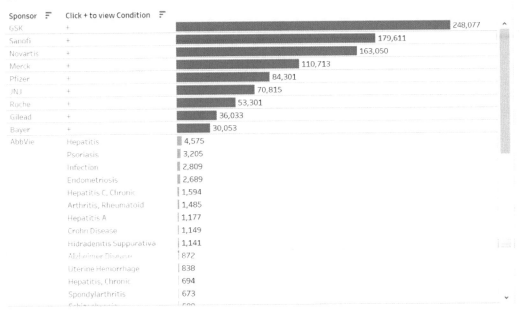

Insight: The Set Action allows the report user to compare the pharmaceutical companies by their total enrollment in completed research studies and to select a desired company and analyze their research studies by the condition categories.

CHAPTER 25

Parameters

Parameters are dynamic inputs that can replace constant values with multiple applications (filters, calculations) and display elements (reference lines, titles) within a workbook. A Parameter Control placed on a dashboard or worksheet allows the report viewer to manage the display for ad-hoc exploration. Parameters enable the addition of flexible interactivity to a report, or experimentation with what-if scenarios by creating values or options not available in the dataset—without making it necessary to alter the design of the view.

This section covers two common Parameter types: Field Swap and Top N. A Field Swap Parameter allows the user to switch between two dimensions or two measures without having to re-create the chart. The Field Swap Parameter illustrated below, for example, permits toggling between Primary Surgeon and Procedure for exploring differing rates of surgical site infections. The second type is a Top N (Number) Parameter, which affords control of the number of top items displayed in the view. The example report (in section 25.2, below) displays the Top N states for cancer death rates.

25.1 Field Swap Parameters

How To: Build a Field Swap Parameter control on primary surgeon and procedure for use in comparing surgical site infection rates and case counts.

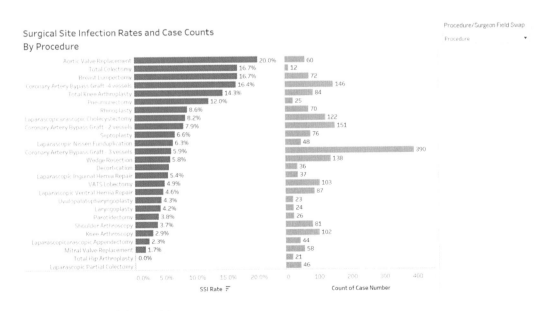

Data Source: De-identified surgical data

About the Data: Surgical data including case counts, surgical site infection counts and rates by operating room, surgeon, procedures, and services.

1 **Create a new worksheet and connect to the data**

» At the bottom of the Tableau workspace, click the icon for a new worksheet.

» In the Data pane, select the "Ch. 25 - Surgical Data" dataset.

2 **Create the chart**

From the Data pane:

» Drag and drop "Procedure" onto the Rows shelf.

» Drag and drop "SSI Rate" onto the Columns shelf.

» Drag and drop "Case Number" from the top section in the Data pane to below the appearing Dimensions/Measures orange divider to change it to a Measure.

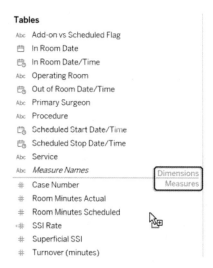

» Drag and drop "Case Number" onto the Columns shelf to the right of the SSI Rate field.

Case Number has the data type "Number (whole)"; as a result, the default aggregation (when Case Number is placed on the Columns shelf) is SUM. This aggregation needs to be changed to COUNT.

» Right-click the "SUM(Case Number)" field.

» From the menu that appears, select "Measures (Sum)"; then from the submenu, "Count."

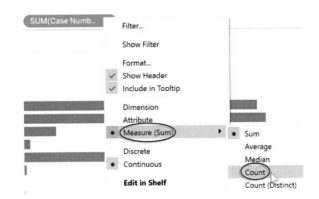

The chart looks like this:

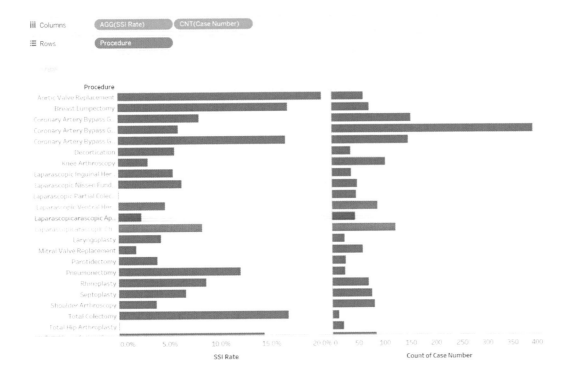

3 Create a Parameter

» Click the caret to the right of the Search window in the Data pane.

» Select "Create Parameter."

◀ Creating and Using Parameters

Create Parameters by following the four steps below:

1. Create the Parameter
2. Show the Parameter Control
3. Use the Parameter in a Calculation
4. Use the Calculated Field in the visualization

In the Create Parameter dialog box:

» To the right of Name, enter "Procedure/Surgeon Field Swap."

» To the right of Data Type, select "String."

» To the right of Allowable values, click "List."

» In the List of values section, select "Click to add new value."

» Enter the following values:

  • "Primary Surgeon" [Press the "Tab" key to move to the next cell; click "Add" to add the next value.]

  • "Procedure"

» Click "OK."

Parameters ▶

Each newly created Parameter appears on a list in the Parameters window, at the bottom of the Data pane. This window is generated by the creation of the first Parameter; if none has been created, no window will be displayed. Parameters can be found on the Top tab of the Filter dialog box, and in the Reference Line dialog box, as well as in the Data pane.

Parameters are global across the workbook and can be used in any worksheet.

》 Right-click the new "Procedure/Surgeon Field Swap" field in the Parameters window.

》 From the appearing menu, select "Show Parameter."

The Parameter is now displayed to the right of the chart.

Parameter Menu Options ▲

The menu for the Parameter opens by way of a caret in the upper right corner of the parameter display and allows the user to customize its appearance. The list of values on the menu can be displayed as a series of radio buttons, a compact list, a slider, or a type-in field. The options shown on the menu depend on the data type of the parameter.

Show Parameter

Parameters appear similar to quick filters in that they contain selections that modify the view; however, each performs different functions. Quick filters enable the user to filter the report data; Parameters permit replacing a static value with a dynamic one for calculated fields, reference lines, bins, and filters. Before it can do the latter task, however, the Parameter must be visible in the workspace. To display it, right-click the parameter field, then select Show Parameter from the menu that appears.

Currently this Parameter displays the drop-down selection, but it is not linked to the target data. The next step is to link it using a new calculated field.

》 Click the caret to the right of the Search window in the Data pane.

》 Select "Create Calculated Field."

》 Change the field name to "Procedure/Surgeon."

》 Enter the following formula:

```
CASE [Procedure/Surgeon Field Swap]
WHEN "Primary Surgeon" THEN [Primary Surgeon]
WHEN "Procedure" THEN [Procedure]
ELSE NULL END
```

Linking the Parameter to the Target Data ▶

A formula must be created to link the string values defined in the Parameter to the field names in the Data source. The formula to the left associates the selected parameter with the related fields. In the Formula Editor, the color purple designates parameters; orange designates field names.

In the Calculated Field shown, the quoted text after the WHEN statements is case-sensitive and **must be identical** *to the text previously defined in creating the Field Swap Parameter.*

```
Procedure/Surgeon                          🗄 16 - Surgical Data (Tablea

CASE [Procedure/Surgeon Field Swap]
WHEN "Primary Surgeon" THEN [Primary Surgeon]
WHEN "Procedure" THEN [Procedure]
ELSE NULL
END
```

» Review the calculation message below the Formula area to verify that the calculation is valid.

» Click "OK."

This new "Procedure/Surgeon" field is now displayed in the Dimensions section of the Data pane.

» Drag the "Procedure/Surgeon" field to the Rows shelf and drop it on top of the "Procedure" field to replace that field.

Test that the Procedure/Surgeon Field Swap Parameter is working correctly:

» Click the caret on the "Procedure/Surgeon Field Swap" Parameter.

» Select "Primary Surgeon."

The chart should adjust to display the data by Primary Surgeon.

» Change parameter control to "Procedure."

4 Format the chart

Adjust the width of the Procedure labels to ensure full display:

» Hover the cursor over the right border of the Procedure/Surgeon headers until it changes to a bi-directional arrow, then drag the border to the appropriate width.

Add labels to the bars:

» Click the framed "[T]" icon on the Toolbar.

Sort on SSI Rate:

» Click the SSI Rate field on the Columns shelf to highlight it.

» Click the Sort Descending icon on the Toolbar.

» Change the Parameter setting to the other Dimension and set the sort for SSI Rate to descending also.

Change the bar color of Count of Case Number to distinguish it from SSI Rate:

» In the Marks card section, click the "CNT(Case Number)" header to select its Marks card.

» Click the Color selector and change to a light gray.

Hide the Procedure/Surgeon field label as it will be included in the title:

» Right-click the "Procedure/Surgeon" field label and select "Hide Field Labels for Rows."

To remove the scroll bar:

» Click the Fit option drop-down on the Toolbar and change to "Entire View."

5 Add a title

» Double-click the Title Row to open the Edit Title dialog box.

» Enter the title, "Surgical Site Infection Rates and Case Counts, By "

» With the cursor in the second space after "By", click the Insert button and select "Parameters.Procedure/Surgeon Field Swap" to reflect the Parameter Control selection.

» Click "OK."

The Parameter selection is now reflected in the title.

6 Rename the worksheet tab and save the worksheet

» Right-click the worksheet tab at the bottom of the workspace, then select "Rename."

» In the highlighted text, enter the new title, "Field Swap Parameter: Procedure/Surgeon," then click "Enter."

» Click the "Save" icon on the Toolbar.

The final chart looks like this:

Surgical Site Infection Rates and Case Counts
By Procedure

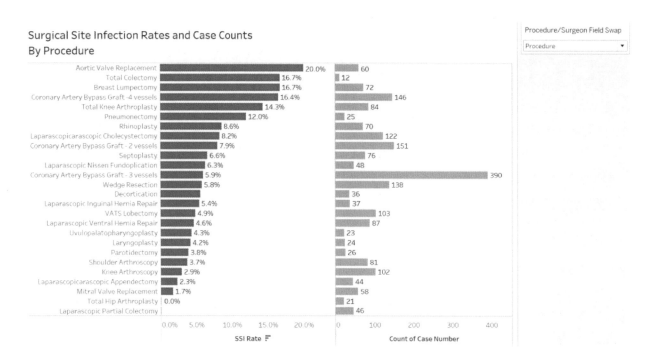

Procedure/Surgeon Field Swap

Procedure ▾

Insight: The Parameter Control allows the report viewer to compare surgical site infection rates and case counts by either of the Dimensions (Primary Surgeon or Procedure) via the drop-down menu, instead of by creating two separate charts.

25.2 Top N Parameters

Another common type of Parameter is a Top N (Number) Parameter, which allows control of the number of top items displayed in the view. This example report displays the top N states for cancer death rates. This is a useful technique to focus the report viewers on the most urgent data while still allowing them the flexibility to see more of the data if desired.

How To: Build a Top N Parameter control for a bar chart display of states with the highest cancer death rates.

Top 10 States with Highest Age-Adjusted Cancer Death Rates for 2017

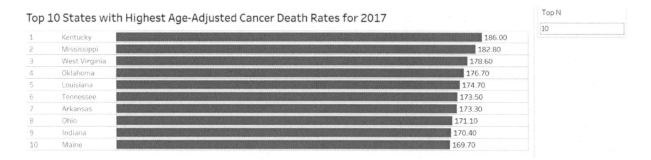

Top N

10

Data Source: Centers for Disease Control & Prevention (www.cdc.gov)

About the Data: 2017 cancer death rates by state (all types of cancer, per 100,000 people)

1 Create a new worksheet and connect to the data

» At the bottom of the Tableau workspace, click the icon for a new worksheet.

» In the Data pane, select the "Ch. 25 - Cancer Death Rates by State (2017)" dataset.

2 Create the chart

From the Data pane,

» Drag and drop "State" onto the Rows shelf.

» Drag and drop "Age-Adjusted Rate" onto the Columns shelf.

» Click the framed [T] icon on the Toolbar.

3 Sort the data by Rank

Rank the states from highest to lowest mortality rates.

» Right-click in any white space of the Data pane.

» Select "Create Calculated Field."

» Change the name to "Rank."

» For the formula, enter "RANK(SUM([Age-Adjusted Rate]))."

» Click "OK."

◄ Rank Function

Signaled by the color blue, RANK is a built-in table calculation, a function that performs a specific task in a calculated field dependent on the data present in the worksheet it is applied to. RANK returns a standard competition ranking, with identical values receiving the same rank. The default ranking is descending; to rank ascending, add 'asc' at the end of the calculation (e.g., RANK(SUM([Age-Adjusted Rate]),'asc').

» Drag and drop the newly created "Rank" field onto the Rows shelf.

As "Rank" is a Measure, it is currently a Continuous (green) field; it should be a Discrete (blue) one.

» Right-click the "Rank" field and select "Discrete."

» Drag "Rank" to, and drop onto, the space before "State" on the Rows shelf.

The chart now looks like this:

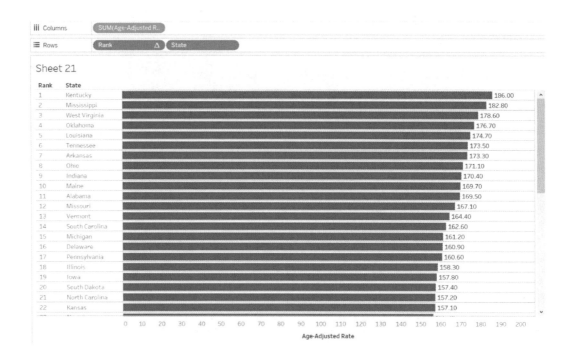

4 Create a Parameter

» Right-click in any white space in the Data pane.

» Select "Create Parameter."

» Name this parameter "Top N."

» Change Data Type to "Integer."

» Change Current value to "10."

» Click "OK."

» Right-click the new "Top N" parameter in the Parameter window and select "Show Parameter."

The parameter control currently is not affecting the number of ranked states in the view. The parameter needs to be used in a calculation.

» Right-click on any white space of the Data pane.

» Select "Create Calculated Field."

» For the title, enter "Top N Filter."

» In the Calculated Field Formula space below, enter this formula: [Rank]<=[Top N]

» Click "OK."

◄ Field vs. Function

Sometimes field names may be the same as a function name. Pay attention to the icon to the left of the label: the italized 'f' represents a Function; a data type icon represents a data field.

Functions, when selected, will be a blue font color in the calculation box; fields will be an orange font color.

» Drag and drop the "Top N Filter" field from the Data pane to the Filters shelf.

» In the Filter dialog box, click to place a checkmark in the "True" box.

» Click "OK."

The chart now looks like this:

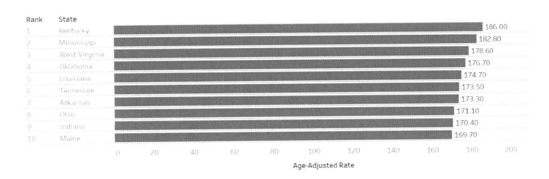

Test the Parameter to ensure it is functioning as expected.

» Enter the desired number in the Parameter window and confirm the chart reflects the selection.

5 Format the chart

» Right-click "Rank" or "State" header on the chart and select "Hide Field Labels for Rows."

>> Right-click the X axis and click "Show Header" to remove its checkmark.

6 **Create a dynamic title**

>> Double-click the Title Row to open the Edit Title dialog box.

>> Enter the title "Top States with Highest Age-Adjusted Cancer Death Rates for 2017."

>> Click to place the cursor between "Top" and "States."

>> Click the caret to open the "Insert" menu.

>> Select "Parameters.Top N" from the menu.

>> Click "OK."

7 **Rename the worksheet tab and save the worksheet**

>> Double-click the worksheet tab at the bottom of the screen.

>> In the highlighted text, enter the new title, "Top N Parameter: Top Cancer Death Rate States," then click "Enter."

>> Click the "Save" icon on the Toolbar.

The final chart looks like this:

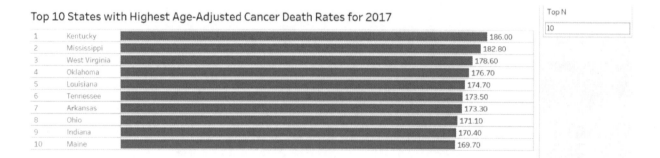

Insight: Ranking and narrowing down the view to the Top 10 (as an example here) shows us that 9 of the top 10 states with the highest age-adjusted cancer death rates are in the South and Midwest.

CHAPTER 26

Data Blending & Cross-Data Source Filtering

Data Blending defines a relationship between common fields in any two separate Tableau data sources as a way to combine data within a single worksheet. Table Joins produce a single Tableau data source; Data Blending queries each data source individually then aggregates the data (to the selected level) and displays the data collectively. Data Blending is useful when the combination of linking fields that create the relationships need to change from sheet to sheet and can be more performant when the data linked and displayed is highly aggregated. Understanding this method of relating common fields across different data sources is also necessary to leverage cross-data source filtering effectively.

How To: Build a multiple-data source dashboard with Data Blending and Cross-Data Source Filtering.

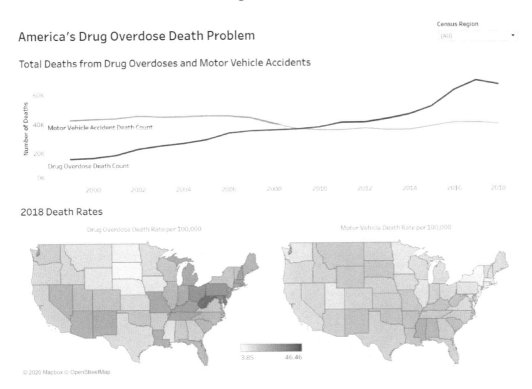

Data Source: *CDC WONDER online databases provide data and analysis to support evidence-based assessment of public health programs and population health trends.*

About the Data: *Centers for Disease Control and Prevention, National Center for Health Statistics. Multiple Cause of Death 1999-2018 in CDC WONDER Online Database. Data are from the Multiple Cause of Death Files, 1999-2018, as compiled from data provided by the 57 vital statistics jurisdictions through the Vital Statistics Cooperative Program. The data are representative of the continental USA.*

Before building out the activity, it is important to understand the mechanics of Data Blending.

26.1 Mechanics of Data Blending

With a single data source, using fields in a worksheet triggers requests for data from that source.

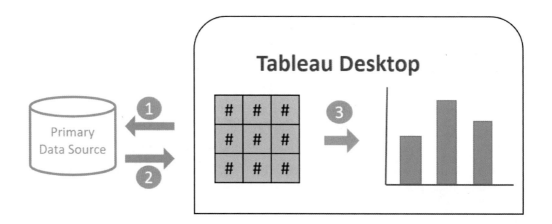

The three numbered arrows above represent the following processes:

1) As fields are dragged and dropped onto the worksheet, requests for data are sent to the primary data source. This process works via Tableau´s proprietary VizQL (Visual Query Language). The first data source used in a worksheet is designated as the "primary data source."

2) The data source carries out the request, including aggregating/summarizing values based on fields present in the worksheet, and returns the results.

3) Tableau uses that results-set to build the visualization. As the visualization is manipulated further, fresh queries are made to the primary data source and the process continues.

During Data Blending, requests are made to 2 or more data sources simultaneously.

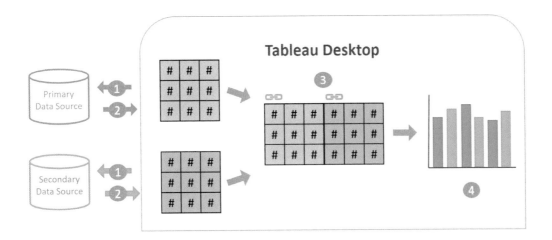

The four numbered arrows above represent the following processes:

1) During Data Blending, Tableau queries two or more data sources simultaneously.

2) All data sources queried return results; all are then aggregated/summarized.

3) The level to which the results are aggregated is set according to the linking field(s). Each data source aggregates its data to that level, and the linking field(s) is/are used to "line up" the tables row by row and merge the data.

4) Tableau uses the resulting merged dataset to generate the visualization.

Important Notes on Data Blending

*   All data values from the primary data source are kept in the final dataset. Data values from the secondary data source(s) are only present in the final dataset if they correspond to matching values in the primary source. Any rows in the secondary data source that do not have matches in the primary source are eliminated, while any values for which the secondary data source has no matches in the primary return Null (a result similar to that in a left table join).

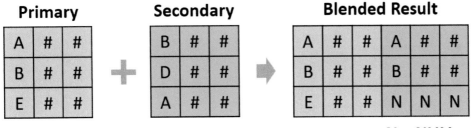

*   With each new worksheet, a new primary data source is selected. A primary data source in one worksheet may be used as a secondary source in another.

- There can be only one primary data source per worksheet; however, multiple secondary data sources may be present in the same worksheet. Similarly, there can be only one set of Measure Names and Measure Values fields for the worksheet; primary data source fields are active, while those in secondary data sources are grayed out.

- Data Blending merges data locally rather than in the underlying data source (this distinction differentiates a Data Blend from a Table Join). Tableau Desktop handles the processing necessary to merge the data during a blend. The level of aggregation for the linking field will determine how resource-intensive the blending process is. If the linking field contains millions of distinct values, hardware resources may run out during the blending process, causing the report to slow or even crash. If Blending results in slow downs and system crashes, another approach should be used. Conversely, if the linking fields are highly aggregated, it is possible for a data blend to perform faster than a very granular table join.

Data Blending Activity

The following training/practice example describes how to define the relationship between two data connections. The datasets used have been taken from the Multiple Cause of Death dataset provided by CDC WONDER (cited above).

The first data source, Drug Overdose Deaths, contains the count of deaths caused by drug overdoses summarized by Underlying Cause of Death Code, State, and Year. The second, Motor Vehicle Incident Deaths, contains the count of deaths caused by motor vehicle incidents summarized by State and Year. While the level of aggregation for each data source is different, the two share common fields (State and Year) that can be used to link the data.

Validation of Blending Results

1 **Establish the primary data source**

» Create a new worksheet and select the "Ch. 26 - Drug Overdose Deaths 1999-2018" dataset.

» Drag and drop *"Drug Overdose Deaths 1999-2018 (Count)"* from the Data pane onto Label on the Marks card. Note: Make sure not to drag "Drug Overdose Death Count" field. The correct field includes the years and is shown in italics on the data pane.

Primary Data Source Indicator ▶

When a field is first placed on the canvas, a blue checkmark appears next to the data source in the Data pane, indicating that it is the primary data source for the worksheet.

2 **Determine the data granularity of the primary data source**

This dataset´s total row count is 15,680. It is critical to understand the lowest level of aggregation present; in other words, what does one row of data represent here? Placing Dimensions in the view disaggregates the data to answer this question. To determine the level of granularity:

» Drag and drop "State" from the Data pane onto the Rows shelf. The text table now shows that there are 320 rows of data per State.

» Drag "Report Date" from the Data pane drop it to the right of "State" on the Rows shelf.

There are 20 years in the dataset; the number of records for each row now decreases to 16.

» Drag " Cause of Death Description" from the Data pane; drop it to the right of "YEAR(Report Date)" on the Rows shelf.

There are 16 causes of death in the dataset; the number of records now drops to 1.

In summary; for the Drug Overdose Deaths dataset,

One Row = One Cause of Death for each Year for each State

State	Year of Report Date	Cause of Death Description	
Alabama	1999	Accidental poisoning by and exposure to antiepile...	1
		Accidental poisoning by and exposure to narcotics...	1
		Accidental poisoning by and exposure to nonopioi...	1
		Accidental poisoning by and exposure to other an...	1
		Accidental poisoning by and exposure to other dru...	1
		Assault by drugs, medicaments and biological sub...	1
		Intentional self-poisoning by and exposure to anti...	1
		Intentional self-poisoning by and exposure to narc...	1
		Intentional self-poisoning by and exposure to non...	1
		Intentional self-poisoning by and exposure to othe...	1
		Intentional self-poisoning by and exposure to othe...	1
		Poisoning by and exposure to antiepileptic, sedati...	1
		Poisoning by and exposure to narcotics and psych...	1
		Poisoning by and exposure to nonopioid analgesic...	1
		Poisoning by and exposure to other and unspecifie...	1
		Poisoning by and exposure to other drugs acting o...	1
	2000	Accidental poisoning by and exposure to antiepile...	1
		Accidental poisoning by and exposure to narcotics...	1

» Remove both the "Report Date" and "Underlying Cause of Death" fields from the Rows shelf before continuing.

3 Establish the secondary data source and create a relationship on "State"

» Select the "Ch. 26 - Motor Vehicle Accident Deaths 1999-2018" dataset.

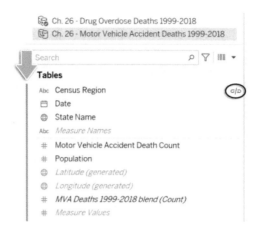

There is now an orange vertical stripe along the left edge of the Data pane. This is a visual cue that it is not the primary data source. There is also a gray broken-link icon to the right of "Census Region" in the Dimensions window. Tableau has identified a matching field in the primary and the secondary data sources for a potential relationship.

»   Drag "State Name" to the Rows shelf; drop it to the right of "State."

An error message appears, stating that a relationship needs to be created between the two datasets.

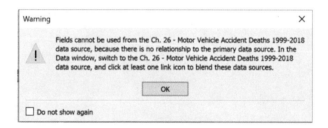

»   Click "OK" to close the Warning dialog box.

There is no established relationship between the two datasets yet. A relationship will now be created between State and State Name.

»   Click "Data" on the Menu bar; select "Edit Blend Relationships…"

»   In the Relationships context dialog box:

• Under Primary data source, ensure that "Ch. 26 - Drug Overdose Deaths 1999-2018" is selected.

• Under Secondary data source, ensure that "Ch. 26 - Motor Vehicle Accident Deaths 1999-2018" is selected.

• Census Region, a field in both data sources, is automatically recognized for a relationship. Leave this as it is. Click the "Custom" radio button.

• Click "Add."

• Select "State" from the primary data source field and "State Name" from the secondary data source field.

• Click "OK." The selections are now displayed on the list.

Click "OK." again.

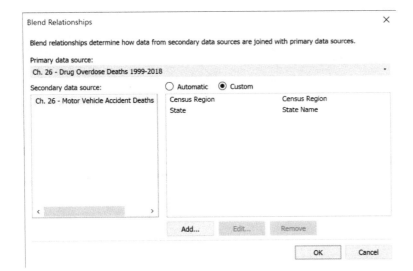

Custom Relationships

If the primary and secondary data sources have field names in common, these fields will be identified as potential linking fields and will show up automatically on the Relationships menu. A custom relationship can be defined between two dimensions with different names as long as they are the same data type. Relationships can only be defined between dimensions.

The State names are now displayed in the text table. In the Data pane of the secondary data source, an orange link icon now appears to the right of "State Name." (The Census Region link remains gray and "broken" because the field is not currently in use in the text table.)

» Ensure the accuracy of the Data Blend by checking that the State Name values align.

» From the secondary data source, "Ch. 26 – Motor Vehicle Accident Deaths 1999-2018," double-click "MVA Deaths 1999-2018 (Count)" to create a text table with row counts from both data sources displayed.

In the secondary data source, there are 20 rows of data per state name.

» Click the "View Data" icon in the Data pane. Notice that the secondary data source contains 20 years of vehicle-death data per state.

» Switch to the primary data source, "Ch. 26 – Drug Overdose Deaths 1999-2018."

» Drag "Report Date" onto the Rows shelf; drop it to the right of "State Name."

The 320 records for the primary data source drop to 16 because it is now broken out by Year in addition to State. Only the 16 rows of various "Underlying Cause of Death" are being aggregated.

» Now switch to the secondary data source, "Ch. 26 – Motor Vehicle Accident Deaths 1999-2018."

» Drag "Date" onto the Rows shelf; drop it to the right of YEAR(Report Date).

Asterisks appear in the cells for the YEAR(Date) column.

State	State Name	Year of Report Date	Year of Date	Count of Drug Overdose Deaths 1..	Count of MVA Deaths 1999-2018 ..
Alabama	Alabama	1999	*	16.000	20.000
		2000	*	16.000	20.000
		2001	*	16.000	20.000
		2002	*	16.000	20.000
		2003	*	16.000	20.000

Linking Field and Aggregation

The linking field indicates the level to which each data source aggregates its values before the resulting tables are merged in a blend.

The asterisks here indicate there is more than one Year value for each row in the secondary data source. Note that this is different than seeing NULL, which would indicate that there are no matching years between the two data sources. Because the data blend occurs only on "State Name," the numeric fields are aggregated to the State level, repeating the same value for all years.

To correct this situation, both "State" and "Year" should be used as linking fields.

4 **Create relationship on "Year"**

» Click "Data" on the Menu bar; select "Edit Blend Relationships..."

» In the Blend Relationships dialog box:

• Under Primary data source, ensure that "Ch. 26 – Drug Overdose Deaths 1999-2018" is selected.

• Under Secondary data source, ensure that "Ch. 26 – Motor Vehicle Accident Deaths 1999-2018" is selected.

• Click the "Add" button.

There are now two Date fields in each column. The Date fields have carets because they can expand to display the possible date parts available for the data blend.

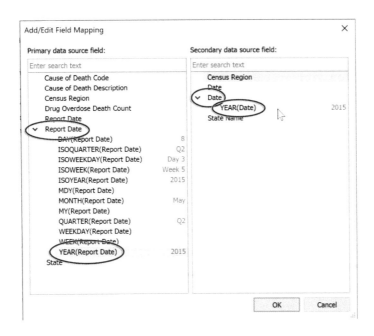

• Click the corresponding carets to expand both fields, then map "YEAR(Report Date)" to "YEAR(Date)" by clicking each option.

• Click "OK."

» Confirm that Year values now match up.

State	State Name	Year of Report Date	Year of Date
Alabama	Alabama	1999	1999
		2000	2000
		2001	2001
		2002	2002
		2003	2003

Asterisks (*) vs. Nulls

During Data Blending, values from the secondary data source can appear with nulls or asterisks when the two data sources are not at the same level of aggregation or do not match.

Secondary data source "NULL" values occur when there is no match between the linking fields in the primary and secondary data sources.

Secondary data source "" values occur when there is more than one discrete secondary data source value on a single partition (column or row) in a worksheet.*

The Count of MVA Deaths 1999-2018 rows is now down to 1, indicating the lowest level of detail for the blended data sources.

» Label the worksheet "Blending Validation" and save.

Build the Analysis

5 **Use the Data Blend to create a line graph showing yearly deaths due to drug over-doses compared to motor vehicle accidents**

» Create a new worksheet.

» Select the "Ch. 26 – Drug Overdose Deaths 1999-2018" data source.

» Drag and drop "Drug Overdose Death Count" onto the Rows shelf.

» Drag and drop "Report Date" onto the Columns shelf.

» Right-click "Report Date" and select "Year" from the date value section of the menu to create a continuous Year Date axis.

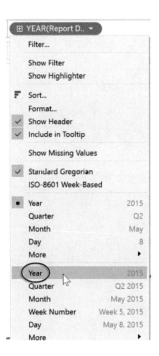

» Select the "Ch. 26 – Motor Vehicle Accident Deaths 1999-2018" data source.

Notice that "Date" has an orange link icon next to it, indicating that it is being used as the blending field. There is a gray broken-link icon next to "State Name" indicating that it is not an active blending field. The "Date" field link is orange because its corresponding linking field "YEAR(Report Date)" is in the worksheet. That is not the case for the "State Name."

» Click the Link icon next to the "State Name" field to reestablish the link so the data are blended correctly. Note: for the current chart, linking "State Name" will not change the displayed results, however this link is important for the following section in order for the calculations to correctly adjust when filtered by Census Region.

» Drag and drop the "Motor Vehicle Accident Death Count" field onto the "Drug Overdose Death Count" axis (the parallel ruler icon will appear to indicate that a shared axis chart is about to be generated).

» Name the worksheet tab "Deaths Timeline."

6 Format the view and edit the title

» Assign the color dark gray to the "Drug Overdose Death Count" line, as it is the focus of the chart. Make the "Motor Vehicle Accident Death Count" line light gray as a reference for comparison.

» Right-click the Y axis; select "Edit axis."

» Change the title to "Number of Deaths."

» Right-click the X axis; select "Edit axis."

» Delete "Year of Report Date" axis title.

» Holding down the Control key (to create a copy), drag and drop the "Measure Names" field currently on Color onto Label on the Marks card.

» Click Label to open its controls.

» Under "Marks to Label, "select "Line Ends," then uncheck "Label end of line."

» Double-click the worksheet title row; change the title to "Total Deaths from Drug Overdoses and Motor Vehicle Accidents."

» Click the "Save" icon on the Toolbar.

The chart now looks like this:

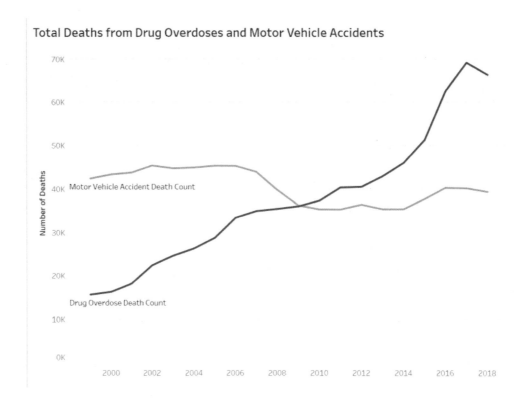

Total Deaths from Drug Overdoses and Motor Vehicle Accidents

26.2 Blended Calculations & Cross-Data Source Filtering

Data Blending can be used to perform complex analytics and achieve advanced interactivity within a workbook. The following exercise shows how to use Data Blending to create:

- Blended calculations that include fields from the primary and secondary data sources.

- A Cross Data Source Filter that affects two primary data sources connected by a relationship already established in the workbook.

Two calculated fields are needed to display the rate of deaths per 100,000 population for Drug Overdose Deaths and Motor Vehicle Incident Deaths. The basic calculation formula is:

`Number of Deaths/Population*100,000`

Each data source contains a field representing its number of deaths; however, only one data source (Ch. 26 - Motor Vehicle Accident Deaths 199-2018) has a Population field. To calculate the rate for Drug Overdose Deaths, a blended calculation is required.

1 **Create calculated fields for death rates per 100,000**

» Create a new worksheet.

» Select the "Ch. 26 - Motor Vehicle Accident Deaths 1999-2018" data source.

» Right-click in the white space of the Date pane; select "Create Calculated Field..."

The first calculated field is for the Death Rate for Motor Vehicle Incidents. This data source contains both fields required for the calculation.

» Name the field "Motor Vehicle Death Rate per 100,000."

» Enter the formula "SUM([Motor Vehicle Accident Death Count]) /SUM([Population]) * 100000" then click "OK."

```
SUM([Motor Vehicle Accident Death Count])/SUM([Population])*100000
```

The second calculated field is for the Death Rate for Drug Overdoses. Because the Drug Overdose Deaths data source does not contain a Population field, a blended calculation is needed.

» Ensure that the primary data source "Ch. 26 - Motor Vehicle Accident Deaths 1999-2018" is selected.

» Right-click in the white space of the Data pane; select "Create Calculated Field..."

» Name the field "Drug Overdose Death Rate per 100,000."

» Enter the formula; "SUM([Ch. 26 - Drug Overdose Deaths 1999-2018].[Drug Overdose Death Count])/SUM([Population]) * 100000".

```
SUM([Ch. 26 - Drug Overdose Deaths 1999-2018].[Drug Overdose Death Count])/
SUM([Population])*100000
```

▲ Blended Calculation

A field drawn from another data source must be labeled with its full name arranged as follows: [Data Source Name]. [Field Name]. The field must be aggregated: when the blend occurs, Tableau requests aggregated tables at the level of the linking field(s) from the applicable data sources. The calculation builds on the merged results set that has already been aggregated.

A quick way to add a field name from another data source into a calculation is to start typing its name, then select the full term desired from the display of field names that appears. Tableau automatically formats the correct name structure and incorporates an aggregate function into the calculation.

2 Build a Map view of 2018 Death Rates

» Ensure that the "Ch. 26 - Motor Vehicle Incident Deaths " data source is selected.

» Double click "State Name" to create a map.

» Hold down the Control key and select the two Death Rate fields, then drag them to the map.

» Drop the fields onto the middle of the map. This automatically generates the Measure Names and Measure Values fields, and creates a Symbol Map with Measure Values on Size on the Marks card.

» On the Marks card, drag and drop the "Measure Values" field from Size to Color. This step converts the view to Filled Maps, showing the death rates as color gradients.

» Move the "Measure Names" field from the Rows shelf to the Columns shelf to position the maps side by side.

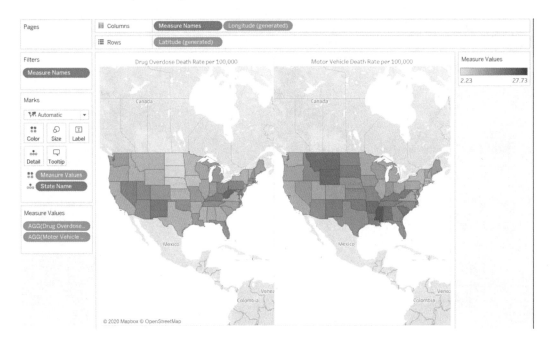

To filter data only for only 2018;

》 Drag and drop "Date" onto the Filters Shelf; choose discrete Years; and select only "2018."

This action causes the color gradients to change. The Motor Vehicle Death Rate map is now a solid color.

Evaluate the blending fields:

》 Select the "Ch. 26 - Drug Overdose Deaths 1999-2018" data source. The link for "State Name" is orange (active); the link for "Report Date" is gray (broken).

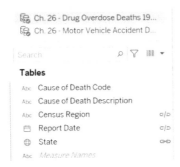

》 Click the linking icon next to "Report Date" to reactivate the link. The colors now vary by death rate.

》 Rename the worksheet title and tab "2018 Death Rates."

Adjust Formatting to simplify the map:

》 Click "Map" on the Menu bar, then select "Map Layers."

》 In the left "Map Layers" pane, under the "Map Layers" section, deselect all but the "Base" option.

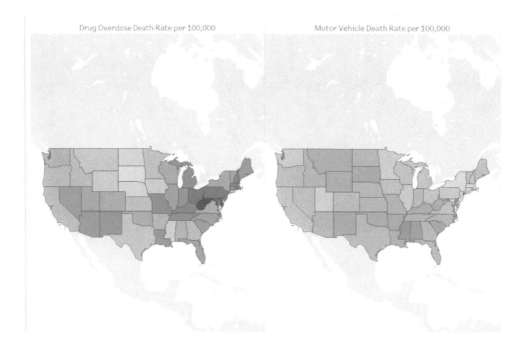

Drug Overdose Death Rate per 100,000   Motor Vehicle Death Rate per 100,000

3 Create a Dashboard with a Cross-Data Source Filter

» Open a new dashboard; rename the tab "America´s Drug Problem."

» Drag and drop the "Deaths Timeline" to the dashboard and position the "2018 Death Rates" worksheet so that it occupies the lower half of the space.

» Drag a Text box to the top of the dashboard; add the title "America´s Drug Overdose Death Problem."

» Change the font to 18-point bold.

» Resize the text box to an appropriate title size.

» Set the dashboard size to the desired size (this example uses size Letter Landscape).

Cross-Data Source Filters

Even if no blending occurs, Cross-Data Source Filters can provide valuable interactivity to compare data from different data sources.

For example, if a dashboard contains several worksheets, each built on its own data source, as long as those sources are related (and those relationships established in the Data > Edit Relationships controls for the workbook), a Cross-Data Source Filter can be created to affect all desired worksheets in the dashboard, or even across an entire workbook.

4 Create a Cross Data Source Filter for the field Census Region

» Navigate to the "Deaths Timeline" worksheet.

» Ensure that the primary data source "Ch. 26 – Drug Overdose Deaths 1999-2018" is selected.

» Drag and drop the "Census Region" field onto the Filters shelf.

» Select all Census Regions, then click OK.

» Navigate back to the "America´s Drug Problem" Dashboard.

» Click the "Deaths Timeline" worksheet to highlight it.

» Click the "More Options" caret at the top right, select "Filters," then "Census Region."

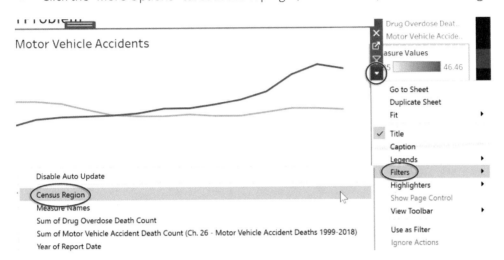

» Click the "Census Region" filter in the right column to highlight, then click the caret near the top right corner.

» Click "Apply to Worksheets" and select "All Using Related Data Sources."

Applying Filters to "All Using Related Data Sources"

When a workbook contains worksheets built from related primary data sources, this option is a quick way to add a filter to all worksheets across that entire workbook.

Most often the filter should apply to all worksheets on a dashboard; but other worksheets using the same data sources exist outside the dashboard, and should not be affected by the filter. In these situations, choosing the Selected Worksheets option allows the user to pick precisely which worksheets the filter should affect.

» Change the filter display format to "Multiple Values (dropdown)."

» Move the "Census Region" filter to the top of the dashboard next to the title.

5 Format the dashboard

» Click the Measure Names color legend in the top right corner to highlight, then click the "X" to remove it. Since the lines are labeled, this color legend is not needed.

» Click the Measure Values color legend to highlight it, then click the caret.

» Select "Floating."

» Move the color legend to float between the two Death Rates maps.

» Click the color legend caret and uncheck "Show Title."

» Click the Deaths Timeline worksheet to highlight it.

» Click the "Layout" tab and select a desired Background color to color the worksheet title.

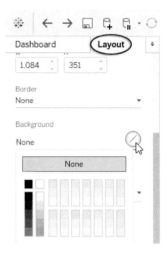

» Perform the same steps for the 2018 Death Rates worksheet title.

The final dashboard looks like this:

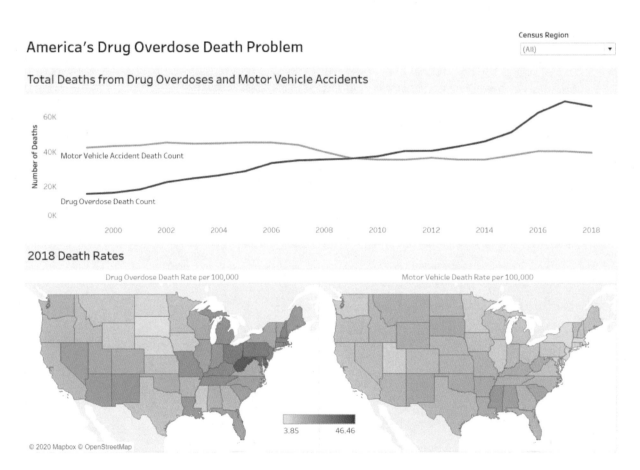

Insight: Nationally, the drug overdose death count continues to rise; it surpassed the motor vehicle accidents death count in 2009. It should further be noted that death rates by state for the most recent year available (2018) reveal regional disparities.

CHAPTER 27

Tips and Tricks

This chapter includes a collection of techniques and nuanced development considerations to improve your understanding of Tableau and assist you in navigating, customizing, and optimizing your Dashboards and Reports.

Navigation and Organization

Below are some quick features to help navigate and annotate a Tableau Workbook.

- **Field finder**. It's not uncommon to have a large number of field names display in the Data pane, which can make a particular field hard to find. To quickly locate a desired field, utilize the Search box above the Tables header in the Data pane. A funnel icon to the right of the Search box, when clicked, aids in narrowing the field listing by Calculation, Dimension, Measure, or Comment.

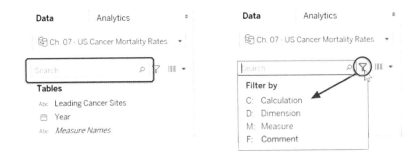

- **View data**. Underlying data can be viewed either in its entirety or down to the aggregation level of a mark.

  - To view an underlying dataset, click the Spreadsheet icon to the right of the Search box in the Data pane.

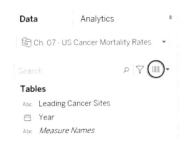

- To view aggregated data for a specific mark, right-click the mark and select "View Data" from the menu that appears.

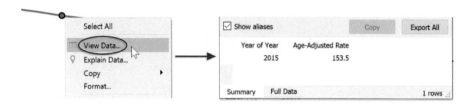

- **Commenting calculated field names**. A custom tooltip can be created to display a field's calculation (or definition), saving time when trying to locate a field with the desired calculation. To copy the formula, right-click the calculated field, then select "Edit" to open the calculated field dialog box. To access the calculated field tooltip and paste the formula, right-click the calculated field name again, and select "Default Properties," then "Comments."

Report/Dashboard Performance Improvement

While no single trick is guaranteed to improve performance, these may help:

- **Performance Recording tool**. Tableau can record workbook performance details (extracts, queries, data blending) to analyze and identify any factors contributing to low speed and poor efficiency. Under "Help" on the Menu bar, choose "Settings and Performance," then "Start Performance Recording." Open a workbook and perform a few sample interactions on the dashboard—click a filter, modify a parameter. When finished, click "Stop Performance Recording." Tableau then generates a Performance Summary identifying any areas contributing to lags or delays.

- **Extract vs. Live connection**. When experiencing poor workbook performance with large file-based data sources, use extracts to take advantage of Tableau´s fast data engine. Live connections to databases can hamper performance due to slower connections and processing speeds. Server-based databases may also benefit from using extracts, however results will depend on the processing power of the database and the size of the extract to be generated.

- **Dataset size reduction**. The number of rows and columns affects speed and responsiveness. Consider the following to reduce the size of the dataset:

- Use Data Source and Extract Filtering. Render data connections more manageable by applying Data Source Filters. Extract data sources have an added benefit as these can be reduced in size via Extract filters.

- Aggregate the dataset to the level necessary for the report to reduce the number of rows.

- **Workbook size**. Simplify workbook elements. Limit the number of worksheets, dashboards, and quick filters. While there is no imposed limit, each additional element can affect performance. To counteract this, consider splitting a workbook into several smaller ones. Reduce the number of quick filters. Quick filters set to show "Only Relevant Values" are particularly performance-intensive.

- **Leveraging the new relationship data model:** Where appropriate, combining multiple tables into a single data source using Tableau's new relationship model can result in faster query times than performing physical table joins. This is particularly true when combining "lookup" tables, or tables used to cross-reference additional fields based on a variable in the main table, into a data source. In short, using a relationship instead of a table join ensures that the table is only queried if fields from that table are actually present in the worksheet, which allows Tableau to write more efficient queries. See chapter 3 for more details on relationships.

Calculation Optimization

The following tips can help improve the performance of calculations:

- **Strings vs. Integers**. Strings are slow; use integers instead.

    - With Functions: `COUNTD([Int])` will be faster than `COUNTD([text])`.

    - With Logical Statements: `IF [Field #] = Integer` will be faster than `IF [Field #] = "text"`.

- **Performance implications of functions**. `SUM()` will be faster than `COUNTD()`. COUNTD tallies the number of unique items in a dataset, comparing every single record against every other record. Consider this formula, for example:

`COUNTD(IF [Age]>60 THEN [Patient_ID] ELSE NULL END)`

For every patient over age 60, the Patient ID will be listed. COUNTD will then count the number of unique records of Patient ID. Assuming one row per patient in the data source, a faster way to do this is:

`SUM(IF [Age]>60 THEN 1 ELSE 0 END)`

This formula will interpret every patient over age 60 as an integer of 1. SUM will then rapidly add up all the integers.

- **CASE / WHEN statements are faster than IF / THEN statements**. When structuring logical calculations, put the most common cases first, so that they are evaluated before less common ones.

- **Leverage speedy mathematical functions**. Imagine a situation where the goal is to create three categories in order to organize Measures in groups for positive, zero, or negative values. One way to illustrate this situation would be:

```
IF [Field]>0 THEN "Positive"
ELSEIF [Field]=0 THEN "Zero"
ELSE "Negative"
END
```

  However, this formula (while accurate) uses strings and requires logic checks, adversely affecting performance. A faster calculation would look like this:

```
SIGN ([Field])
```

  This calculation will group the field into 1's, 0's, and -1's very quickly. If needed, rename these values with more descriptive aliases (1="Positive," 0="Neutral," -1="Negative," for example).

- **Boolean calculations**. Instead of writing an IF / THEN statement to create two Dimension buckets, use a Boolean calculation, then create aliases. For example:

```
IF [Total Patient Falls Rate] < 1.5
THEN "Good"
ELSE "Poor"
END
```

  This formula uses strings and logic checks. Instead, use a Boolean calculation:

```
[Total Patient Falls Rate] < 1.5
```

  The values can then be renamed with descriptive aliases (TRUE = "Good" and FALSE = "Poor").

Order of Operations

Tableau performs operations in a specified order. Understanding this order ensures that analytics perform as intended, and can help troubleshoot any unexpected results. The diagram to the right conveys the order in which Tableau performs its operations (filters are in blue text; calculations and functions in black). A full understanding of the upstream effects of the steps preceding an operation is crucial to its success. For example, if a FIXED Level of Detail calculation is not returning the desired result, it is likely being affected by an Extract, a Data Source, and/or Context Filters, so check those first.

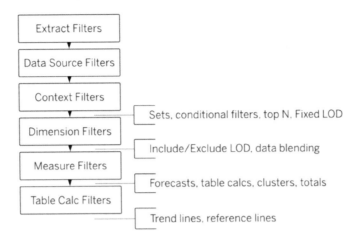

Diagram taken from Tableau Online Help Manual at: https://help.tableau.com/current/pro/desktop/en-us/order_of_operations.htm

Alternative Data Connection Methods

- Open Excel or CSV file in Tableau. Before opening Tableau, locate the desired Excel or .csv file. Drag it to the desktop and drop it onto the Tableau icon there. This action simultaneously launches Tableau and opens the file.

- Copy/paste Excel. Copy a selection of cells from an Excel spreadsheet and paste them into Tableau, generating a new data source. After copying the Excel selection, open Tableau, select "Data" from the Menu bar, and click "Paste."

- Web Data Connectors. Are open source and offer a great short cut to new data connections.

Custom Colors & Shapes

- **Custom shapes** can be added to the Tableau Shapes menu. Navigate to the local Tableau Repository and add the image file(s) to the Shapes folder there. To find the Tableau Repository, click "File" on the Menu bar, then "Repository Location..."

- **Custom color palette**. Categorical, sequential, and/or diverging custom color palettes can be added to Tableau by editing the Preferences.tps file in the Tableau Repository. The palettes then appear on the Select Color menu. Tableau´s Knowledgebase Articles provide clear, detailed instructions for creating these palettes.

Other Visual Techniques

- **Leverage Layout Containers:** Layout containers can be tricky for beginner Tableau developers to leverage effectively, however they are a powerful tool to use to ensure various dashboard objects align as intended. A layout container is either horizontally or vertically oriented; all objects inside the container follow the same orientation (unless another layout container is nested within it). In this example, a horizontal layout container (containing Objects 5-8) is nested inside a vertical layout container (containing Objects 1-4 and the horizontal layout container):

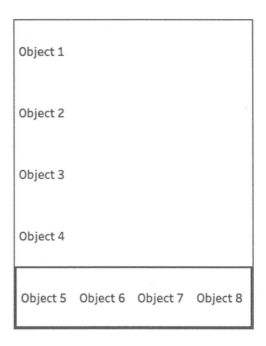

Layout Containers have several benefits and features:

a. All objects inside a layout container can be evenly distributed for uniform display, or set to specific pixel height/width to achieve precise spacing:

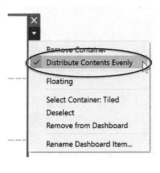

b. Objects, such as charts displaying varying amounts of data (due to interactive filtering), can be configured to dynamically adjust, removing unneeded white space.

c. Floating layout containers can incorporate a Show/Hide Button to dynamically expand and contract objects within the layout container. This provides endless possibilities to hide and show filters, annotations, text boxes, and even additional charts within a dashboard.

- **Move discrete column header to the top of a chart**. Click "Analysis" on the Menu bar, then select "Table Layout," and "Advanced." In the Table Options dialog box, uncheck the option "Show innermost level at bottom of view when there is a vertical axis."

- **Replace field reference**. If the name of a field in a chart is modified for any reason, Tableau is unable to find the correct destination for updated data. It flags this mismatch with a red exclamation point. To correct this error, right-click the invalid field in the Data pane and select "Replace References." In the dialog box that appears, select the replacement field name.

Accessibility and Distribution

351

CHAPTER 28

Accessibility & Distribution

28.1 Accessibility

Tableau supports several features that comply with U.S. Section 508 and WCAG (Web Content Accessibility Guidelines) to ensure users with physical, sensory or mental disabilities can access or view, navigate, and understand reports and dashboards published to Tableau Server, Tableau Online, or Tableau Public. To achieve accessibility in this inherently visual medium, it is necessary to combine the technical capabilities of the tool with accessible design best practices. In reviewing these features and techniques, it is helpful to consider the different accessible audiences and the specialized accommodations they require.

At a high level, consider how the strategies below serve the following audiences:

- Users who have vision loss may not be able to read small fonts, read data or text with low contrast backgrounds, distinguish all or certain color palates, or see small navigation buttons.

- Users who are blind that depend on a screen reader (a browser or file-based tool used to read webpage, .csv files, and excel documents out loud) to listen to and interpret titles, headers, and data.

- Users with intellectual disabilities that benefit from simple explanation with clear titles, headers, and word choices.

- Users with physical disabilities that require accessible equipment that often only supports navigation with keystrokes instead of a mouse.

Tableau supports the following features and resources to enable accessible report creation:

- **View Data window:** displays a visualization's underlying data in a text table format that can be read by a screen reader or exported to an excel or .csv file.

- **Keyboard navigation:** allows users to navigate without a mouse to support the selection of different workbook tabs, charts, and drop-down or list filters. As of this writing, actions and parameters cannot be engaged without the use of a mouse.

- **Compliance with contrast standards and color-blind color palette:** supported when compliant colors are used by report developers.

- **Screen reader support:** titles, captions, workbook tabs, categorical legends, captions, and objects with alt-text, including text, webpage, image, and buttons can be read by a browser supported screen reader.

- **Authentication:** when signing into Tableau Server for visualizations embedded on a webpage.

For additional details and considerations, please refer to the Accessibility FAQ in the Tableau Community Forums (https://community.tableau.com/s/question/0D54T00000C6nsjSAB/faq-accessibility).

The following Best Practices will help to meet compliance with Accessibility principles:

The Data:

- Aggregate the data wherever possible and emphasize the most important data. Heavily detailed data is difficult to interpret from a screen reader. Additionally, more than 1,000 marks in a chart will initiate a shift to the server to render the data, which is not yet supported for WCAG compliance (the number of marks can be viewed in the bottom left corner of Tableau Desktop's window).

- Enable the permission to view summary data (and underlying data if desired).

- Do not rely solely on color to distinguish marks; add shapes and labels.

- Use the color-blind palette or ensure there is enough contrast in the selected colors.

- Limit the number of colors and shapes in a single view.

- Use filters to reduce the number of marks in the view at a given time. List and Drop-down List filters are the views that are currently supported for WCAG compliance.

- Maps should not be used as they currently are not WCAG compliant.

Supportive Text:

- Using plain language, ensure titles, labels, legends, filters, and supportive text are descriptive as possible. Any interactive element text should describe its purpose. Use text to describe what is being displayed and how they relate. Links should be explained as to what they are and where the user will be navigated to.

- Avoid using sensory descriptors such as color or location.

- Use captions to supplement the description of the data. These can be displayed by clicking "Worksheet," then "Show Caption," on the Menu Bar.

- Legends: the title should list the associated chart.

- Add alt-text to Image Objects and tooltip text to Button Objects explaining what they are.

- Ensure text color contrast is 4.5:1 (if using large text, ratio should be 3:1). A contrast checker (https://webaim.org/resources/contrastchecker/) is a useful tool to evaluate contrast and legibility.

Dashboard Layout:

- Include the use of tablet and mobile versions.

- Set sensible focus order for dashboard zones. Focus order is the sequence that determines in what order a screen reader will read or keystroke navigation will highlight objects in a dashboard. The focus order of views and objects in a dashboard is set by the order they were added during the dashboard creation. If this is not the desired order, the Tableau workbook XML can be edited. To learn more, refer to the Tableau Community Forum (https://community.tableau.com/s/question/0D54T00000C6USYSA3/how-can-i-set-the-focus-order-of-the-views-and-objects-in-a-dashboard).

- Add an image object with a link to Tableau's keyboard navigation instructions: https://help.tableau.com/current/pro/desktop/en-us/access_keyboard_navigation.htm. Set the tooltip for the image explaining what the link provides.

- Dashboard Extensions enable the addition of new performance options outside of what has been built into Tableau. Extensions are HTML pages hosted in a dashboard Web Page Object—if the HTML page user-interface is accessible, then this extends to the dashboard. An example of a dashboard extension that can be used for accessibility is "DataTables Extension for Tableau" created by Toan Hoang. This provides a way to display the underlying data in a useful table format.

28.2 Report & Dashboard Distribution

So far, this book has presented information on how to create data visualizations using Tableau Desktop. This section guides the reader to the best product offerings for sharing reports and dashboards based on the most common types of audience and distribution situations.

Consider the questions that follow to select the appropriate tool to develop and distribute your visualizations. A comparison chart and in-depth analysis of each product come later in the chapter, further clarifying features and design.

- **Connectivity:** What data sources do you need to access?
- **Distribution:** How do you intend to share your dashboards and reports, and control who can see them?
- **Automation:** Do your reports need to be automatically refreshed?
- **Security:** Does your data need to be HIPAA-compliant? Do you require on-premise security, or can your work be saved to the cloud?

Report Development Products: Tableau Desktop Variants

- **Tableau Desktop: Professional Edition** - connects to almost any data source via 75+ connectors. Compatible with Tableau Public, Tableau Server, and Tableau Online.

- **Tableau Desktop: Tableau Public Edition** - connects to Microsoft Excel, Microsoft Access, multiple text-file formats, statistical files, Google Sheets, and Web Data Connectors. Files may be saved only by taking extracts of the data source(s) and publishing them to Tableau Public. (This process makes an internet connection mandatory.)

Tableau Option	Cost	Data Sources	Comments
Reader	Free	Data extracts and local data files	• No built-in security • No ability to refresh data automatically • Workbooks can be viewed and interacted with, but not altered or developed
Public	Free	Data extracts and live Google Sheets	• Storage space is limited to 10 gigabytes per named user • Data source maximum size is 15,000,000 rows of data per workbook • Workbooks can be viewed by anyone. However, the option to download workbooks and their underlying data sources, while on by default, can be turned off.
Server	Paid	Any supported data source	• Enhanced security • Requires data-center space, server purchase, and IT support
Online	Paid | Hosted version of Server	Data extracts and live connections to some sources	• Secure (not publicly viewable), with limited security features • Live connections to some data sources, both hosted in the Cloud and on site via the Tableau Bridge client. While this syncing product offers some security for the transition, it may cause slight transfer delays and is not currently HIPAA compliant. • 100 GB storage

Tableau Reader

As the name implies, Tableau Reader is a read-only application, available at no charge from the Tableau website. Once installed, Tableau Reader enables a user to open visualizations and interact with them by filtering, sorting, and examining data. However, Tableau Reader does not permit the creation of visualizations.

Tableau Reader can open only Tableau Packaged Workbooks (.twbx files). As explained in Chapter 2, these files contain visuals as well as the extracted data sources.

Tableau Reader has two significant limitations: security and automation. Anyone with a .twbx file can un-package it and access the underlying data; there is no built-in security for the distribution of a packaged workbook. Additionally, any such workbooks opened in Tableau Reader cannot make real-time connections to databases or be scheduled to refresh data extracts automatically.

Tableau Public

Tableau Public is a free, hosted service that lets anyone publish Tableau Packaged Workbooks to the Web. Any version of Tableau Desktop can be used to publish Tableau Packaged Workbook files to Tableau Public. If a user has not purchased Tableau Desktop, a free desktop product (Tableau Desktop Public Edition) can be downloaded and used to create workbooks based on Tableau Data Extracts and to publish them on the Web. The limitation to using the Tableau Desktop Public Edition is that all work developed with this free software can be saved only to the Tableau Public cloud.

Tableau Public is an open sharing platform. It is possible to toggle on and off the ability for others to download a published workbook, but all data and worksheets posted are fully viewable and accessible by the public, making this an unsuitable choice for proprietary business data or protected health information (PHI). There are also limitations on the amount of data that may be included in each workbook and a total storage cap per user. It is worth repeating: Tableau Desktop Public Edition saves work to Tableau Public Web servers, not locally on the user´s computer. To save workbooks to Tableau Public, choose Server > Tableau Public > Save to Web. Bloggers, non-profit organizations, and periodicals are typical users of Tableau Public. However, any organization looking to enhance its website with interactive data visualization using public data could also find it useful.

Tableau Server

Tableau Server provides a central repository for all Tableau workbooks accessible by an organization´s business users via a Web browser. Server also offers two significant advantages; a data-refresh feature and the ability to keep data and workbooks onsite to satisfy robust security protocols. New products have emerged to deploy Tableau Server hosted on a cloud platform (Amazon Elastic Compute Cloud | EC2, Azure Virtual Machines, and Google Compute Engine, among others).

This enterprise-class business analytics platform can scale up to vast numbers of users. The server can connect live to databases or automatically refresh data extracts published to Tableau Server by scheduling updates from their original source. Tableau Server provides enhanced security and permits users to customize access to reports with specifications defined by the server administrator. Tableau Server is ideal for large companies that need to share live content with a high degree of security.

Tableau Online

Tableau Online is similar to Tableau Server but is hosted via a third-party Tableau partner. This product retains the advantages of cloud distribution and automatic refreshes but is hosted offsite. This arrangement can lead to security challenges in some cases.

Tableau Online provides ease of use, speed, and security without the need to manage the physical infrastructure of a server network. It is well suited to small companies that lack an IT department (or larger companies with overloaded IT departments).

Tableau Online´s big differences are security and data transfer. Access to content is controlled by the user´s set-up in the Tableau Online interface. Tableau Online is unable to publish workbooks with a live connection to data behind an organization´s firewall; instead, the data can be "pushed" (manually or on an automated schedule) or connected to certain cloud-hosted data environments like Amazon Redshift and Google BigQuery. (The exceptions to this limitation include data sources that are already cloud-based.) Tableau Online requires additional per-user licensing, even if those users already have access to Tableau Desktop.

Tableau and HIPAA

HIPAA, the Health Insurance Portability and Accountability Act, sets the standard for protecting patient data. Any company that deals with protected health information (PHI) must ensure that all required physical, network, and process security measures are in place and active. Note particularly, however, that Tableau is not a Business Associate, and Tableau Online is not HIPAA-compliant. Tableau Server is the only option for a distribution system of PHI that can be made HIPAA-compliant.

Tableau Server and Tableau Online: License Types

When leveraging Tableau Server or Tableau Online, organizations can purchase different licenses with features based on their users' capabilities and needs. There are three license types: Tableau Creator, Tableau Explorer, and Tableau Viewer.

- **Tableau Creator:** This is the only license with access to Tableau Desktop, the tool taught in this book. Creator enables the user to connect to any supported data source, construct and promote published data sources to Tableau Server/Online, and develop and publish reports to Tableau Server/Online. As of this writing, this license also comes with access to Tableau's companion tool, Tableau Prep, for producing more complex data sources and workflows.

- **Tableau Explorer:** This license allows the utilization of data sources and reports that have been published to Tableau Server/Online. It is solely web-based. A user connects to a published data source or workbook to build/edit and share reports through Tableau Server/Online's "web-editing" interface. The primary limitation with this license is its inability to create new data sources.

- **Tableau Viewer:** This license is intended solely for the consumption of Tableau reports already published to Tableau Server/Online. It is not for report developers. If permissions are provided by the report publisher (Creator or Explorer), the user can also download the underlying or summary data from the report or export the content as an image or pdf.

Publishing Reports to Tableau Server or Tableau Online

While Tableau Reader and Tableau Public have limited security capabilities, Tableau Server and Tableau Online allow distribution of reports and dashboards with a large degree of control over what is visible. Below are the general steps to publishing a workbook once Tableau Server has been deployed at a company. This walk-through assumes that users, groups, and projects have already been configured.

» Finalize reports and dashboards and ensure that all reports to be published have descriptive tab names. These names will be visible to users.

» Select Server > Publish Workbook and type in server name and credentials.

» Type information into all required fields in the publishing menu.

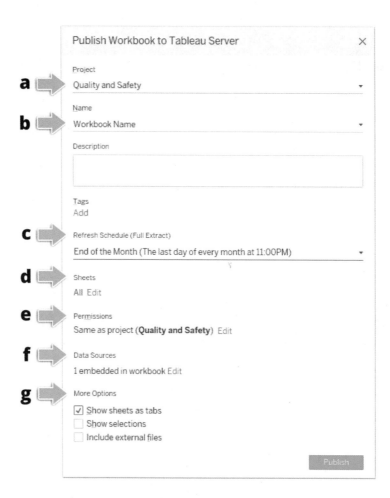

a. Select a project to keep the reports organized.

b. Give the project workbook a descriptive name.

c. Schedule an Extract Refresh (for packaged workbooks only).

d. Select the dashboards and worksheets to publish by checking or unchecking the appropriate tabs.

e. Assign and add permissions for users or groups. Select viewer, interactor, and editor for predefined permissions settings, or customize permissions for greater precision. See image below for permissions details.

f. Decide on an authentication method for the data sources; embedding the database connection credentials or having the report prompt the user.

g. Select additional options to display tabs across the top for easy navigation.

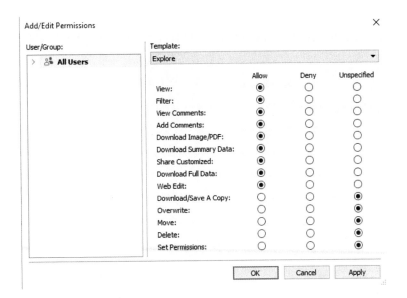

Best Practice

Be very careful when specifying who can see more than just the displayed data. Certain permission options (Web Edit, Download Full Data, and Download/Save a Copy, for example) allow end-users to see all data underlying a report.

SECTION 8

Gallery

CHAPTER 29

Gallery of HealthDataViz Dashboards

A software application alone cannot enable even the most technically savvy person to create reports and dashboards that bring out the story in the data, and thereby both urge and empower users to take action. For this to occur, designers and developers require an entire toolbox of skills, including subject-matter expertise, data familiarity, awareness of design and data visualization best practices, and intense curiosity that pushes them to find and bring to light what is most crucial to grasp.

We offer here five examples of dashboards and reports designed by HealthDataViz that build on these skills along with many of the Tableau techniques and best practices discussed throughout this book. Each example is prefaced by an explanation of the healthcare requirement and design approach used, and illustrated by call-outs of specific Tableau techniques used to develop the view.

- Hospital CEO Dashboard

- Syndromic Surveillance

- Hospital Operating Room Utilization by Day

- Hospital Patient Care Financial Margins by Payor

- US Healthcare Expenditures

Hospital CEO Dashboard

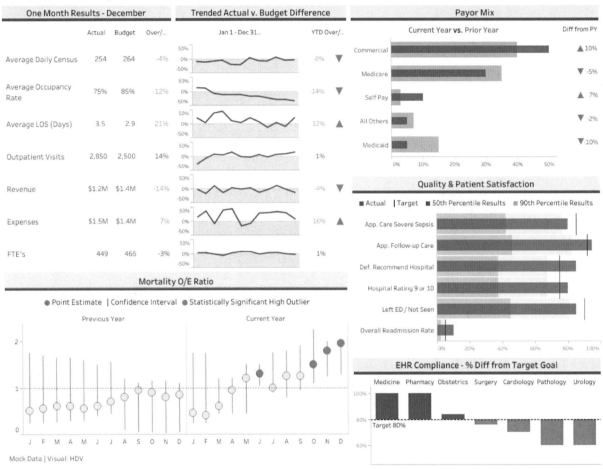

Hospital CEO
YTD Performance: January 1 to December 31

This dashboard was designed to address the scope, role, decisions, and current environment in which a hospital chief executive officer (CEO) has to navigate—an environment shaped by value-based purchasing (VBP) and public reporting, where financial, clinical, information technology, and patient satisfaction results are all inextricably linked. The concept of VBP and the underlying driver of the information that hospital CEOs require to be successful is that healthcare purchases (payors, patients) should hold healthcare providers (hospitals, doctors, etc.) accountable for both the cost and quality of care they deliver. This prototype dashboard is included in the revised edition of data visualization expert Steve Few´s book, *Information Dashboard Design*, and HealthDataViz's own book, *Visualizing Health and Healthcare Data*.

- Industry-standard metrics on the hospital´s occupancy rate and average daily census along with high-level financial results—revenue and expenses—all compared to budget. Up and down icons alert the CEO to areas that may require further inquiry, along with sparkline deviation graphs that feature direct variances of actual performance to budget for the preceding 12 months.

- The Payor Mix section allows the CEO to easily monitor any changes of the current year's payor mix from the previous year.

- The Quality and Patient Satisfaction sections display composite results for categories of mandated performance measures using a bullet graph. The hospital's results (the teal bars) are compared to internally set targets (the vertical black lines). Two comparative national results are displayed in the background using different gray color gradients to show different percentile results.

- Departmental EHR compliance is displayed with a deviation bar chart to easily and quickly identify which departments are not meeting their targets.

- Special initiatives in the bottom left corner with a simple horizontal bar graph to encode year-to-date performance compared to target or goal.

- The hospital´s mortality observed-to-expected (O/E) ratio, utilizing a point to display the point estimate and a vertical line representing confidence intervals, are color-encoded to highlight statistical significance for a particular month.

Tableau Techniques Used

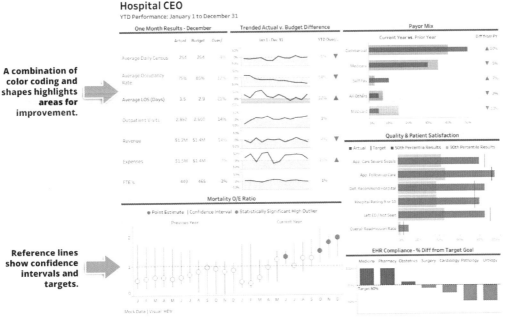

A combination of color coding and shapes highlights areas for improvement.

Reference lines show confidence intervals and targets.

IN GENERAL:

The data-to-ink ratio is maximized to decrease distractions and highlight the story.

Custom images are floated to create intuitive keys.

Actions and Quick Filters are intentionally omitted, so that the executive audience can gather insights as quickly as possible.

367

Syndromic Surveillance Dashboard

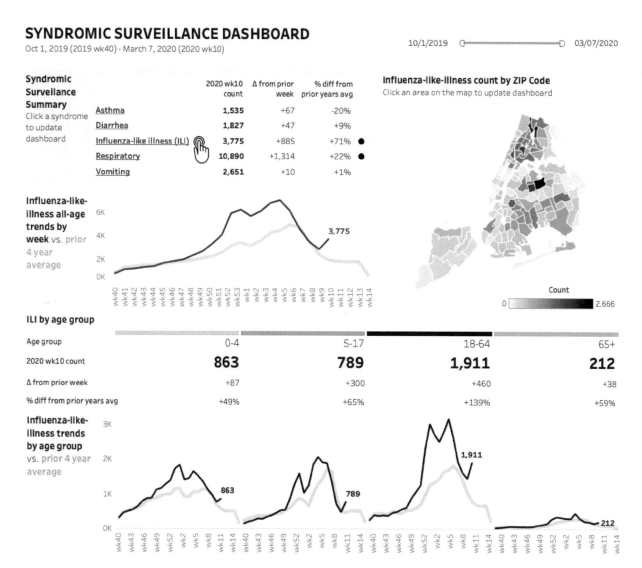

This example dashboard was designed to help public health department leaders and managers who are responsible for monitoring syndromic surveillance data and protecting the public health of communities. Using publicly available data from the NYC Department of Health and Mental Hygiene (DOHMH) captured at the beginning of the COVID-19 pandemic presents an opportunity to demonstrate the power of a simple, easy to understand and use dashboard that allows people to rapidly monitor critical public health data.

- A table of summary data by syndromic categories are displayed to appear like hyperlinks signaling to users if they click on them, an action will occur—changes to the graphs to show data and information of the selected category.

- A small dot icon on the table and thin bars above the age groups of different red color saturations, representing the percent change, is designed to leverage pre-attentive attributes.

- The line graph in the top section displays the number of reported cases for the selected date range; the line graphs in the bottom section are stratified by age groups.

- An interactive map shows case counts by zip code—clicking an area on the map filters the display to just that area.

- To view additional public health data from the NYC DOHMH, check out their "EpiQuery" tool designed by HealthDataViz: https://a816-health.nyc.gov/hdi/epiquery/

Tableau Techniques Used

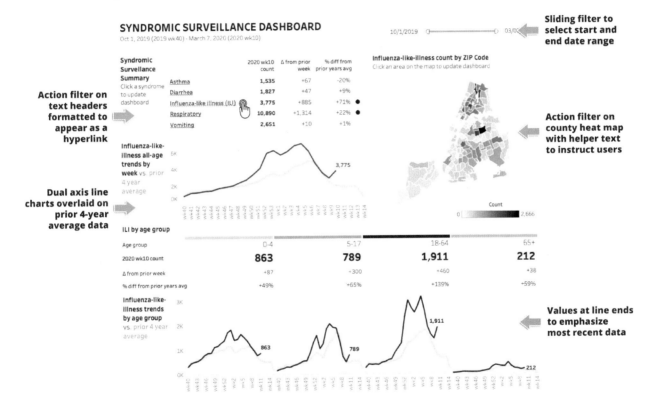

Hospital Operating Room (OR) Utilization by Day

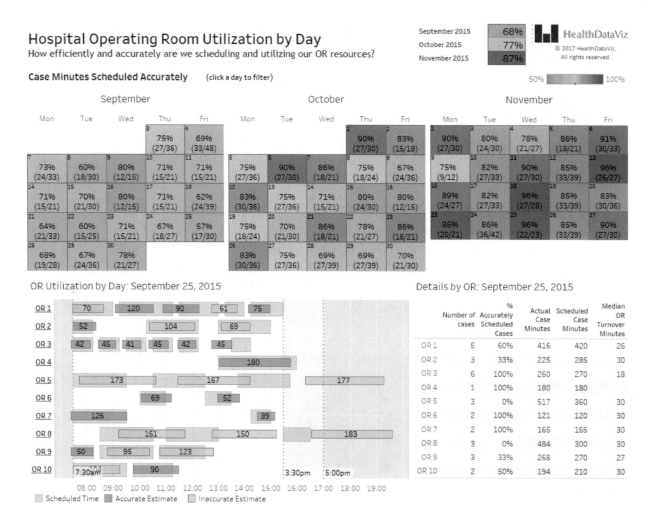

Extensive research by HealthDataViz on surgical outcomes makes it clear that high-quality, cost-effective surgical care stems in large part from efficient and productive use of operating rooms. The Hospital Operating Room dashboard above, created by HealthDataViz and showcased in *The Big Book of Dashboards: Visualizing Your Data Using Real-World Business Scenarios* (Steve Wexler, et al., 236-245), makes it easy to see how effectively procedures are scheduled and OR resources used.

This dashboard displays surgical case and OR scheduling information to help OR managers, other staff, surgeons, and anesthesiologists identify potential opportunities to improve. They can then build strategies for more efficient deployment of facilities and resources. Note the following particularly useful features of this dashboard´s design:

- The calendar view displays the percentage of cases that were scheduled accurately for each day. Blue signals higher accuracy; orange, lower.

- A click on any one day makes associated data on the Gantt chart and text table change to display that day´s information, providing even greater levels of detail

- The combination of summary data in the calendar heat maps and detailed data in the Gantt chart and text table makes it possible to identify any scheduling or use patterns. Contextual details help foreground opportunities to improve.

Tableau Techniques Used

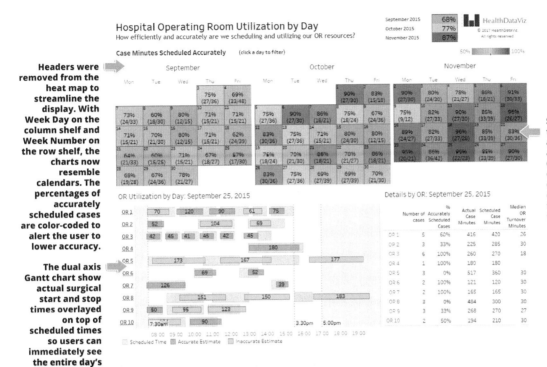

Headers were removed from the heat map to streamline the display. With Week Day on the column shelf and Week Number on the row shelf, the charts now resemble calendars. The percentages of accurately scheduled cases are color-coded to alert the user to lower accuracy.

The dual axis Gantt chart show actual surgical start and stop times overlayed on top of scheduled times so users can immediately see the entire day's activity

Selecting a day on the calendar activates an action filter that displays (in the charts below the calendars) all cases occurring on that day across the page

Hospital Patient Care Financial Margins by Payor

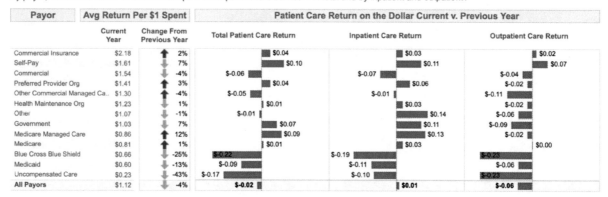

Hospital Patient Care Financial Margins by Payor

What is the surplus or deficit by payor in total and by inpatient and outpatient services to our hospital's financial bottom line?

The importance of Payor Mix ("who´s paying the bills?") for any provider delivering healthcare services cannot be overstated: the slightest change can greatly impact an organization's bottom line. Healthcare-service purchasers pay at different levels, and patients require different types and amounts of services. An increase in private insurance versus Medicare, for example, or compared to Medicaid or uncompensated care, can make the difference between profit and loss.

How each payor contributes to (or compromises!) a provider´s financial health can be powerfully displayed in a well-designed report like the one above. Note the design elements that contribute to clarity, flow, and impact:

- The top half displays the example hospital´s payor mix, and how it has changed from the previous fiscal year.

- The arrow icons are gray (rather than a more "emotional" color such as red or green); the change is noted, but not judged, and the icons are visible to all, including the 10% of males who are red-green colorblind.

- Three deviation graphs display revenue after expenses both in total and broken out for inpatient and outpatient care.

Tableau Techniques Used

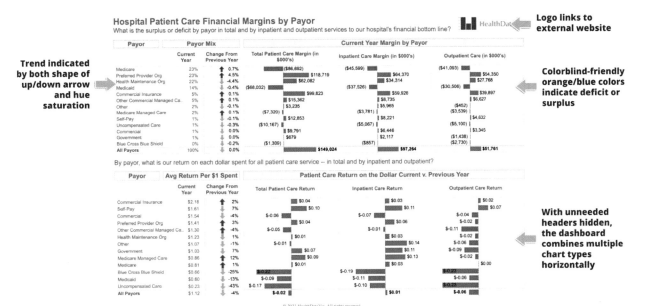

Trend indicated by both shape of up/down arrow and hue saturation

Logo links to external website

Colorblind-friendly orange/blue colors indicate deficit or surplus

With unneeded headers hidden, the dashboard combines multiple chart types horizontally

U.S. Healthcare Expenditures

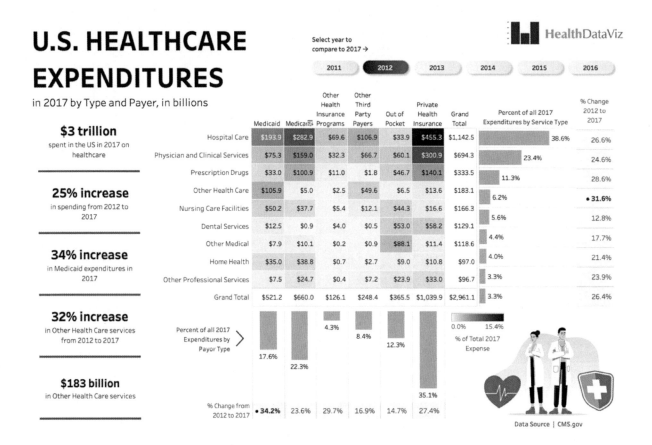

This interactive display designed to showcase U.S. healthcare expenditures by service type and payer uses data from CMS.gov. The following design elements emphasize the story in the data:

- Summary metrics sized to emphasize their importance are placed at the left side of the dashboard, utilizing many (but not all) people's mental model of reading left to right.

- A heatmap/highlight table allows the viewer to quickly identify the highest values. (This chart may look familiar; it's the same chart created in the Highlight Table/ Heat Map exercise in Chapter 8, shown here now fully incorporated in a dashboard display.)

- Marginal histograms are used to display the overall distribution of the values for Type of Service and for Payer.

- Additional functionality in the form of a parameter action allows viewers to select comparison years to display changes in values.

Tableau Techniques Used

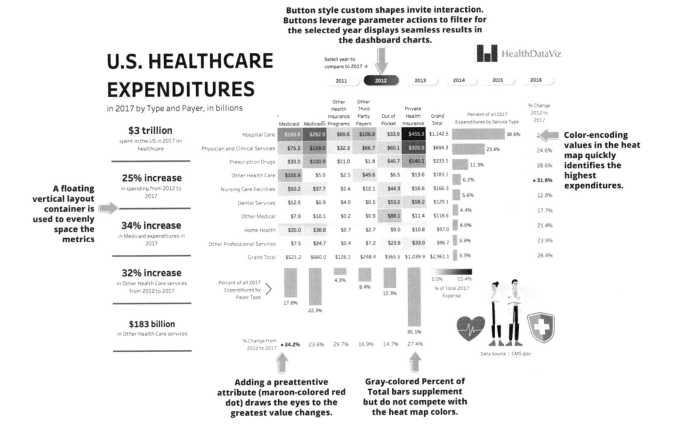

Button style custom shapes invite interaction. Buttons leverage parameter actions to filter for the selected year displays seamless results in the dashboard charts.

U.S. HEALTHCARE EXPENDITURES

in 2017 by Type and Payer, in billions

$3 trillion
spent in the US in 2017 on healthcare

25% increase
in spending from 2012 to 2017

A floating vertical layout container is used to evenly space the metrics

34% increase
in Medicaid expenditures in 2017

32% increase
in Other Health Care services from 2012 to 2017

$183 billion
in Other Health Care services

Color-encoding values in the heat map quickly identifies the highest expenditures.

Adding a preattentive attribute (maroon-colored red dot) draws the eyes to the greatest value changes.

Gray-colored Percent of Total bars supplement but do not compete with the heat map colors.

Here´s the bottom line: the key to creating an effective dashboard is to understand the people who will use it and the decisions they need to make. Once you know this, you can build dashboards that deliver both big-picture and detailed versions of current performance and desired goals, giving users the vision and the tools to see problems and solve them fast and well.

References

Books

Few, Stephen. *Information Dashboard Design: Displaying Data for At-a-Glance Monitoring.* Analytics Press, 2nd edition, 2013.

Few, Stephen. *Show Me the Numbers: Designing Tables and Graphs to Enlighten.* Analytics Press, 2nd edition, 2012.

Lidwell, W, Holden, K, Butler, J. *Universal Principles of Design, Revised and Updated: 125 Ways to Enhance Usability, Influence Perception, Increase Appeal, Make Better Design Decisions, and Teach through Design.* Rockport Publishers, 2nd edition, 2010.

Rowell, K, Betzendahl, L, Brown, C. *Visualizing Health and Healthcare Data.* Wiley, 2020.

Tufte, Edward R. *Envisioning Information.* Graphics Press, 1990.

Ware, Colin. *Visual Thinking for Design.* Morgan Kaufmann, 1st edition, 2008.

Ware, Colin. *Information Visualization: Perception for Design.* Morgan Kaufmann, 4th edition, 2020.

Online Help

Tableau Help: https://help.tableau.com/current/pro/desktop/en-us/default.htm

Data Sources

Area charts

Centers for Medicare & Medicaid Services, National Health Expenditures by Type of Service and Source of Funds; CY1980 to 2015. Retrieved from: https://www.cms. gov/Research-Statistics-Data-and-Systems/Statistics-Trends-and-Reports/NationalHealthExpendData/NationalHealthAccountsHistorical.html

Connecting to Data: Relationships and Table Joins

Massachusetts Department of Transportation, Crash Query and Visualization web application. Crash data with injury for 2018 by County. Retrieved from: https://apps.impact.dot.state.ma.us/cdv/.

Massachusetts Trauma Hospital Destinations. Retrieved from: https://www.mass.gov/service-details/trauma-hospital-destinations.

Connecting to Data: Reshaping Data Files

World Health Organization. (2012). Health Statistics and Information Systems. Projections of mortality and causes of death, 2015 and 2030 > Mortality 2015 and 2030 - Baseline Scenario > WHO regions. Retrieved from: http://www.who.int/healthinfo/global_burden_disease/projections/en/

Data Blending

Centers for Disease Control, National Center for Health Statistics. CDC WONDER Online Database. Motor Vehicle Accidents Deaths by State and Drug Overdose Deaths by State, 1999-2018. Drug Overdose Deaths codes include X40 – X44, X60 – X64, X85, Y10-Y14.

Highlight Tables/Heat Maps

Centers for Medicare and Medicaid Services. https://www.cms.gov/Research-Statistics-Data-and-Systems/Statistics-Trends-and-Reports/NationalHealthExpendData/NHE-Fact-Sheet. NHE Tables download.

Line Charts

Centers for Disease Control, Flu Portal dashboard. Influenza positive tests reported to Clinical Labs for flu seasons 2016 to 2019. Retrieved from: http://gis.cdc.gov/grasp/fluview/fluportaldashboard.html

Maps

Massachusetts Department of Transportation, Crash Query and Visualization web application. Crash data with injury for 2018 by County. Retrieved from: https://apps.impact.dot.state.ma.us/cdv/.

Massachusetts Trauma Hospital Destinations. Retrieved from: https://www.mass.gov/service-details/trauma-hospital-destinations.

Running Total

Centers for Disease Control and Prevention, National Center for Health Statistics. Multiple Cause of Death 1999-2015 on CDC WONDER Online Database. UCD-ICD-10 113 Cause List > Accidents > Motor vehicle accidents. Retrieved from: wonder.cdc.gov/mcd.html

Set Actions

Taken from Harvard Dataverse. Hey, Spencer, 2019, "Data for "A Bird's Eye View of Pharmaceutical Research and Development. https://dataverse.harvard.edu/dataset.xhtml?persistentId=doi:10.7910/DVN/S8C77Q

Small Multiples Charts

Trust for America's Health. The State of Obesity; Better Policies for a Healthier America, Sep 2016. Issue Report. Retrieved from: https://www.tfah.org/report-details/the-state-of-obesity-2016/

Stories

Centers for Disease Control and Prevention, National Center for Health Statistics, Multiple Cause of Death 1999-2018 on CDC WONDER Online Database. ICD-10 Codes: T40.1 for Heroin and T40.4 for Other Synthetic Narcotics.

Tooltips

Centers for Disease Control and Prevention, United States Cancer Statistics, Mortality Rate, 1999-2016. Retrieved from: https://wonder.cdc.gov/cancermir-v2016.html

Top N Parameter

Centers for Disease Control and Prevention, United States Cancer Statistics. 2013. Retrieved from: https://www.cdc.gov/cancer/npcr/uscs/download_data.htm

About the Authors

Daniel Benevento, AB

Dan Benevento is a principal and technical lead at HealthDataViz, passionate about using health and healthcare data to save the world. He collaborates with business stakeholders and IT professionals nationwide to design and develop timesaving, high-impact reports and dashboards throughout the health and healthcare sector and to develop staff to communicate their data clearly. When not working to create better data visualizations, he spends his time climbing cliffs, paddling rivers, strumming guitars, savoring fancy cheeses, and doting on his new daughter.

Katherine S. Rowell, MS, MHA

Kathy Rowell is co-founder and principal of Katherine S. Rowell & Associates and of HealthDataViz, a Boston firm that specializes in helping healthcare organizations design and present data displays that effectively inform decisions and bring decisive action. She advises providers, payers, policymakers, and regulatory agencies on aligning systems, designing reports, and developing staff to make clear to all concerned what needs to be done—soon— and why. Kathy and her colleagues Lindsay Betzendahl and Cambria Brown also authored Visualizing Health and Healthcare Data, published by Wiley and available on Amazon.

Janet Steeger, MEd, RN

Janet Steeger is a clinical and educational consultant with over 20 years of experience in curriculum design and implementation in healthcare quality improvement, electronic medical records, and Tableau software. When she steps away from computer and classroom, her Belgian Malinois and Dutch Shepherd dogs become her students in training for competition in the protection sport of French Ringsport. Making it clear how thoroughly she understands the way learning works, Janet would say that they teach her at least as much as she teaches them—probably more.

About HealthDataViz

HealthDataViz specializes in designing and developing data visualizations that inform decisions and drive action. Our public health and healthcare experience and expertise, deep understanding of the science of human cognition, and our expertise in business intelligence technologies guide every client engagement, transforming data into compelling stories and people into compelling storytellers.

Design and Communication

HealthDataViz harnesses the best practices of data visualization to craft dashboards, reports, and infographics that display health and healthcare data accurately, clearly, and compellingly. Our solutions solve complex problems, improve care and its delivery, reduce errors and loss, and inform the public and policymakers.

Do the statements here drain your resources and prevent your teams or stakeholders from making informed decisions? We can help!

- Reports make no sense.
- Data displays for the general public are difficult to understand and do not use plain language.
- Good decisions are compromised by bad | missing information.
- Viewers can´t find the opportunities in the data.
- Dashboards look like ransom notes; fragmented, confusing, scary.

Data Literacy Training

Staff competence in the use, interpretation, and reporting of healthcare data varies widely. HDV adapts customized training programs for each organization´s individual levels and situations, to improve knowledge, understanding, and capabilities, and enable the production of extraordinary reports. Its meticulously tailored curricula meet the needs and reporting requirements of each particular client with in-person and real-time virtual courses on:

- Data Visualization Workshops
  - » Communicating Healthcare Data with Tables and Graphs
  - » Dashboard Design for Communicating Healthcare Data
- Tableau for Healthcare Workshops
  - » Beginner|Intermediate
  - » Intermediate|Advanced

Public Workshops

Best practices of data visualization guide the creation of these hands-on, interactive sessions—including the tremendously popular and well-attended "Tableau for Healthcare" two-day course, the genesis of this book. Visit www.HealthDataViz.com for full details and a calendar of upcoming workshops.

Write us at *info@healthdataviz.com*!

380

Other HealthDataViz Books

Visualizing Health and Healthcare Data: Creating Clear and Compelling Visualizations to "See how You're Doing" is a one-of-a-kind book for health and healthcare professionals to learn the best practices of data visualization specific to their field. It provides a high-level summary of health and healthcare data, an overview of relevant visual intelligence research, strategies and techniques to gather requirements, and how to build strong teams with the expertise required to create dashboards and reports that people love to use. Clear and detailed explanations of data visualization best practices will help you understand the how and the why.

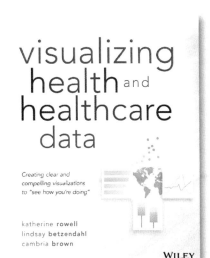

- Learn how to build beautiful and useful data products that deliver powerful insights for the end user.

- Follow along with examples of data visualization best practices, including table and graph design for health and healthcare data.

- Learn the difference between dashboards, reports, multidimensional exploratory displays and infographics (and why it matters).

- Avoid common mistakes in data visualization by learning why they do not work and better ways to display the data.

This book is meant to serve as a resource for both seasoned professionals in and newcomers to the healthcare industry, a resource that provides concise but thorough descriptions of select clinical classification systems and select healthcare databases. We have followed a very simple format. Each entry on a named system or database presents a general description of its current state, followed by a timeline of key points in its evolution. Finally, a summary section describes present structure and terminology. This arrangement will, we hope, help the reader understand the antecedents and evolution of these systems and databases, and thereby help guide the choice of exactly the right such resources for a particular project.

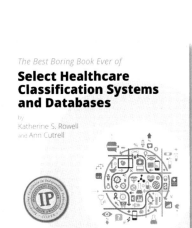

Index

385